War, disability and rehabilitation in Britain

MANCHESTER
1824

Manchester University Press

Cultural History of Modern War
Series editors

Ana Carden-Coyne, Peter Gatrell, Max Jones, Penny Summerfield and Bertrand Taithe

Already published

Christine E. Hallett *Containing trauma: nursing work in the First World War*

Jo Laycock *Imagining Armenia: Orientalism, ambiguity and intervention*

Juliette Pattinson *Behind enemy lines: gender, passing and the Special Operations Executive in the Second World War*

Jeffrey S. Reznick *Healing the nation: soldiers and the culture of caregiving in Britain during the Great War*

Jeffrey S. Reznick *John Galsworthy and disabled soldiers of the Great War: with an illustrated selection of his writings*

Michael Roper *The secret battle: emotional survival in the Great War*

Penny Summerfield and Corinna Peniston-Bird *Contesting home defence: men, women and the Home Guard in the Second World War*

Colette Wilson *Paris and the Commune, 1871–78: the politics of forgetting*

Centre for the Cultural History of War

War, disability and rehabilitation in Britain

'Soul of a nation'

JULIE ANDERSON

Manchester University Press

Published by Manchester University Press
Altrincham Street, Manchester M1 7JA, UK
www.manchesteruniversitypress.co.uk

British Library Cataloguing-in-Publication Data is available

Library of Congress Cataloging-in-Publication Data is available

ISBN 978 1 7849 9349 8 *paperback*

First published by Manchester University Press in hardback 2011

This edition first published 2016

Printed by Lightning Source

For my parents,
Pat and Duncan Anderson

Contents

Acknowledgements *page* viii
List of illustrations x
List of tables xi
Epigraph xii

Introduction 1

1 *Unfortunates*: disability, 1900–1939 14
2 *Attitude*: disabled ex-servicemen after the First World War 42
3 *Soul*: rehabilitation in the Second World War 72
4 *Fit*: the process of rehabilitation 102
5 *Men*: masculinity and rehabilitation 130
6 *Revealed*: women and rehabilitation 152
7 *Nation*: rehabilitation and the post-war State 176

Conclusions 210
Select bibliography 217
Index 235

Acknowledgements

Due to the nature of academic books, without professional assistance and the efforts of colleagues, family and friends, it would be impossible for an academic writer to finish any project.

Throughout this project I have worked with a number of archivists and librarians at various libraries around the country. I would like to thank the librarians at the National Archives in Kew, London; the British Library, London; the Newspaper Archive at Colindale; the Wellcome Trust Library; the RNIB and RNID libraries; the library at the Royal College of Surgeons, and the John Rylands Library at the University of Manchester. Neil Young and Rod Suddaby at the Imperial War Museum were hugely helpful, as was Helen Alper at Roehampton. I would like to thank the Wellcome Trust for their continuing support and interest in the history of disability.

I would like to thank all my colleagues at the Centre for the History of Science, Technology and Medicine at the University of Manchester, especially Emm Barnes, Aya Homei, Vladimir Jankovic, Vicky Long, Gillian Mawson and Stephanie Snow. Elizabeth Toon was never too busy to read my work and provide insightful comments. Neil Pemberton, sharer of office space for a number of years, was always around to encourage me in my endeavours. My sponsor Flurin Condrau provided guidance, useful advice and explained the necessity of flat shoes.

My editor extraordinaire Roy McLeod took time to read the draft manuscript in his endeavour to make me a better writer and I hope he will be pleased with the result. I would also like to thank Joanna Bourke, who has been such a source of support, and Penny Summerfield for her inspiration and guidance. Ana Carden-Coyne provided many lively debates about the history of disability and war and has always given generously of her time. Neil Carter regularly sent useful finds in archives I may never have got to. I would like to thank the other 'History Barbies', Heather Perry and Beth Linker, who made conferences so much more enjoyable and provided much appreciated support. Other people who have added to this project in no small way include Virginia Berridge, Peter Catterall, Dion Georgiou and Steve Ickringill.

Rima Apple has been a superb mentor; Martin Atherton has been a generous and kind friend; Wendy Gagen has provided steadfast support; Graeme Gooday has tempered his sage advice with good humour from across the Pennines; Kara McKechnie has been co-president of clubs and her encouragement and friendship have sustained me; Lisa O'Sullivan has given me projects and warm friendship; Jonathan Reinarz's efforts have seen me through some difficult times; Walton Schalick, Natasha Winters-Schalick and little Zara made me feel part of their family no matter where we all were; Steve Sturdy provided wise counsel, and Helen Valier has given me staunch support, both as an academic and friend.

Lee Hamer has probably had to hear much more about rehabilitation than he ever wanted to and I thank him for his forbearance in so many ways and the calm technical assistance he was always able to provide when he was confronted with unreasonable demands.

To my publisher at Manchester University Press, Emma Brennan, I owe more than a debt of gratitude for her humour, patience and intelligent guidance. I would also like to thank her for her friendship and the establishment of some long-standing, much enjoyed rituals. The editors in the Cultural History of War series, Penny Summerfield, Bertrand Taithe, Peter Gatterall, Max Jones and Ana Carden-Coyne, have always been supportive of my work and I would like to thank them for putting my book into their series. I would also like to thank the three anonymous reviewers who actively engaged with the manuscript – their efforts certainly improved the finished product. Despite the assistance I received, any errors or omissions are wholly owing to me.

Finally, I would like to dedicate this book to my parents, Pat and Duncan Anderson. This is really all I have to offer them after all their years of steadfast support; sharing my highs and comforting me through my lows, and I do so with love and gratitude.

List of illustrations

1.1 Patients and nurses in the sun, Woodlands Hospital, Birmingham, 1926 (reproduced with permission of the Royal Orthopaedic Hospital Trust, Birmingham) *page* 21
1.2 War identifies poor physiques (reproduced with permission of the Wellcome Library, London) 30
2.1 Soldiers with artificial limbs at Queen Mary's Roehampton, First World War (reproduced with permission of the Imperial War Museum) 45
3.1 Soldier being walked outside at Oswestry, Shropshire 1944 (reproduced with permission of the Imperial War Museum) 82
3.2 Amputees exercising in the gymnasium, Queen Mary's Roehampton, 1944 (reproduced with permission of the Imperial War Museum) 88
4.1 Rehabilitation in the Air Force (reproduced with permission of the Wellcome Library, London) 105
4.2 Football Match 'Knees vs. Ankles' (reproduced with permission of the Wellcome Library, London) 107
5.1 Stoke Mandeville Bed Cycle 1949 (reproduced with permission of the Science Museum, London) 137
7.1 Outdoor exercises at a miners' rehabilitation centre, 1950s (reproduced with permission of the Chartered Society of Physiotherapy) 191
7.2 Bed cricket at the Royal Orthopaedic Hospital, Birmingham, 1949 (reproduced with permission of the Royal Orthopaedic Hospital Trust, Birmingham) 200

List of tables

4.1 Injuries and diseases treated in RAF orthopaedic centres, 1941–44 (D-Day) *page* 109
4.2 Number of aircrew plastic surgery cases treated at Queen Victoria Hospital, East Grinstead, 1939–44 114

'The greatness of a nation is in its fit men, but the soul of a nation is revealed in its attitude to its unfortunates'

George Tomlinson
Parliamentary Secretary – Ministry of Labour, 1944

Introduction

> The greatness of a nation is in its fit men, but the soul of a nation is revealed in its attitude to its unfortunates.

In this speech, George Tomlinson, Joint Parliamentary Secretary to the Ministry of Labour and National Service speaking at The Ex-Services' Society Annual Medical Conference in 1944, epitomised the contemporary attitude of the wartime government toward the rehabilitation of disabled ex-servicemen during the Second World War.[1]

While not seen as destructive as the First World War, the Second World War was still a devastating conflict. More than half a million British servicemen and women and civilians died, and more than 300,000 were injured. The damage, through techniques of modern warfare, was delivered with even more devastating efficiency in the Second World War than the First. Additionally, civilians were exposed to the physical dangers posed by war, experiencing nightly bombing raids on major cities around Britain.

The onslaught of a second large-scale conflict of the twentieth century, while not welcomed by those who remembered the destruction of the First, was nevertheless entered into, and preparations were made to receive large numbers of casualties as the nation prepared itself for war. To those that had experienced the destruction of the First World War, preparations for large numbers of damaged bodies were made, as the nation prepared itself. Inter-war developments in medicine provided new ways for injured bodies to be treated. Experience of mass warfare from the First World War was disinterred from medical journals and mingled with new medical practices and innovations.

This book investigates the culture of rehabilitation and the institutions which practised it. In particular, it focuses on the nature of injured and disabled bodies in relation to the rehabilitative practices established in Britain. In an effort to maintain a strong military force, rehabilitation became the overarching system adopted by the military and the State. Slogans such as 'Make Do and Mend', which exhorted housewives to use the resources that they had at their disposal, were applied to many aspects of life in wartime Britain. Indeed, this attitude of using available resources extended to melting saucepans that re-emerged as Spitfire aircraft. Military expediency was applied in a number of different ways. Essentially, the theory behind rehabilitation was that seriously injured and permanently disabled servicemen could be reconstructed and reused in different contexts. Severely disabled men were not to be left on the scrapheap.

At this time, the State, in consultation with the medical profession and other experts, developed and perfected theories and systems that dealt with the large numbers of men and women disabled, whether in the short term or permanently, who were far more likely to survive their injuries than had been the case in the First World War. The practice of rehabilitation was adopted by the State and consisted of a system where a soldier/patient was hospitalised and prescribed a regime, which consisted of a combination of medical, occupational, sporting and social therapy. Notions of competitive masculinity drove the rehabilitation system. The ultimate rehabilitation occurred when the serviceman returned to his combatant duties, or if the impact of the residual disability was too great, to other non-combatant employment in the Services, or, in fewer cases, was discharged to work in industry.

Bodies were essential for rehabilitation. The notion of the 'body' has been imbued with a number of meanings and is culturally and historically conceptualised. Constructed environments, institutions, expectations, class and gender are just some of the ways that bodies are understood. Wartime bodies are different from those in peacetime environments. The body moves between peacetime and wartime spaces; it is subject to the rigour of military practice and discipline at times of war. Bodies can be altered by war, permanently and irrevocably. The body, as a weapon of war for the State, took on different guises as it was put through the rehabilitative system. When an ex-serviceman was wholly rehabilitated, his body returned to its status as a war weapon. If there was residual disability, his body could still be an instrument of war, albeit in a different guise. Discharge from military service was not always the result for those who could not take an active role in combat. The body was not diminished, despite disabling injuries, for the State to use it to fight in the war. In addition to the requirement for many bodies to fight on many fronts, technical expertise and specialised knowledge ensured that corporeality as expressed through the ability for physical combat was not the only value of a fighting body. The importance of the body in its many manifestations to work for the warring State was not underestimated as Britain immersed itself in a long total war. The idea of the Military Revolution, in which the investment of the State in its soldiers owing to more complicated technologies and tactics means that they become more valuable to the State and therefore the State becomes more active in and concerned for their health and welfare, was evident in military thinking in this conflict.[2] The focus on the investment in technical training is more evident in rehabilitative practices in the Second World War than it is in other wars. Historians Ana Carden-Coyne and Wendy Gagen have written on rehabilitation in the First World War, but I contend that the constructions and meanings differ vastly between the two conflicts.[3] The requirement for a substantial number of men who were highly trained to be on hand to fight ensured that rehabilitative practices were taken seriously by the War Office. It was important to return these men to the field of battle and for those who were unable to fully regain their function, for them to be relocated to another part of the war effort, either in an altered combatant role, or a civilian one, in administration or in the production area. Disabled bodies were also constructed by social and cultural forces in different times and places, and rehabilitation restored and re-evaluated their usefulness to the State, the military and society.

Rehabilitation was based in medical practice and was a result of new and existing therapies, combined with the need to repair an injured fighting force as quickly as possible. Medical treatment during war has been a topic of interest for historians of medicine. There have been some excellent studies of medical treatment in the Second World War, recently Mark Harrison's *Medicine and Victory*.[4] This book is a detailed account of medical treatment for servicemen during the war; it does not reflect on what happened to injured men and women who were redeployed or discharged. What happened to servicemen after they left the hospital is less researched than the medical care provided for them during battle. I argue that the focus on disabled ex-servicemen and women can tell us more about the nature of British medical practice during that period. There is still some debate surrounding whether or not war was 'good' for medicine; however, medicine and war are certainly closely associated and practitioners were required to mend the maimed from battle.[5] Medical innovations were developed to meet the requirements of war, including the mass production of penicillin, therapy for tropical diseases and surgical treatment during the Second World War. These innovations in techniques and technology had important ramifications for the severely injured because of their ability to save life, which increased numbers of disabled people. This book delves into the complexity surrounding injury and does not end when the period of hospitalisation is over. Rather, it follows servicemen from the hospital to the rehabilitation unit, and seeks to understand the meanings, processes and practice of rehabilitation for those disabled in war.

The story of the Second World War and its social, political and economic aftermath has been told by historians. Indeed the development of the welfare state and its concentration on full employment, housing, education, social welfare and the National Health Service (NHS) were a pivotal moment in post-war British history although, as Peter Hennessey points out, like many western nations, Britain 'had been laying the foundations of some kind of welfare state in the interwar years' and war had given 'the process a shove'.[6] But it would be simplistic to confine this change to work on government policy and statutes. The change was much more overarching than that. The impact of rehabilitation on the post-war State was unequivocal. Rehabilitation became an all-encompassing term; it was used to describe the reconstruction of Europe's infrastructure, the restoration of people displaced by war, and the rebuilding of emotional lives of children following their experiences of war. By the 1960s, the word 'rehabilitation' was used principally to describe the system of care associated with more extreme behaviour; criminals and young offenders were usually rehabilitated. It continues to be used in medicine, usually to describe the recovery process of stroke victims, and is used less in relation to people with disabilities.

Disability history

Disability can have a number of causes; a result of birth defects, war, working in industry, poor health care and poverty. Although disabled people have always been a part of society throughout the centuries, large-scale conflicts, a low standard of health provision, numbers of poor people and unsafe industry increased numbers of disabled people at specific points during the twentieth century. Even in times of peace, improved medical care has prevented premature death or prolonged the lives of disabled people but has not always led to improved life chances or social acceptance. The nature of the various transformations and changes between 1918 and 1956 is an important component in understanding disability. The book will demonstrate that both the shifting nature of disability and disablement itself were influenced by different cultural ebbs and flows. It also highlights the ways in which attitudes toward the nature of different disabilities have changed, and that this was not linear. Some disabling illnesses have simply disappeared. Stomach ulcers are no longer a disabling condition owing to the refinement of medications to control the condition; nevertheless, stomach ulcers were one of the most common reasons for military discharge in the Second World War.[7]

It is equally important to understand the role of charitable associations that worked on behalf of disabled servicemen within this period. It would seem obvious that an argument could be made that the focus of different Ministries, particularly the Ministry of Labour and National Service and the Ministry of Pensions, in addition to the development of the welfare state ended the need for charities for disabled war veterans. Similarly to the First, the Second World War actually led to the development of new charities and voluntary associations to assist in caring for the war disabled where the State's provision was lacking.

Medical treatment and health issues, although often dismissed by those who study disability politics as the 'medical' model of disability, can be an important way to gain insight into disabled people's lives. The medical model is defined as the domination of medical experts and medical treatments of disability. The social model differs in that it defines disability as the barriers erected, altitudes toward and exclusion of disabled people by society.[8] Over the past decades, a dialectic has been constructed between the medical and social models as scholars have attempted to 'rescue' disabled people from the perceived overarching dominance of medicine. While the social model continues to have considerable support within contemporary disability activism and disability studies in the UK, more recently critiques have emerged, challenging the dominance of the social model. If the medical model is seen as problematic by many disability activists and theorists, the strong political overtones of the social model have limited its use as a tool for understanding disability in an historical framework. In fact, both models are essentially contemporary in their focus. I would argue that new approaches in social and cultural history which are more sensitive to power dynamics and inequalities, and agency and patient–practitioner interactions offered in this book are a useful way to capture the embodied experience of disability. It is not clear how social approaches to the understanding of disability that attempt to dismiss or sideline the role of medicine in the construction of the 'disabled person' can be used to describe situated historical stories without ignoring that individual's experience. Rehabilitation, with its focus on the reconstruction of a body to serve the wartime State in any capacity, provides another historical example of the relationship between disabled bodies and medicine. For the disability historian, the priority is to describe, contextualise and understand the experience of those in the past.

Disability history is becoming a well-established field and, largely owing to the industry of historians, the history of disabled people cannot be said to be 'hidden' anymore. Paul Longmore, Catherine Kudlick, Rosemarie Garland Thompson, Zina Weygand, Walton O. Schalick, Henri-Jaques Stiker and many others are producing more historically and culturally contextual studies of disabled people.[9] Research that has focused on disability and war has been produced by Joanna Bourke, Ana Carden-Coyne, Wendy Gagen, Heather Perry, Beth Linker, Deborah Cohen and David Gerber.[10] Other areas of academic research explored disability before it became the focus of professional historians. In the field of public policy, disabled people have been strongly represented by writers in the UK including Colin Barnes and Michael Oliver.[11] Their books generally deal with the subject of disability politics, and they explain the rise of groups representing disabled people and the nature of disability politics from the 1960s. Insofar as they do delve into the history of disabled people, the result has been superficial, relating the history of disabled people to their marginalisation within wider society. There is, according to some researchers in the public policy field, a reason for this. Jane Campbell and Michael Oliver's *Disability Politics* argued that the study of the history of disabled people was not 'feasible' as their life experiences had been too neglected.[12] As they see it, the use of personal experience is the only way to write a history of disabled people. Nevertheless, historians have managed to research and write histories of disabled people, and while it is a long-neglected field of study, it looks set to grow further as more historians try to make sense of disability using different historical methodologies. As we see in the case of rehabilitation, the multitude of relationships that exist between disabled and able-bodied people is much more complex than simply one of marginalisation by one group of the other. The full range of issues that reflect the history of disability need to be explored, so that the result is a more balanced and historically accurate story, and this book will hopefully add to the scholarship in the history of disability so that a more contextual story can be constructed.

The remit of this book is both broad and complex. There is a wide range of different types of disability explored here, but such a work cannot hope to cover all of the varying types of disabilities that existed. The study concentrates predominantly on those servicemen, women and civilians who were physically injured and blinded. Although we will see that the morale of the injured and disabled servicemen was important, as it was understood that attitude had an effect on their 'will to get well' and depression surrounding injury was a barrier to wellness, the book does not tell the story of those with psychiatric disorders such as battle fatigue.

Chapter outline

The first chapter, *Unfortunates*, focuses on Britain before the First World War and provides important historical background in understanding the nature of disablement. Britain's disabled fell into three distinct groups: the war disabled, the industrial disabled and civilian disabled, which included children. The evolution of care for disabled people, such as it was, was generally focused on those disabled in war and less frequently on civilians who had been born with their disability or become disabled through disease or birth defect. Charitable support for disabled ex-servicemen freed the State to provide for disabled workers through the National Insurance Act, although industry continued to maintain much fiscal responsibility for disabled workers and their rehabilitation and care when injured. Civilians were another question altogether, but the State, through public health reforms, made attempts to improve the health of poorer children to ensure that disability caused through disease and poverty was lessened. The chapter examines the evolving state of disabled people and suggests that the period did result in some change in attitudes to disability and support for disabled people, as a result of the overarching need for change in relation to social welfare and the establishment of new Ministries such as the Ministry of Health in 1919.

The First World War exposed the public to disability on a grand scale, exposing them to large numbers of men with shattered senses, limbs and nerves. The second chapter, *Attitude*, focuses on the changing view of the disabled ex-servicemen from the First World War. While many ex-servicemen disabled in the First World War were not especially well supported by the State, which has been highlighted by historians such as Deborah Cohen, attitudes toward the war disabled as heroic and self-sacrificing were promulgated by various interest groups.[13] The function of the emerging welfare state was essentially given over to war veterans; the Ministry of Pensions which was formed in 1916 exclusively administered pensions for the war disabled. Charitable giving, which was an important component of support for disabled people, focused on war charities, and agencies for disabled ex-servicemen such as the British Legion were set up. Others were established during or just after the war, such as St Dunstan's, a home for blind ex-servicemen, and the Star and Garter Home, both of which feature in the chapter as examples of ways that disabled men from the war were reinforced in the public's consciousness. While State provision was difficult to procure and lacking in generosity, levels of public support for the war disabled from the Great War shifted the emphasis away from civilians and onto these 'more deserving' war veterans.

The third chapter, *Soul*, explains how the shifting boundary of the battle-front transformed the nature of combatants and altered perceptions of disabled people. For the first time, the Home Front was an integral part of the war, as were all the various workers who were required to actively participate in the defence of mainland Britain. Many people were permanently disabled through enemy action and industrial accidents, and joined those injured as a result of active service in the new system of State-sponsored rehabilitation. The scale of disability during the Second World War led to the creation of medical facilities and institutions to rehabilitate injured men and women. The chapter explains how the system developed, the process of rehabilitation from injury and wounding to the point of redeployment in the workforce or the Services. Britain was short of manpower during and immediately following the war, and many people who had previously been thought of as unemployable through disability were drafted into the workforce.

The key aim of the process of rehabilitation was to bring people to a level of fitness where they could be redeployed as workers or combatants. The fourth chapter, *Fit*, interrogates how notions of fitness differed between the various branches of the Armed Services. It will also assess in what ways the 'fit' body was transformed by the demands of war. Using the Royal Air Force (RAF) as a case study, the chapter will show that in a more mechanised war, with its emphasis on technical knowledge, the body becomes a locus of expertise and therefore its value did not always manifest itself physically. This was particularly important for the RAF.

The pilots were highly and expensively trained, and their role as bastions to the German bombing of mainland Britain was the stuff of legend and a propagandist's dream. Additionally, those bodies trained to fly, service aircraft, navigate planes and other functions specific to aircraft were also valuable assets to the State. Of particular value to the RAF were the civilian consultant surgeons who saw to it that the RAF maintained its preferential status, and that its injured were provided with the best rehabilitation possible, which was unique to the Service. The nature of injuries in the RAF meant that much rehabilitative work focused on orthopaedics. Burns associated with flying were also an associated danger. The chapter juxtaposes the tough, physical methods employed in orthopaedic centres with the social rehabilitation practised in burns units.

The fifth chapter, *Men*, examines the masculine characteristics of the disabled and rehabilitating man, and the ways in which different establishments endeavoured to keep this notion of self intact. Men's wartime identity was partly the perception of themselves as weapons of war, their bodies strong, fit and essentially masculine. A disabling injury or condition was therefore an emasculating experience, robbing a man of this identity and stripping him of his masculine self. The authorities were aware how important it was to quickly restore this physical notion of manhood, and believed that if this could be done the individual's sense of self would follow. This was bound up in the notion that in this more technological war, the corporeal identity of the body was not their only value, that knowledge and technical expertise gained were also an important asset to the war effort. However, rehabilitation was all about the physical body, and although the notion of mental health was important, as centres were to be 'impregnated with enthusiasm',[14] this was done through a concentration on the physical self. The chapter focuses in particular on the regime at Stoke Mandeville. If the body was rehabilitated the mind would follow suit. Rehabilitation harnessed the competitive nature of masculinity in order both to rebuild bodies and restore a sense of the male self. This was done mainly through sport and exercise, but competitions were made from many aspects of daily life at rehabilitation centres.

For the first time women as participants in war, outside the nursing profession, were valued and therefore were also subject to rehabilitative practices which were similar to those provided for men. The next chapter, *Revealed*, exposes the nature of rehabilitative practices for women during the Second World War. The chapter reflects on the role of women and their responses to the essentially masculine physical rehabilitative process, and suggests it quickly became obvious that women could not be turned into men, nor were rehabilitative practices, with their emphasis on competitive sport and physical exercise, suitable for women.[15] Disabled women were also able to take advantage of the relaxation of limitations for employment opportunities due to the doubly disadvantageous problem of their perceived lack of ability and their gender, and participate in a range of wartime activities alongside able-bodied people. The chapter examines the way that the threat of permanent disablement was expressed in gendered arguments about compensation for women performing wartime duties which were equal to that of men. In addition, the chapter discusses provisions made for disabled women once they were rehabilitated or discharged, and their newly negotiated relationships with various State agencies.

The final chapter, *Nation*, examines the ways that central government responded to the challenge of large numbers of war disabled in the context of the new welfare state. In particular, it reflects on various pieces of legislation such as the Disabled Persons (Employment) Act 1944 and the National Assistance Act 1948, passed during and after the war which benefited disabled people, particularly those who were injured on active duty. The central argument of this chapter is that the State, through various different government departments including the Ministry of Labour and National Service, and Ministry of Pensions, placed a value on the fighting man and non-combatant woman's body as instruments of war, and accepted fiscal and social responsibility for men and women injured as a result of the fighting. During the war, this system of care and rehabilitation had by necessity produced a large-scale bureaucracy that tended to the needs of the war disabled, which was carried over to peacetime Britain. The State was responsible for structures and organisations that would oversee medical care, vocational rehabilitation and eventual redeployment in the workforce. There were problems inherent in an infrastructure this size; jobs protected for disabled ex-servicemen were considered insufficiently skilled, but on the whole the legislation benefited disabled people. There were complaints that civilians did not benefit from the legislation as well as ex-servicemen. Much of the legislation was geared toward getting disabled people back to work, as the more disabled people who could be made 'fit' and redeployed, the lower the welfare bill, which was vital to an economy reeling from six years of war.

The book concludes by looking briefly beyond the Second World War, to assess the ways that the treatment of disabled ex-servicemen more broadly informed post-war attitudes in the arenas of health, rehabilitation, welfare and disabled rights through to 1956. Not only did it alter many social, political and economic conventions that had previously been applied, but its aftermath altered the face of State provision and contemporary attitudes to war veterans and the civilian disabled. The book demonstrates the ways that disabled bodies were rehabilitated, reintegrated and redeployed during and after the war. Indeed, rehabilitation was the cornerstone of a system that ensured that bodies (and minds) were repaired and reused.

The development of the welfare state in the post-war period, and its associated focus on ex-servicemen, meant that rehabilitation and the care of the war disabled were cornerstones of the post-war rebuilding of the State. Improvements in medical treatment during and after the Second World War had an impact on the rehabilitative process. Increased centralisation – all servicemen with the same injury treated in central locations, such as spinal injuries at Stoke Mandeville – and specialisation; the best specialists were brought together to work and advance their field, for instance treatment of airmen's burns at East Grinstead, had a definite impact on residual disability. In focusing on the experience of the disabled ex-servicemen, this book will demonstrate that the impact of the Second World War was more profound, significant and long lasting than the First in the changing arenas of health care, welfare, social attitudes, disability rights and legislation. Essentially, the nation itself was rehabilitated in its ability to reconstruct not just bodies, but to construct a whole system which altered public perception, social welfare, employment legislation and medical practices. More generally the book demonstrates how important the men and women of the Services – and those civilians – disabled in the 1939–45 period were. The unique and formative experience of men and women disabled during the Second World War was profoundly different from that of the First World War. By focusing on medical and welfare developments, reconstruction as well as changing public attitudes informed by disabled war heroes and the work of charities, this research demonstrates how disabled people moved into the post-1945 era in a radically new environment. A key legacy of the Second World War was the creation of a generation of physically disabled people, and the concomitant shift in cultural, social and State attitudes toward that group.

Notes

1 Address by George Tomlinson, Ex-Services' Welfare Society Annual Conference, Tuesday 8 February 1944, Research Board of the Correlation of Medical Science and Physical Education SA/RBC C.7/5, Wellcome Trust, London.

2 See Jeremy M. Black, *A Military Revolution?: Military Change and European Society 1550–1800* (London, 1991).

3 See Ana Carden-Coyne, *Reconstructing the Body: Classicism, Modernism and the First World War* (Oxford, 2009); Wendy J. Gagen, 'Remastering the Body, Renegotiating Gender: Physical Disability and Masculinity during the First World War, the Case of J.B. Middlebrook', *European Review of History*, Vol. 14, No. 4 (2007), 525–41.

4 Mark Harrison, *Medicine and Victory* (Oxford, 2007).

5 Roger Cooter, 'Medicine and the Goodness of War', *Canadian Bulletin of Medical History*, Vol. 7 (1990), 147–59.

6 Peter Hennessey, *Never Again: Britain 1945–1951* (London, 1993), 121. See also Kenneth O. Morgan, *The People's Peace: British History Since 1945* (Oxford, 1999); Rodney Lowe, *The Welfare State in Britain Since 1945* (Basingstoke, 1999); Nicholas Timmins, *The Five Giants: A Biography of the Welfare State* (London, 1996).

7 Zantac is used to control the symptoms and effects of stomach ulcers.

8 For definitions of, and support for the social model idea see Jane Campbell and Michael Oliver, *Disability Politics* (London, 1996), 36–8.

9 Paul K. Longmore, *Why I Burned My Book: And Other Essays on Disability* (Philadelphia, 2003); Catherine J. Kudlick, 'Disability History: Why We Need Another "Other",' *American Historical Review*, Vol. 108, No. 3 (June 2003); Rosmarie Garland Thompson, *Extraordinary Bodies: Figuring Physical Disability in American Culture and Literature* (New York, 1997); Walton O. Schalick, *Childing the Cripple and Crippling the Child: Children with Physical Disabilities in France, Germany, the United Kingdom and the United States, 1800–1905* (forthcoming); Zina Weygand, *The Blind in French Society from the Middle Ages to the Century of Louis Braille* (Palo Alto, 2009); Henri-Jacques Stiker, *A History of Disability* (Ann Arbor, 2000).

10 Joanna Bourke, *Dismembering the Male: Men's Bodies, Britain and the Great War* (London, 1996); Ana Carden-Coyne, *Reconstructing the Body*; Gagen, 'Remastering the Body, Renegotiating Gender'; Heather Perry, 'Re-arming the Nation: Artificially Rebuilding the State and Society in World War One Germany', in Katherine Ott, David Serlin and Stephen Mihn (eds), *Artificial Parts Practical Lives: Modern Histories of Prosthetics* (New York, 2002), 75–101; Beth Linker, *The Roots of Rehabilitation: Reconstructing Disabled Soldiers in World War I America* (Chicago, forthcoming); Deborah Cohen, *The War Come Home: Disabled Veterans in Britain and Germany 1914–1939* (Berkeley, 2001); David Gerber (ed.), *Disabled Veterans in History* (Ann Arbor, 2000).

11 See Colin Barnes, *Disabled People in Britain and Discrimination* (London, 1991); and Michael Oliver, *Understanding Disability: From Theory to Practice* (Basingstoke, 1996).

12 Campbell and Oliver, *Disability Politics*, 17.

13 See Deborah Cohen, *The War Come Home: Disabled Veterans in Britain and Germany 1914–1939* (Berkeley, 2001).

14 Ludwig Guttmann, 'The Treatment and Rehabilitation of Patients with Injuries of the Spinal Cord', in Zachary Cope (ed.), *History of the Second World War* (London, 1953), 499.

15 See Julie Anderson, 'British Women, Disability and the Second World War', *Contemporary British History*, Vol. 20, No. 1 (March 2006), 37–53.

1

Unfortunates: disability, 1900–1939

> Much of our population is stigmatised as C3, and, so closely do the two co-operate, that this reproach applies not only to our bodies, but also to our uninspired minds.[1]

In her article on 'National Fitness', Prunella Stack highlights the obsession with fitness that had concerned a number of agencies, both private and government, since the nineteenth century. Prior to the Second World War, a concentration on fitness culminated in displays possessing military overtones which were held all around the country. As we can see from this quote, bodily health was associated with fitness of mind. Despite efforts to improve the nation's fitness, there were still significant numbers of people who were deprived and who suffered from poor health; and the threat of disability through disease, illness or accident remained high. Work was dangerous, as there was little safety provision accidents were common, and children lacking a safe environment in which to play were exposed to the dangers of increasing levels of traffic on the roads.

This chapter will explore these issues in the inter-war period, and examines children, the industrial disabled and civilians. A key aspect of this chapter, and an important defining concept for this book, is the endeavours to 'cure' disabled people. Whether by medical intervention, exercise or sport, the need to 'cure' or 'limit' disability and its effects is a common theme for disabled people in this period, as concerns were expressed surrounding notions of degeneration and the rise of eugenics. The ability to ameliorate disability related to children in particular, as children were seen as malleable, both physically and mentally.

Additionally, dependence on charity and low levels of government assistance were persistent themes in this period, although new developments in early social welfare in medicine, housing and support by the State preview later developments after the Second World War.

The chapter demonstrates how the State failed to take a uniform approach, both medical and social, to issues surrounding disabled civilians. This is not to argue, however, that civilian groups were comprehensively marginalised in favour of disabled ex-servicemen, although, as we will see, the war wounded did enjoy preferential treatment. The State developed, in the context of broader welfare reforms, strategies for coping with disabled children and civilians, while a range of charities and voluntary groups played a key role in their care. Such charities were developed for disabled people in the nineteenth century. The British Foreign Blind Association for Promoting the Education of the Blind was founded in 1868, and the British Deaf and Dumb Institute was established in Leeds in 1890.[2] There were other agencies that catered for physically disabled children such as the Invalid Children's Aid Association, which was set up in 1888.[3] Others followed in the early twentieth century, including the Central Council for the Care of Cripples and numbers of other specialist voluntary organisations.[4] By 1914, over 40 voluntary agencies had been formed just to aid children with disabilities.[5]

Disabled people endeavoured to fit into social and economic life, and much of this was supported through voluntary associations. In addition to work, disabled people also took part in sport and games, adapting themselves to social norms associated with recreation, and reflecting the nation's renewed interest in fitness. The chapter discusses the complex set of relationships between government and voluntary interests, the role of medicine and, for a select group, the nature of agency, which demonstrate the complex and interwoven experiences of disabled groups during the inter-war years.

Health, disease and disability

Before the First World War, the Liberal government's programme of social legislation slowly began to have a positive effect on the population's health. Attempts to solve problems caused by substandard housing were partially rectified by the Town Planning Act, which persuaded local authorities to build more dwellings.[6] Community benefits arrived in the shape of pensions for elderly people, which were paid by 1909, and there were attempts to improve children's health.[7] Indeed, there was a renewed interest in the nation's health, mainly because, as Helen Jones reminds us, 'there was one primary concern that dominated health reforms and that was the fear of the decline in the health of the British population'.[8] The disappointing physical condition of recruits who volunteered to fight in the South African War in 1899 shaped the debate surrounding degeneration. More than 35% of all volunteers in Britain were rejected as unfit for any type of military service.[9] Concerns surrounding poor levels of fitness resulted in the establishment of the Inter-departmental Committee on Physical Deterioration which reported its findings in 1904. These stated that children were born healthy but owing to a number of factors, including neglect, poor housing and inadequate medical care, their condition deteriorated and they became unfit.[10] This coincided with a growing rise in popularity and organisation of eugenics. The British Eugenics Education Society was established in 1907 and attempted to influence legislation to curb the reproduction of those deemed unfit, usually on account of 'mental deficiency'.[11]

After the First World War, the Ministry of Health was established in 1919, and its increasing responsibilities included caring for disabled people's health and the welfare of blind people.[12] An enquiry set up to advise the newly formed Ministry resulted in the Dawson Report of 1920, which recommended a State-administered medical service for the whole nation.[13] Later, post-war legislation tackled further problems associated with housing, public health, food, drugs and workers' compensation. However, the threat to those who were deemed unfit throughout the 1920s and 1930s was still very real, particularly for those deemed mentally unfit, as Sharon Morris highlights in her article on the inter-war debate on sterilisation, noting 'the general mood was becoming less tolerant, less disposed to improvement and more towards imposing restrictions'.[14]

A system of preventative medicine for children became popular after the First World War. The Ministry of Health under George Newman concentrated heavily on this holistic approach and areas of medicine such as orthopaedics aligned themselves with this new direction in policy.[15] Newman was highly influential as he held the office of Chief Medical Officer to the Ministry of Health and the Board of Education.[16] Newman was a pragmatist; he advocated alterations to the curriculum for children with learning difficulties, so that they might be taught to earn a living, as opposed to teaching them how to read and write.[17] The school medical inspection, which was inaugurated in 1907, together with school clinics, provided a means to practise this type of preventative medicine. Newman wrote:

> Medical inspection led to medical treatment or at least amelioration, and it is true to say that some millions of impaired or diseased children have been mended or healed. Thus disease and its results in childhood have been checked or restricted.[18]

In inspecting, monitoring and treating, Newman presented a triumvirate of methods to deal with the problem of disabled children.

Disease, danger and disability for children

A key issue in post-war health reform was the well-being of children; a desire to reduce effects of chronic illness and disability from disease. After the First World War, poverty still had a significant effect on a newborn's life expectancy; they were exposed to diseases or poor conditions which could cause disability or ongoing poor health. Mothers in poor physical condition were more likely to have babies weaker than those born to mothers in a better state of health, so working-class mothers were instructed to breast feed babies, or if they were unable, to feed them cow's milk, not the cheaper condensed milk.[19] Diseases like tuberculosis and rickets were relatively common; the Medical Research Council concluded in 1918 that 'in most civilised countries, rickets is one of the most common diseases of childhood'.[20] Rickets was caused by a lack of Vitamin D, which softened developing bones and was characterised by bowed legs. The same report also included findings showing that children with access to fresh air and exercise had less chance of developing rickets.[21]

Tuberculosis continued to cause concern, although its threat decreased through the 1930s. It was highly contagious and pulmonary TB had high numbers of fatalities. The disease could also settle in the spine, hip and joints, which weakened bones and reduced mobility.[22] By 1937 the government had introduced legislation to reduce the public's chances of contracting tuberculosis. The Tuberculosis (Attested Herds) Scheme was designed to test every herd in Britain to cull cows carrying it, but still had low impact by 1939 when TB remained responsible for the majority of deaths in 15–24 year olds.[23] Adherence to the tried methods of isolation and sanatoria, coupled with a public suspicious of vaccination and the numbers of doctors involved in the treatment of TB meant that take-up rates of the BCG vaccine, developed at the Pasteur Institute in the 1920s, were very low.[24]

Children and babies were affected by other diseases which had disabling effects. In 1910, an epidemic of cerebro-spinal meningitis caused deafness in a number of children.[25] More common causes of deafness in children were measles and scarlet fever.[26] Rheumatic fever, usually a result of scarlet fever, put a child at risk of becoming blind or deaf. Ophthalmia neonatorum, caused by bacteria passed from mother to child during birth, caused large numbers of blind children.[27] The infection was often due to undiagnosed or untreated gonorrhoea in the mother which infected the child during delivery.[28] Silver nitrate dropped in the infant's eyes effectively eliminated ophthalmia neonatorum, but diseases like measles were difficult to treat. By the 1930s, the death rates from these childhood diseases had fallen, as had the infant mortality rate, which had slipped to 57 per 1,000 births in 1935.[29]

Disease was not the only threat to children, the possibility of injury with permanently damaging effects could be just around the corner. The street as a playground provided exciting yet dangerous spaces for children. With new technology came added dangers, and an increase in the numbers of civilian disabled. As the number of cars on the road grew, poorer children in particular had to share their playground space, which was usually the street, with these dangerous companions. In 1909 there were 26,091 recorded injuries from cars.[30] Poorer children did not have access to a safe garden to play in, so they were more likely to be run over by cars.[31] As car ownership increased through the 1930s, so did numbers of pedestrian accidents. From 1930–38, there were 182,834 automobile injuries reported, mainly to pedestrians.[32] Between 1927 and 1937, 14,000 children were killed on the roads.[33] The speed limit, abolished in 1930, was re-introduced in 1934 in the Road Traffic Act, but set ten miles an hour higher. In the interests of safety, in the 1930s pedestrian crossings were introduced.[34] Accidents in industry remained high, but for children their playground environment could be a dangerous and disabling space.

Education for disabled children

With growing numbers of disabled children, and the developing charity and welfare culture of late nineteenth and early twentieth century Britain, attention focused on how children with disabilities should be educated. Essentially, education was to provide ways for these children to become useful within society, usually at low skilled jobs. Legislation which provided access to education had begun in the eighteenth century, but it was not until the nineteenth century that the number of educational establishments increased and disabled children were able to go to school in greater numbers.[35] Education became compulsory for children between 5 and 10 years old by 1880.[36] In 1893, the Elementary Education (Blind and Deaf) Act was passed and local authorities were charged with providing and maintaining schools for blind and deaf children. The Elementary Education (Defective and Epileptic Children) Act was passed in 1899.[37] One key aspect of the 1899 Act was that it separated epileptic children from those with mental difficulties.[38] This legislation, however, defined 'defective' children and placed no onus on local authorities to provide them with education. Although it was not compulsory, 116 schools were established for children with mental difficulties.[39] Moreover, there was significant variation in the number of establishments and standards provided for children with differing disabilities. During 1915–17, regulations were added to the Mental Deficiency Act to ensure that deaf children were not certified as having a learning difficulty.[40] The 1918 Education Act made schooling for disabled children mandatory; however, the Act was not fully enforced until the mid 1920s.[41] Disabled children were usually enrolled in 'special' or segregated education, where authorities believed their needs were catered for and effects of disabilities reduced or even cured.

Many children did not receive schooling specific to their needs. 'Special' schools educated children with a wide range of disabilities and were funded by voluntary and government agencies. In 1900, a child unable to walk would get minimal schooling; so legislation was enacted to ensure that disabled children received a certain standard of teaching.[42] The Education Act of 1918 entrusted local authorities with responsibility for teaching disabled children, but children continued to depend upon charities for support. The Invalid Children's Aid Association provided funds and schools for children affected by tuberculosis and those with physical disabilities.[43] By 1921 there were 308 institutions across Britain, providing day and residential facilities for attendees.[44] Unlike their able-bodied counterparts, disabled children were compelled by legislation to stay in school until they were 16. While at school, they were provided with medical care, including massage, remedial exercises and instruction in hygiene. Similar to blind and deaf children, they were accepted into institutions from a very young age. Chailey in Sussex admitted physically disabled children from 1 month to 16 years old.[45] The alternative was a place in mainstream education. Some local schools allowed disabled children to attend, but others did not. Children with cerebral palsy were effectively refused admittance on the grounds that they would upset other children. Other children could not go because they were unable to physically get to school, and for some because there was little by way of provision when they got there.

One of the more popular forms of hygienic education in the early twentieth century was open-air schools. This theory was not new in Britain; Hugh Owen Thomas, an orthopaedist in Liverpool, had placed babies in orange boxes outside the hospital where he worked.[46] The first school was established in Charlottenberg, Germany in 1904 and the first one was opened in Britain in 1907.[47] These schools removed children with tuberculosis and rickets and the sickly and malnourished from mainstream education and placed them in what was deemed to be a healthy environment. The regime consisted of outdoor classrooms, afternoon rest and an improved diet and was believed to be highly beneficial for children with poor health.[48] Removal merely from their unhealthy, crowded home environment often improved these children's health. However, the regime could be harsh. Children were compelled to sit in blankets in open-sided classrooms in winter and to endure afternoon naps outside wrapped in blankets.[49] Despite this Spartan regime, children's health improved, mainly due to better food, rest and exercise. By 1921, there were 55 open-air schools in England and Wales, and numbers increased throughout the 1930s.[50] By 1934 there were 95 day and 52 residential open-air schools with 14,701 students.[51] As these therapies enjoyed some success, other environmental cures increased in popularity, and gathered a following by adults. The Sunlight League was established in 1924 by Dr Caleb Saleeby. It advocated the benefits of sunshine, opening up Lansbury Lido in Hyde Park and starting a craze for bodily exposure to the elements. Sunlight did not have to be natural to improve health. The effects of sunlight were believed so beneficial that artificial sunlight treatment was given to children and adults.[52]

Some physically disabled children attended mainstream school, although generally blind and deaf children were sent to schools specifically catering for them. There were a higher proportion of residential facilities for blind and deaf children than for other disabilities as they had specific educational requirements.[53] The theory behind both removal from the home and segregation was that parents did not possess skills necessary to provide a solid education for a sensory deprived child.[54] Blind children were taught Braille by specially trained teachers, which was another reason for separate educational establishments. Segregation started early. Sunshine Schools for Blind Babies were opened from 1918, and provided a home and teaching facilities for children aged two to five years from low income homes, and for illegitimate children from birth.[55] The

Figure 1.1 Young children on Lorenz frames to correct bone deformities with nurses at the Royal Orthopaedic Hospital, Birmingham, 1926. Therapy consisted of exposure to sunshine and fresh air (reproduced with permission of the Royal Orthopaedic Hospital Trust, Birmingham)

Blind Persons Act of 1920 and the Education Act of 1921 legislated that blind children were schooled from 5 to 16 years old. Educational services for blind children were most advanced. Many schools concentrated on preparing students for the job market, often concentrating on music, either playing instruments or tuning pianos, and massage, as it was felt that blind people compensated for their blindness by heightened senses of sound and touch.[56] There were 67 schools for blind children by 1921; in addition a public school system for blind children had emerged. Worcester College, a public school for blind boys, opened in 1917. Unlike some physical disabilities which were associated with poverty, blindness cut across all classes. Chorleywood College for Blind Girls opened in 1921, which provided blind girls with higher standards of education.[57] While education for blind children was more advanced, there were more schools and a prescribed teaching method, deaf children's education was hampered by controversy surrounding teaching methods.[58] There was much debate surrounding oralism and signing from the nineteenth century which progressed throughout the twentieth. Deafness presented a particular problem for doctors as they were not able to judge whether or not hearing aids would help. Many deaf people purchased hearing aids that were useless.[59] Early hearing aids were cumbersome and not transportable, so deaf people had to sit in a room to use them. There was no government assistance for purchasing hearing aids before the National Health Service in 1948, and many hearing aids were imported from America, so they were expensive.

Essentially, the purpose of special schools, while providing a rudimentary education, was to prepare disabled children for different types of low skilled work.[60] One of the best known of these institutions was Chailey Heritage Craft School in Sussex.[61] At Chailey, children learned crafts; girls were taught weaving, knitting and needlework, and boys carpentry and shoe repair.[62] Once they left school, they were subject to the vagaries of the job market. There was no government-sponsored, organised system of sheltered workshops for civilians, although there were some for disabled ex-servicemen, until Remploy was established after the Second World War.[63] Prospects for disabled children were dependent, to a large extent, on social class. Class did not protect children from disability, but it did make dealing with its effects easier. Life opportunities for a disabled child were better if they were middle or upper class, as they were for children without disabilities. Should a child be disabled the better-off family could afford to pay for aids such as wheelchairs, private tutors and quality nutrition. Better diets and opportunities for health care ensured that middle-class disabled children withstood periods of illness. Education was not limited to the State system as private tutors were hired. As for work, it could be found in a protected environment and was not always low skilled or low paid, and was not always necessary for upper- or middle-class children.

Generally, diagnoses of disability were made by doctors. As medical practitioners began to understand more about disabilities, generally held assumptions such as the association between physical and mental disabilities gradually eroded. In addition, this led to suggestions that the educational system might be altered to benefit children with disabilities. Medical orthodoxy had long argued that hygiene was important for good health. Such thinking became a key issue in children's education and welfare. Good health was provided by a combination of fresh air, exercise and good nutrition. Medical inspections of children were established in 1907, and the School Meal Service provided the nation's poorer children with a daily meal.[64]

Regardless of class, disabled children often experienced extended periods of hospitalisation. As physicians experimented on disabled children's bodies, provision was made for their education. A key example of an institution such as this was Agnes Hunt's Home, in Baschurch, Shropshire, opened specifically for physically disabled children. In 1903, Hunt began an association with influential contemporary orthopaedic surgeon, Robert Jones.[65] The *Cripples' Journal*, a quarterly magazine published by Hunt and Jones from 1924, detailed the work of the hospital and examples of experiments in orthopaedic surgery.

Disabled workers

Working in factories and other heavy industry was dangerous. Accidents could lead to permanent disablement. Although there were significant improvements in working conditions since the nineteenth century, by the early twentieth century there was still little safety provision and no equipment to protect workers from hazards such as chemical spills or loud noise. The National Insurance Act of 1911 was an important piece of legislation, as it enabled workers to insure themselves against unemployment caused by accidents.[66] Although the State provided the means with which people could insure themselves, the government did not provide insurance, instead relying on a group of 'approved or friendly societies to assist the insured with benefits'.[67] According to statutes, the law decreed that an injured worker be paid 30 shillings a week, but there was no notion where this money would come from should a company find itself unable to pay its bills. Government did not provide any capital for benefits.[68] Coverage included health care and visits to the doctor, but this was only for insured workers. Other anomalies existed within the system. If a worker required substantial aids such as crutches or an artificial limb, these were considered 'additional benefits', to which the claimant was not usually entitled. Workers had to apply to charities such as the Royal Surgical Aid Society for these items.[69] Charities which provided limbs and surgical appliances had numbers of standard items, which often did not fit, as limbs were not specifically designed for the wearer. While National Insurance benefit paid for a period of recovery while a worker was ill or recovering from an accident, it did not provide for long-term disablement. For those whose sickness extended beyond the regulation 26 weeks, benefits were reduced by half.[70] The practice of persuading injured workers to sign away rights to compensation for a cash payout continued. Workers did not have bargaining strength if they suffered disabling injury; compensation was insufficient, and if the main earner was incapacitated the household could plunge headlong into poverty. People with disabilities were not given the opportunity to work. One article called for an Industrial Training Workshop for Cripples as it argued that cripples did not know anything about industry and employers knew nothing about cripples as workers.[71]

The exception to insufficient provision for seriously and permanently injured workers was the mining industry. Mining was one of the most dangerous occupations and workers' safety had long been an issue. In 1911, the Coal Mines Act established rules to protect miners from specific injuries and conditions associated with mining.[72] In addition to obvious dangers of working underground, there was added risk of pneumoconiosis, a lung condition caused by inhalation of dust.[73] A variety of conditions, such as 'beat' hand, knee or elbow, where the skin became swollen and infected from the constant use of equipment used to dig out coal were also common.[74] Serious cases of this condition sometimes required amputation. In 1924, the Medical Research Council examined mining at the 'insistence' of the Mines Department, which wished to reduce numbers of compensation causes associated with mining. The report noted, 'although general mortality is low, (miners) suffers more from occupational diseases which are subject to compensation than any other industry in the country'.[75]

In 1920 the Mining Industry Act supplied funding from a levy on coal to provide additional facilities for miners' recreation and education. In 1926, further legislation was enacted to install pithead baths, so miners could wash before they went home.[76] There were also special hospitals and medical services for miners at Berry Hill near Mansfield, which were largely a result of trade union activity.[77] While the State did not provide miners with the range of benefits for war wounded, mining was vital to the economy, so its workers warranted special treatment and concessions.

Whether workmen were well compensated or not, resources were not being put into a system of rehabilitating those injured in industry in the early part of the century.[78] By the middle of the 1930s steps were being taken to provide workers with facilities for rehabilitation. In 1935, the Delevingne Committee was set up to report on the established systems to repair workers' industrial injuries and make recommendations regarding rehabilitation, which was the first time that the term had been used in an official capacity by the government. It submitted its final report regarding injured workers 1939. The report concentrated principally on fractures, as a badly healed fracture could result in a lifetime of disability, and the establishment of an organised fracture service. It emphasised that remedial training for workers who sustained fractures remained inadequate, and underlined that it was a cause of residual disability.[79] It suggested that services in existence for ex-servicemen be expanded to include injured workers. The report referred specifically to artificial limbs and suggested the expertise of limb fitters at Roehampton, who made and repaired limbs solely for disabled ex-servicemen, be used to benefit injured workers. The system of curative workshops in hospitals and fracture clinics to minimise disablement ought to be available in hospitals throughout the country. However, the Committee did not suggest that the government fund this service; rather that money should be available under the Poor Law should patients qualify for assistance.[80]

During the 1930s, the government funded investigations into the effects of types of work, such as the Committee on Industrial Pulmonary Disease. There were queries about death rates and costs of compensation, which was said to be £100,000 in one year.[81] Recommendations were made, but no legislation to force companies to provide adequate standards of safety and welfare for workers.[82] The Workman's Compensation Act of 1937 made health and safety a priority.[83] Gradually expertise provided to disabled ex-servicemen became available to a select group of civilians; for example in 1936, some disabled workers were provided with artificial limbs from Roehampton. They were disabled in industry, primarily railways and mining, although a few non-industrial cases were accepted.[84] Although provision was made, often it was sub-standard in relation to provision for ex-servicemen, even though ostensibly the civilians were offered the same expertise as their Service counterparts. Ron Moore, a young civilian amputee noted: 'Roehampton delivered one pair of legs to me; there was no advice, no help, just the usual "good luck mate". The artificial legs rubbed blisters where they joined the tops of my legs and they often bled.'[85] The complicated fitting process and prolonged period at Roehampton for training in using a limb provided for disabled ex-servicemen were not offered to him.

Disabled civilians

The State and voluntary associations combined to care for disabled ex-servicemen and, to a lesser extent, children. Children with disabilities were seen as deserving of assistance, and there was a social responsibility in providing them with education. However, disabled adults found assistance difficult to obtain, as government and private enterprise were reluctant to shoulder responsibility for them. They did not have representation from organisations, nor did they benefit from emotive notions of sacrifice which surrounded the war disabled. Associations such as the Central Council for the Care of Cripples, established in 1919, felt there was too much emphasis on ex-servicemen, and disabled civilians were not getting the assistance to which they were entitled. But the government did little to alter this before 1939, and many people supported this stance. The President of the Central Council for the Care of Cripples, Fredrick Watson agreed:

> It is most desirable that so far as possible our social services are not under official jurisdiction. Their removal from the political arena has given them a direct touch with the working classes, which is of the highest possible importance. It holds the door open to co-operation in a sense that State-paid; State-aided control can never perform except at a further enormous increase on national debt and bureaucracy.[86]

Disabled civilians would have to wait for the establishment of the welfare state before they could expect some level of support from the State.

Children were viewed as redeemable and trainable. Adults, not of school age, and without the advantage of education, presented a 'considerable economic problem'.[87] The Central Council for the Care of Cripples began to tackle issues surrounding disabled adults in 1925.[88] In 1927, when the Voluntary Orthopaedic County Associations surveyed numbers of cripples in England by visiting homes around the country, they found many disabled adults living in family homes, hidden from the outside world and curiosity of local communities.[89] In his book on caring for disabled people published in 1930, Fredrick Watson noted, 'the houses of the poor in slums and country cottages revealed pitiful secrets of grown or partially grown men and women, usually quite unlettered, quite useless, quite hopeless and often incurable'.[90]

Efforts to highlight the plight of physically disabled civilians living in poverty were made by private individuals. Pamphlets were produced which tried to raise public awareness of the individual difficulties experienced by disabled people. One of these publications was the *National Cripples' Journal*, which was first published in 1930.[91] Unusually, it was written by disabled people, and not by groups of social reformers or medical professionals. It was sold door to door, and brought physically disabled people's experiences to public attention. Each issue stated their objective:

> We want to get national recognition for crippled people in the same way it is given to the blind, our comrades in distress. We do not want to be dependent on charity, but want National Workshops with a living wage for partially disabled cripples, and for the poor cripple in the spinal carriage we want a small weekly pension instead of Poor Relief. It is dreadful to be totally disabled and also in distress.[92]

The *National Cripples' Journal* was particularly concerned with problems of daily living which affected disabled people.[93] The *National Cripples' Journal* highlighted the realities for civilians, lacking in significant charitable support. At issue were problems securing work, which was a constant problem for disabled men and women. A conference in 1921 noted, 'Every cripple must eventually compete in the labour market with healthy rivals and unless he has been educated and taught a trade his position is hopeless.'[94]

Other special interest and health journals were published. *Sunlight*, the publication of the Sunlight League, was specific in its recommendation of sun as healthy. The *Cripples' Journal* produced by Robert Jones and Agnes Hunt was particularly directed at parents and also as a promotional tool for orthopaedic work at Oswestry.

In an effort to tackle problems, institutions to train disabled people for work were set up by the Ministry of Labour, in the 1930s, after some pressure from the Central Council for the Care of Cripples. The Queen Elizabeth Training College for the Disabled was established at Leatherhead in 1935.[95] Others soon followed; two years later St Loyes College, Exeter, for the Training and Rehabilitation of the Disabled opened.[96] The 1930s saw a burgeoning of curative workshops and residential factories, like Cripplecraft, where local authorities would fund places for disabled people to be trained for work.[97] Some workshops were closely associated with a hospital. The Stanmore Enterprise was linked to work with patients at the Royal National Orthopaedic Hospital, Stanmore, outside London. In 1937, the Enterprise opened and accepted young crippled men, paid for by their local authority, for training in trades including boot making, upholstery, sign writing, tailoring and watch repair.[98] Other training facilities were established, such as the Surrey Voluntary Association for Cripples in 1935. However, this was a private charity, and not provided with central funding. These workshops, whether paid for by donation or provided with State grants, supplied new sources of labour, which was important as Britain began to prepare for war in the latter stage of the 1930s.

The establishment of these workshops, so that disabled people could be trained for work, was important as employment remained one of the ways that disabled people were accepted by wider society. Not only was work fiscally rewarding, it provided disabled people with equality and reduced the stigma of being a 'burden'. It was important for people to see disabled people as useful members of society, not reliant on help wholly from State or charitable provision. The nature of work was fluid. The Central Committee for the Care of Cripples worked to achieve recognition for disabled civilians by promoting products they made. This method was not innovative; exhibitions and sales of work were used to promote products made by disabled ex-servicemen after the First World War. As exposure had provided the war disabled with new markets, the Committee organised four international exhibitions of 'Cripples' Work' in Exeter in 1929, Nottingham in 1931, Bristol in 1934 and Edinburgh in 1937.[99] Exhibitions were also organised at local level. Groups such as the Leicester Guild of Cripples made artificial flowers in order to support their services and to demonstrate to the public that disabled people could do a day's work.[100]

Agency and protest

Since disabled people received little support, and were often recipients of charitable donations which were irregular and dependent on public whim, it may be assumed that disabled people were a quiescent group. In many cases this was true. Public demonstration was not the province of disabled people, but for some it proved an effective method of highlighting conditions. Blind people were the most politically active disabled group during the immediate post-war period.[101] In April 1920, a group of 250 blind men from all over the country marched to London to insist that government 'accept responsibility for the direct maintenance of the Blind from Public Funds'.[102] In many ways their protest was a fait accompli as Parliament had already legislated for the Blind Persons Act of 1920. The more favourable conditions that blind people were given by legislation were in stark contrast to other disabled groups.[103] One reason why this action was so successful was that blindness was an acceptable and recognisable disability and many people were highly sympathetic to those without sight.[104] The overcoming of odds by the blind men of St Dunstan's, as we will see, had been promoted with great success, and blind institutions had usually been supported through the nineteenth century. However, it is notable that no blind war veterans from St Dunstan's participated in the march. St Dunstan's men were essentially a privileged group, who received many concessions and charitable donations, owing to a shrewd publicity campaign which made much of their status as 'heroic' war blind. There are a few seconds of film of the march in 1920 and grainy footage shows Trafalgar Square erupting with cheers as blind men walk into the centre of London. The march was repeated in 1936, with similar aims to those in 1920, and many men from workshops mainly from the north marched on London, this time with less fanfare. The Blind Marches of 1920 and 1936 were not a celebration or public display of blind workers' fitness. Quite the contrary, many participants were unable to walk all the way to London, despite having passed a fitness test in order to be included.[105] As reported in a National League of the Blind report: 'this was only to be expected in view of the fact that normally blind people do very little walking and most of the workshop occupations are more or less sedentary'.[106]

Sport, disability and charity

The exhortation 'Be fit – be fit! For Honour's sake, be fit' in Rudyard Kipling's book for boy scouts and girl guides to become fit and maintain standards of bodily health highlighted concerns surrounding fitness, particularly in the period following the First World War.[107] After the war, the State and various voluntary and medical bodies remained concerned about the nation's health. From the 1930s, the concentration on fitness, as a personal goal and a way to represent the nation's strength, was not limited to military training. In fact, the military had only embraced physical training from 1861.[108] The establishment of fitness clubs and workplace exercise in addition to government legislation made British people more aware of their bodies. Positive reports of fitness regimes in countries such as Germany further reinforced British desire to take its place as leader of nations in physical fitness. Poor results in Olympic Games throughout the 1920s and 1930s made the British population aware of bodily shortcomings in those purporting to represent the nation's fitness. It was not just a personal goal; it became a national responsibility, and by the outbreak of the Second World War fitness was a key aspect of individual war readiness. Mark Harrison notes, 'it therefore seemed reasonable to expect the dutiful citizen to keep him or herself fit to serve the country in whatever capacity might be deemed necessary'.[109]

Like work, playing sport and games was another way that disabled people could subscribe to society's norms. Sport was considered very important for children with disabilities as it strengthened them. Drill was conducted in schools, and gymnasiums were often put to use to

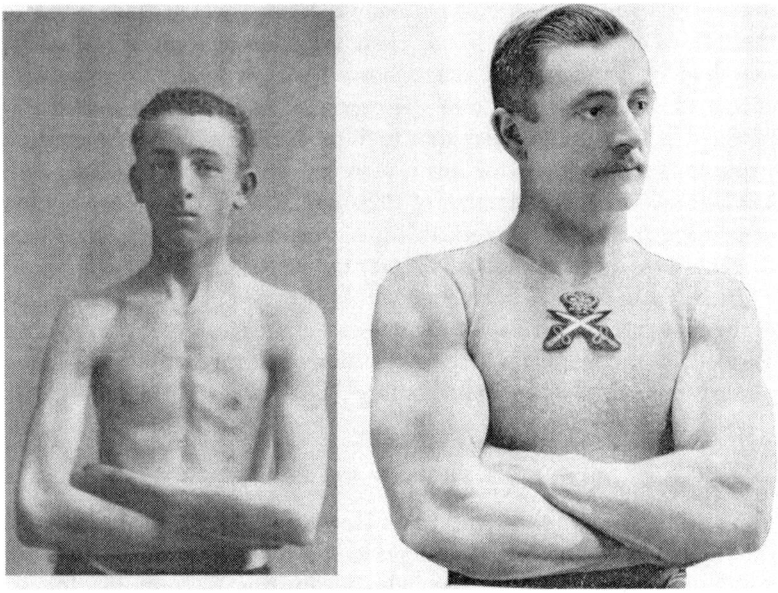

Figure 1.2 Prussian bodybuilder Eugen Sandow (1867–1925) was often used as an example to expose the number of men with poor physiques in Britain, and to inspire them to emulate the bodybuilder's physique (reproduced with permission of the Wellcome Library, London)

exercise the body and mind. Often charities provided disabled children with sporting equipment, as it was difficult to play sport because their clothing and footwear were often unsuitable.[110] Appeals for sports equipment became a regular feature of institutions. In the 1930s, the *Manchester Guardian* collected for its 'sports gear appeal'; it included schools for disabled children. A school thanked the *Manchester Guardian* for bats and balls it had received: 'The letters show that games, and rhythmic exercises, for which balls are required, play an important part in the lives of crippled children.'[111] Philanthropy involved provision of sporting facilities on a larger scale. In 1938, a playing field and cricket pavilion were presented to the Boys Heritage School at Chailey.[112] Charitable acts were not limited to gifts of equipment; schools organised local children to play games against disabled children. Girls from the famous public girls' school, Roedean and St Mary's Hall played stoolball against pupils from Chailey Heritage School.[113] Whether donations or activities were large or small, sport was a regular focus of charity for disabled children.

While disabled ex-servicemen, particularly those who were institutionalised, took part in sport, as we will see in the next chapter, and children in special schools did drill and played games as part of the curriculum, the sporting needs of disabled civilians were not well supported or catered for. Most activities organised for disabled civilians were done so by voluntary services. It was important, not only because of the benefits derived from a fitter body, but for a social function, as events provided an opportunity for disabled people to get together and enjoy recreational activities.

A Sports and Social Club was established by the National Institute for the Blind in 1919.[114] Exercises were taken up by blind civilians, including Margaret Morris's dancing and remedial exercise to music, which was more interesting than repetitive drill.[115] Blind people at the National Institute held a display of marching and physical exercise in London in 1927.[116] Social events were less prominent and fitness and games were concentrated upon when the National Sports' League for the blind was established in 1930, which limited events to swimming and rowing. However, eventually programmes were extended to include other activities.[117] In addition to sporting competitions, games nights were held in which people played draughts, chess and card games.[118] Dances were also popular, and meant physical proximity, which was one of the first steps to sexual contact. Sporting events were not limited to men. Blind women also took part; throwing the hammer and running races at several events in Manchester in 1936.[119] The National Institute held many sporting competitions that featured rowing, swimming and tennis, and activities such as rambling, but these were activities of blind civilians and not activities of war veterans, so there was little public interest in or support for them.

Gradually, disabled people began to take full advantage of the fitness craze that swept the nation, and began to establish themselves as players of games. Numbers of disabled people played golf; one-armed golfers had been playing on the courses of Britain since the late nineteenth century.[120] The Association of One-Armed Golfers was officially established in 1932, and the first championship for them was held the next year.[121] In 1934, an international one-armed tournament between Scotland and England took place.[122] Prior to that inaugural match, competitions were held at Hoylake and other golf courses, which pitted one-armed golfers against each other. Blind people were able to adapt golf in order to take part. A report in *The Beacon* told of a blind officer who played golf with the aid of his caddy, who rang a bell, allowing him to aim the ball in the correct direction.[123] Another report detailed a combination of disabilities when a blind golfer used a limbless caddie when he went around a course in Newcastle.[124]

However, despite efforts to include blind people in activities to make them fitter, it is evident that many blind people took very little exercise. For the *National Cripples' Journal*, one of its purposes was to appeal to Christians to assist local disabled people by subscribing, but another group singled out as potential benefactors were sportsmen 'who enjoy games we cannot'.[125] Since the journal had to rely for funds on door-to-door sales and subscribers sympathetic to the plight of physically disabled people, sales may have been reduced if articles were published about disabled people robustly enjoying games and sporting pursuits.[126] Indeed, many disabled people did not have the means to enjoy participating in sports and games.

While organisations for blind people established games and activities, other disabled groups engaged in activities providing a social and physical outlet. These efforts were mainly local; for example, in 1938 a social club for physically disabled people was established in Coventry, which organised a series of games with a group of disabled people from Leicester.[127] Named the Enterprise Club, it was originally for boys unable to join in physical forms of exercise played in boys' clubs. Many early games were played indoors and included billiards and archery. Owing to transport difficulties, competitions between cities were not as regular as participants may have wished, but whenever possible social and sporting competitions were organised.[128]

While the *National Cripples' Journal* steered away from sport, possibly from fear that it would affect donations, sports competitions were used by charities to raise money for disabled people. Raising money could take several forms. We will see in the next chapter how homes and hospitals used sports days for disabled ex-servicemen as fundraisers, and sought donations for sports equipment and facilities. Able-bodied sporting events also raised money for disabled people. Publicity awakened people's interest in institutions; in some cases, famous sporting personalities would visit and provide extra impetus for giving. Famous sportsmen lectured to disabled children on sport. Gus Platts, a leading boxer in the 1920s, went to the Sheffield School for the Blind to give students instruction in boxing.[129] Civilian disabled groups organised their own charity sporting events. These were usually small scale, yet they succeeded in making money; for example, the Enterprise Club in Coventry raised £100 from a boxing tournament.[130] Facilities were provided for disabled people using local community effort. The Courageous Comrades Club of Belfast, comprising students from Queen' College, assisted in laying hard tennis courts at a residential home for deaf people.[131]

Like the majority of the population, disabled people enjoyed watching sport. Ex-servicemen had more opportunity to attend sporting events as spectators, which we will see in the next chapter. War veterans were often provided with free tickets to see football matches, but there is little evidence to suggest that football clubs' largesse extended to other disabled groups. Occasionally, school children were taken to local matches.[132] The editor of the *National Cripples' Journal*, Len Inskip, wrote a letter to the *Star* newspaper in 1936, suggesting that disabled civilians be admitted without charge to football matches.[133] Like many other requests regarding transport concessions, the suggestion was not taken up by any football club.

Technology improved disabled people's lives and one of the most important in the inter-war period was radio, providing entertainment and a window on the world to a wide range of people. It could be particularly important for those who had difficulty with mobility. In addition to entertainment programmes, broadcasts included radio commentary of sports competitions.[134] The National Institute for the Blind wrote to the BBC in 1931 requesting that it did not curtail running commentaries of sports events.[135] Blind people were particularly keen listeners to radio broadcasts, so a Christmas Appeal for Wirelesses for the Blind was inaugurated in 1930; and many blind people had their own radio by the outbreak of the Second World War.[136] The ability to know the score in a football match was another way that people with disabilities were able to integrate themselves into cultural life.

Conclusions

Prior to the outbreak of the Second World War, 'disability' was a complicated conglomeration of different conditions. As this chapter has shown, disability took many forms and was a product of birth, disease, accident, poverty, work and war. Poor health and disability was of particular concern, as it reflected the health of the nation. Britain appeared to be falling behind its western counterparts and the rise of eugenics echoed the nation's concern with national fitness.

While war and work provided significant numbers of disabled people, the two groups were treated very differently, as we will see in the following chapter. Those disabled in war were given pensions, benefits and significant charitable support. The same could not be said for the industrial worker. As Bentley Gilbert reminds us, 'the nation gave a pension to a soldier but not to a man who served his country by a life of honest industry'.[137] After the First World War, the State was most fiscally supportive of disabled veterans, leaving disabled civilians to voluntary services and charity. However, it did not ignore the needs of disabled people completely. Indeed, its awareness surrounding disabled people grew throughout the 1930s, and with it developments in material aid, albeit at varying and low rates. During the 1930s, Factory Acts and medical committees concerned themselves with workers' health and accident prevention.

Children were better off as they were provided with education, of varying quality, even if it was only to prepare them for work, and were more likely to receive charitable support due to a combination of vulnerability and adaptability to training. They also responded well to medical interventions, mainly fresh air and exercise, which became standard methods of treatment from early in the twentieth century. The State recognised that through these preventative methods, some disabilities could be avoided or their impact on a disabled child's life greatly reduced. One of the key features of restoring disabled children's health was using sport and physical exercise. The ideology of exercise and sport as a way of maintaining a healthy body and creating good character was popular and promoted after the First World War. The certainty of another war in the 1930s also led to increased concentration by the State and voluntary services to improve the fitness of potential soldiers. This fitness mantra filtered into schools and factories, and disabled people with physical difficulties were believed to benefit from it. As this chapter has demonstrated, children at disabled schools found physical exercise and drill a part of their educative process.

Broad developments observed in schools and homes for disabled children echoed across all disabled groups. Disabled civilians developed their own recreations, reflecting the interest in exercises and sport across the whole nation. In doing so, disabled people, while still objects of charity and some State support, established their own sporting and social networks; yet their endeavours integrated them into cultural life while still leaving them on the perimeter of social and economic reality during the inter-war years.

Notes

1 Prunella Stack, 'National Fitness', in Joseph Mayers and Bernard Spiers (eds), *Where Do We Go From Here?* (London, 1938), 129.

2 The British Foreign Blind Association for Promoting the Education of the Blind became the Royal National Institute for the Blind (RNIB). The National Bureau for Promoting the General Welfare of the Deaf was established in 1911 and eventually became the Royal National Institute for Deaf People (RNID).

3 Kate Rackham, *The Invalid Children's Aid Association: The First Ninety Years* (London, 1977), 5.

4 The Central Council for the Care of Cripples was formed in 1919. See Joan Anderson, *A Record of Fifty Years' Service to the Disabled 1919–1969* (London, 1969); Frederick Watson, *Civilization and the Cripple* (London, 1930); and Roger Cooter, *Surgery and Society in Peace and War: Orthopaedics and the Organisation of Modern Medicine 1880–1948* (Basingstoke, 1993), 155–7.

5 Anne Borsay, 'Disciplining Disabled Bodies: The Development of Orthopaedic Medicine in Britain, c. 1800–1939', in David M. Turner and Kevin Stagg (eds), *Social Histories of Disability and Deformity* (Abingdon, 2006), 100.

6 Only 11,000 houses were built between 1909 and 1915. Bentley B. Gilbert, *British Social Policy 1914–1939* (London, 1970), 138.

7 The Royal Commission on the Aged Poor submitted its report in 1895. P.H.J.H. Gosden, *Self-Help: Voluntary Associations in the Nineteenth Century* (London, 1973), 280–81.

8 Helen Jones, *Health and Society in Twentieth Century Britain* (London, 1994), 21.

9 Anne Hardy, *Health and Medicine in Britain Since 1860* (Basingstoke, 2001), 40.

10 Jane Lewis, 'Health and Health Care in the Progressive Era', in Roger Cooter and John Pickstone (eds), *Companion to Medicine in the Twentieth Century* (London, 2003), 85.

11 Dorothy Porter, *Health, Civilization and the State: A History of Public Health From Ancient to Modern Times* (London, 1999), 168.

12 W.M. Frazer, *A History of English Public Health 1834–1939* (London, 1950), 350.

13 Roy Porter, *The Greatest Benefit to Mankind* (London, 1997), 642.

14 Sharon Morris, '"Human Dregs at the Bottom of Our National Vats": The Interwar Debate on Sterilization of the Mentally Deficient', in Turner and Stagg (eds), *Social Histories of Disability and Deformity*, 154.

15 Borsay, 'Disciplining Disabled Bodies', 111.

16 Steve Sturdy, 'Sir George Newman', *Dictionary of National Biography*, on-line.

17 J.S. Hurt, *Outside the Mainstream: A History of Special Education* (London, 1988), 144–5.

18 Sir George Newman, *The Building of a Nation's Health* (London, 1939), 213.
19 Jones, *Health and Society in Twentieth Century Britain*, 24.
20 Medical Research Council, *A Study of Social and Economic Factors in the Causation of Rickets* (1918), FD 4/20, National Archives, London, 9. In 1919 it was estimated that 80% of children in London schools had rickets. Frazer, *A History of English Public Health*, 407.
21 Medical Research Council, *A Study of Social and Economic Factors in the Causation of Rickets*, 72.
22 Thomas Dormandy, *The White Death: A History of Tuberculosis* (London, 1999), 335.
23 The testing scheme continued, but by 1939 was testing only 3% of all herds. Medical Research Council, *Report of the Committee on Tuberculosis in Wartime* (1942), FD 4/246, National Archives, London, 5.
24 Hardy, *Health and Medicine in Britain Since 1860*, 101.
25 M.G. McLoughlin, *A History of the Education of the Deaf in England* (Gosport, 1987), 193.
26 Medical Research Council, *Hearing and Speech in Deaf Children* (1937), FD 4/221, National Archives, London, 3.
27 Ian Fraser, *Whereas I was Blind* (London, 1942), 85.
28 It was estimated that more than half the cases of blindness in children aged 7–16 was caused by venereal disease in the parents. *The Lancet* (4 April 1925), 717.
29 Newman, *The Building of a Nation's Health*, 311.
30 Sean O'Connell, *The Car in British Society: Class, Gender and Motoring 1896–1939* (Manchester, 1998), 115.
31 Ibid., 119.
32 For every fatal accident there were 30 non-fatal ones. *The Lancet* (16 November 1935), 1117.
33 C.V. Godfrey, *Roadsense for Children* (Oxford, 1937), 8.
34 Joe Moran, 'Crossing the Road in Britain, 1931–76', *Historical Journal*, Vol. 49, No. 2 (2006), 478.
35 McLoughlin, *A History of the Education of the Deaf*, 46.
36 Anne Borsay, *Disability and Social Policy in Britain Since 1750* (Basingstoke, 2005), 106.
37 Seth Koven, 'Remembering and Dismemberment', *American Historical Review* (October 1994), 1172.
38 'The Evolution of Special Schools', *Special Schools Quarterly*, Vol. 1, No. 2 (March 1911), 4.
39 D.G. Pritchard, *Education and the Handicapped 1760–1980* (London, 1983), 195.
40 McLoughlin, *A History of the Education of the Deaf*, 47.
41 Anderson, *A Record of Fifty Years' Service*, 59.

42 In 1900 if a child received any education from the authorities it was a 20 minute session twice a week provided by an 'untrained visitor'. Many did not learn how to read or write. Rackham, *Invalid Children's Aid Association*, 27.

43 TB Homes and open-air schools were opened in 1909, 1913 and 1914 for boys and girls by the Invalid Children's Aid Association. Rackham, *Invalid Children's Aid Association*, 15.

44 These included children who were blind (67), epileptic (6), deaf (50), physically disabled (75), tubercular (55), and those in open-air establishments (55). Board of Education, *Annual Report of the Chief Medical Officer of the Board of Education* (London, 1921), 117.

45 C.W. Kimmins, *Chailey Heritage 1903–1948* (London, 1948), 7.

46 Watson, *Civilization and the Cripple*, 18.

47 Albert J. Green, 'Open Air Schools for Delicate Children', *Special Schools Journal*, Vol. XX, No. 2 (June 1930), 39.

48 Lewis Williams, 'Open-Air Schools', *Special Schools Quarterly*, Vol. 3, No. 2 (June 1913), 34.

49 Some children complained that during a nap session they had to lie on their right side only – if they lay on their left side or their back they were beaten. Frances Wilmot and Pauline Saul, *A Breath of Fresh Air: Birmingham's Open-Air Schools 1911–1970* (Chichester, 1998), 194.

50 Five of these schools were residential and 50 were day schools. Board of Education, *Annual Report of the Chief Medical Officer of the Board of Education* (1921), 132.

51 Ralph P. Williams, 'Open-Air Schools for Delicate Children', *Special Schools Journal*, Vol. XXIV, No. 1 (February 1934), 16.

52 'Commemoration of Death of Dr Saleeby', *Sunlight*, Vol. 5, No. 1 (Summer 1943), 4.

53 Out of a total of 67 schools for the deaf, 21 were residential and 29 were day. This is in contrast to the physically disabled, where out of 75 schools, 60 were day. Board of Education, *Annual Report of the Chief Medical Officer of the Board of Education* (1921), 122.

54 Ida Mann and Antoinette Pirie, *The Science of Seeing* (London, 1946), 199.

55 RNIB Archives, *National Institute for the Blind Reports 1946–1951*.

56 W.H. Illingworth, *History of the Education of the Blind* (London, 1910), 47, 53.

57 *The Lancet* (23 July 1921), 214.

58 For an example of the controversy see Iain Hutchison, 'Oralism: A Sign of the Times? The Contest for Deaf Communication in Education Provision in Late Nineteenth Century Scotland', *European Review of History*, Vol. 14, No. 4 (December 2007), 481–502.

59 Deaf people were warned to ensure that they were buying their aids from a reputable dealer as dishonest suppliers had duped many.

60 One of the first of these was the Cripples' Home and Industrial School for Girls, Winchmore Hill, Buckinghamshire in 1851. The first one for boys was Wright's Lane Home for Crippled Boys, Kensington. Watson, *Civilization and the Cripple*, 113.

61 Chailey was formed from a group in London originally established by Grace Kimmins which was called the League of the Brave Poor Things. See National Archives files ED 62 and MOH 102 for further details on Chailey Heritage School.

62 Kimmins, *Chailey Heritage 1903–1948*, 82.

63 J.L. Edwards, 'Remploy: An Experiment in Sheltered Employment for the Severely Disabled in Great Britain', *International Labour Review*, Vol. 77 (1958), 147.

64 John Welshman, 'Physical Education and the School Medical Service 1907–1939', *Social History of Medicine*, Vol. 9, No. 1 (April 1996).

65 He became the Home's doctor that year and by 1907 the small concern had re-established itself as a hospital. Agnes Hunt, *Reminiscences* (Shrewsbury, 1935), 119, 123.

66 The benefits did not start until January 1913. Gilbert, *British Social Policy*, 103.

67 Gosden, *Self-Help*, 282.

68 J.L. Smyth, 'Industrial Accidents and Rehabilitation', in Invalid Children's Aid Association/Central Council for Care of Cripples, *The Welfare of Cripples and Invalid Children* (London, 1935), 91.

69 The charitable organisation, the Royal Surgical Aid Society provided items such as spectacles and artificial limbs to those unable to afford them. Ursula Keeble, *Aids and Adaptations* (London, 1979), 23.

70 Charles Webster, 'Health, Welfare and Unemployment During the Depression', *Past and Present*, No. 109 (1985), 211.

71 Cecil E. Kny, 'Rehabilitation of Cripples', in Invalid Children's Aid Association/Central Council for Care of Cripples, *The Welfare of Cripples and Invalid Children*, 83.

72 Donald Hunter, *The Diseases of Occupations* (London, 1978), 223.

73 Ninety per cent of cases of paraplegia in the twentieth century can be attributed to accidents in mines during peacetime. Ibid., 1116.

74 Medical Research Council, *Report on Miners 'Beat Knee', 'Beat Hand' and 'Beat Elbow'* (1924), FD 4/98; Medical Research Council, 'Chronic Pulmonary Disease in South Wales Coalminers' (1924), FD 4/243, National Archives, London.

75 Medical Research Council, *Report on Miners 'Beat Knee', 'Beat Hand' and 'Beat Elbow'*.

76 Hunter, *Diseases of Occupations*, 226. See also Barry Supple, *A History of the British Coal Industry*, Vol. 4 (Oxford, 1987).

77 Cooter, *Surgery and Society in Peace and War*, 207.

78 *The Lancet* (6 April 1935), 817.

79 *British Medical Journal* (19 August 1939), 418.

80 Ministry of Health, *Final Report of the Inter-departmental Committee on the Rehabilitation of Persons Injured by Accidents* (London, 1939) (Delevingne Committee).

81 Medical Research Council, *Physical Methods for the Estimation of Dust Hazard in Industry* (1935), FD 4/199, National Archives, London. The year in question is not detailed, but the Committee on Industrial Pulmonary Disease was established in 1930, so presumably this cost occurred between 1930 and 1934.

82 Ibid. Lomax and Whytlaw-Gray recommended that stone masons should not work in enclosed spaces, respirators should be used and dust should be swept off stones regularly. Jones, *Health and Society in Twentieth Century Britain*, 71.

83 See Peter Bartrip, 'The Rise and Decline of Workmen's Compensation', in Paul Weindling (ed.), *The Social History of Occupational Health* (London, 1985), 157–79.

84 From October 1936 to October 1943 there were 3151 civilian cases dealt with as well as an unspecified number of private cases. Commemorative leaflet *Queen Mary's (Roehampton) Hospital 1915–1943.*

85 Steve Humphries and Pamela Gordon, *Out of Sight: The Experience of Disability 1900–1950* (Plymouth, 1992), 124.

86 Watson, *Civilisation and the Cripple*, 107.

87 Ibid., 34.

88 Anderson, *A Record of Fifty Years' Service*, 13.

89 Robert Jones and Agnes Hunt, *The Heritage of Oswestry 1960–1961* (Oswestry, 1961), 70.

90 Watson, *Civilisation and the Cripple*, 36.

91 It was renamed *The Voice of the Disabled* in 1969, and was published until 1980.

92 *National Cripples' Journal*, No. 7 (January 1931), 1.

93 One of their campaigns was to persuade the railway companies to cease charging a disabled person more than double the normal fare when they travelled with their invalid chair. *National Cripples' Journal*, No. 17 (1933), 6.

94 *The Lancet* (6 August 1921), 305.

95 Anderson, *A Record of Fifty Years' Service*, 15.

96 Lord William Beveridge, *Voluntary Action: A Report on Methods of Social Advance* (London, 1948), 244.

97 Cripplecraft was a workshop in Sevenoaks where disabled people made toys. Joan Simeon Clarke, *Disabled Citizens* (London, 1951), 176–7.

98 *British Medical Journal* (17 July 1937), 129.

99 The fifth exhibition, scheduled for 1939, was cancelled due to the outbreak of war. Anderson, *A Record of Fifty Years' Service*, 26.

100 Derek Seaton, *From Strength to Strength: The History of the First 100 Years of the Leicester, Leicestershire and Rutland Guild of Disabled People 1898–1998* (Leicester, 1998), 46.

101 Even previously, the blind organised in a way that other disabled groups did not. In 1899 workshops for blind people were registered as independent trade unions; in 1902 they affiliated with the Trades Union Congress and in 1909 the Labour Party. Campbell and Oliver, *Disability Politics*, 47.

102 Letter from the General Secretary of the National League of the Blind of Great Britain and Ireland, to all sub-sections of the League (no date, presumably 1936), MH 55/590, National Archives, London.

103 These included Old Age Pensions provided for the blind at age 50, and the local authority was given responsibility to provide for blind welfare. Southern Regional Association for the Blind, *Chronological Summary: Legislation Relating to the Blind* (London, 1965), 6.

104 As a comparison, here are two quotes from the same source. 'Blindness is a handicap so severe that it has long gripped the sympathy of civilised peoples.' Contrast the previous statement with, 'Deaf intelligent children can grow into an adult with attributes so nearly normal that he can take his place amongst ordinary citizens.' Clarke, *Disabled Citizens*, 24, 99.

105 No women were selected to go on the march. *North Mail* (23rd September 1936).

106 Memo from V.L. Harkness to Mr Roundell, GI District re: Blind Marchers (1936), MH 55/590, National Archives, London.

107 Rudyard Kipling, Preface to *Land and Sea Tales for Scouts and Guides* (London, 1923).

108 Newman, *The Building of a Nation's Health*, 269.

109 Mark Harrison, *Medicine and Victory* (Oxford, 2008), 25.

110 *Special Schools Journal*, Vol. 24, No. 3 (October 1934), 65. See also Welshman, 'Physical Education and the School Medical Service', 41.

111 *Manchester Guardian* (30 May 1935).

112 Kimmins, *Chailey Heritage*, 31.

113 Ibid., 82.

114 *The Beacon*, Vol. 4, No. 43 (July 1920), 10.

115 Margaret Morris described her movements as 'A method of Physical Education and Creative Dance combining therapeutic and aesthetic values'. Margaret Morris, *Creation in Dance and Life* (London, 1972), preface. See also Margaret Morris, *My Life in Movement* (London, 1969) and Joan W. White, *Margaret Morris: A Prophet Without Honour* (Glasgow, 1980).

116 *The Beacon*, Vol. 9, No. 122 (February 1927), 14.

117 *The New Beacon*, Vol. 14, No. 160 (April 1930), 65.

118 Ibid., Vol. 14, No. 166 (October 1930), 210.

119 *Manchester Guardian* (2, 27 June 1936).

120 *Golf* (25 March 1892), 20.

121 *Royal and Ancient Golfer's Handbook* (London, 1998), 949.

122 Webster Evans, *Encyclopaedia of Golf* (London, 1971), 156.

123 *The Beacon*, Vol. 4, No. 43 (July 1920), 14.

124 *Newcastle Evening Chronicle* (October 1933).

125 *National Cripples' Journal*, No. 7 (January 1931), 1.

126 Before the Second World War there are no articles in the *National Cripples' Journal* about disabled people playing sport. This is interesting as Len Tasker, of the Enterprise Club in Coventry, was involved in the *National Cripples' Journal*, becoming its editor on Len Inskip's death in 1955, and was heavily involved in organising sports and games before the war.

127 *The Coventry Cripples' Social Club* (1943), 8.

128 Interview with Len and Peggy Tasker, April 1998.

129 *The Beacon*, Vol. 4, No. 41 (May 1920), 9.

130 *The Enterprise Club: 50th Anniversary Brochure* (1980), 5.

131 *British Deaf Times*, Vol. 31, Nos 367–8 (July–August 1934), 89.

132 Occasionally disabled children at the Wingfield-Morris Orthopaedic Centre were taken to sporting matches in their spinal carriages by hospital visitors. W.B. Foley, 'The Cripple Child', *Journal of State Medicine*, Vol. 41 (1933), 724.

133 There is no further mention of the response to the letter, so presumably it did not have the desired effect. *National Cripples' Journal*, No. 30 (1936), 10.

134 Sporting commentaries were only commenced in 1927 when the BBC changed from a company to a corporation because of restrictions on agreements with news agencies. John Ford, *This Sporting Land* (London, 1977), 223.

135 *The New Beacon*, Vol. 15, No. 173 (May 1931), 108.

136 Lord William Beveridge and A.F. Wells, *The Evidence for Voluntary Action* (London, 1949), 220.

137 Bentley B. Gilbert, *The Evolution of National Insurance in Great Britain: The Origins of the Welfare State* (London, 1966), 71.

2

Attitude: disabled ex-servicemen after the First World War

The First World War was a catalyst in increasing the public's awareness of disabled people. The steady realisation of the levels of brutality on the Western Front was accompanied by visible signs of war; men returned home without sight, hearing, limbs, faces or minds. The general spirit of war remembrance, and a sense of society's debt to the sacrifice of its male youth, moved these men into a privileged place in the nation's consciousness, albeit within a context of usual standards of care, treatment and support.

This chapter examines the early inception of rehabilitative therapy as it was practised during the First World War and discusses its implications in relation to disabled servicemen. In particular, the chapter will highlight the role of sport as a type of physical and mental therapy. When historians discuss bodies disabled in war they often explain the ways in which war-disabled bodies were made heroic and deserving as a result of their sacrifice. The ways in which disability was caused had important ramifications for its place on the hierarchy of disablement, and the public's perceptions of such disability as deserving. The blind body is in the majority a whole one, unlike that of the amputated body, and therefore elicited different responses. In order to make sense of all this we must first understand the way that disabled ex-servicemen were seen, categorised and recognised by those around them. Disability cannot be seen in cultural isolation, but only in reference to the majority of able-bodied. It is these people, the broad society, who judge the ways in which disabled bodies are 'useful'. Society was paternalistically driven by an altruistic need to combat the deprivations of disability in its war wounded. This meant that disabled ex-servicemen occupied a charitably constructed place in the public's sympathy, which was culturally constructed in an inequitable fashion. A society that had been through the horrors of war, and its associated loss and feelings of guilt, was driven by the belief in rebuilding. For such a society the pathetic remains of ex-servicemen (whether limbless, mad, dirty, drunken or vagrant) that were seen begging on the street were a horrific and embarrassing sight. What more pleasant for a society faced with the fallen heroes in the gutter than the sight of the upright, rehabilitated and hard-working disabled war veteran?

Joanna Bourke reminds us that bodies in the First World War were intended to be mutilated.[1] Mutilation could take various forms; thousands were blinded, deafened, lost limbs or faces, while others lost their sanity.[2] The First World War exposed the combatants to maiming and wounding on an unprecedented scale, producing huge numbers of disabled men. Young, fit men were monstrously disabled. These returning victims of war had a significant impact on the public. Disabled ex-servicemen could not be easily hidden or segregated in schools.

As more and more maimed, deaf, blind and disfigured soldiers were discharged, support services were established to care for and provide services and training. Some of these services were well organised and funded, ready to help disabled ex-servicemen to a life of usefulness and activity.[3] Their main function was to provide support for the men and in doing so help to renegotiate their masculine identity. This chapter will present patient experiences in two different institutionalised settings. St Dunstan's was a long-term training centre for blinded servicemen and the Star and Garter Home was established to house disabled ex-servicemen. These two institutions were not hospitals that provided medical treatment for the wounded, as detailed in Jeffrey S. Reznick's account of the Shepherd's Bush Military Hospital; rather, they provided an environment where medical and social restoration was practised, and endeavoured to make these efforts successful in the longer term.[4] Both the Star and Garter and St Dunstan's utilised sport to enforce normal standards of masculinity, and the chapter concentrates heavily on the sports and games played and what they meant for the men at these institutions and the public who watched them.

As we will see, while there was no established system of rehabilitation in the First World War, there were some features that formed the basis of rehabilitation, but I would argue that much of this stayed within medicine. Some military doctors realised that it was not feasible, nor was it desirable, for soldiers to be operated on once and be sent back to the front lines. In some cases they required more surgery or more therapy to make an improved recovery. One of the hallmarks of rehabilitation is the systematised approach, which requires a number of services to work together with one goal in mind. Where we see the beginning of rehabilitative therapy is in the cooperation between doctors, voluntary associations or charities and the War Office. While the seeds of rehabilitation were sown, it was not until the Second World War that a modern, organised system of rehabilitation came into being.

Medicine and war

In the First World War, conditions at the front were horrific. Soldiers injured by machine guns and shells were prone to infection and gas gangrene, so amputations were common.[5] Without the benefit of modern antibiotics, large flesh wounds took a long time to heal.[6] A badly set femur meant a soldier would have a permanent limp; a constant reminder of his war service. The effect of injury was exacerbated by delays in treatment caused by slow horse-driven ambulances used during the early stages of the conflict.[7] In addition, privations of war also exacerbated hidden illnesses. It was impossible to effectively screen those with TB, and such an infectious disease meant that many soldiers contracted it during their service.

While injuries were shocking and severe, advances were made in medicine to combat their scale and seriousness. Hospital trains were in use by 1915 and treatment was carried out in more hygienic surroundings where possible.[8] Treatment became specialised. X rays became 'the eyes' of the war surgeon and as portable types were designed, meant that surgeons could identify the location of shrapnel and bullets.[9] By 1915, the Thomas splint was in general use and prevented the residual effects of badly set bones.[10] At his unit in Aldershot, Harold Gillies developed maxillofacial surgery for soldiers whose faces had been shattered by gunshot wounds and shrapnel.[11] The pressure to return wounded soldiers to the front as quickly as possible resulted in numbers of badly repaired facial injuries, and Gillies insisted that his patients be provided with a number of operations so that they would be able to look at the public without them turning away.[12] Mobile hygiene units ensured that the health of soldiers was less affected by preventable disease.[13] In establishing specialist fracture wards and convalescent depots, men recovered to provide the endless supply of bodies required for mass warfare. Despite medicine's best efforts and scientific and technological progress, many servicemen were invalided out of the Forces with permanent disabilities.

Figure 2.1 Soldiers practising walking in frames with their new artificial limbs at Queen Mary's Roehampton during the First World War. This hospital was a specialist centre that treated the majority of the amputees from the First World War (reproduced with permission of the Imperial War Museum)

For the 41,050 men who lost one or more limbs, artificial ones were provided. The majority were manufactured and fitted at Queen Mary's at Roehampton, which opened the same year as St Dunstan's, and was the main limb-fitting hospital for ex-servicemen in England.[14] Huge numbers of ex-servicemen with amputations swelled numbers of beds.[15] Soldiers were taken to Roehampton where the new limbs were made, fitted and recipients were trained in their use.[16] Training in many types of craft, including limb making, were faught and the employment bureau at Roehampton helped amputees find work. Patients' stays were temporary until they were deemed fit enough to return home.[17]

State support for disabled ex-servicemen

The Ministry of Pensions was established in 1916 and its main function was to provide war wounded with pensions. By 1918, 400,000 ex-servicemen received pensions.[18] Amounts awarded to men varied; pension rates were higher for those disabled in the First World War than for previous conflicts.[19] Pensions were calculated by percentages. The loss of one arm and one eye, two or more limbs or severe facial disfigurement qualified as 100% disability.[20] A Constant Attendance Allowance was available to those who required permanent care.[21] Pensions were also awarded when military service caused diseases such as tuberculosis, or if a previous condition was exacerbated by war service.[22]

Local War Pensions Committees were responsible for organising training and medical treatment after discharge.[23] In addition, benefits extended to ex-servicemen's wives and children, and were provided using a complicated set of rules.[24] Awarding disability pensions was controversial, as government wanted to minimise costs. Ex-servicemen turned down by Local Committees, known to be dubious about the effect of ex-servicemen's disability on their earning capacity, had recourse to the Appeals Tribunals, which rarely overturned Committees' views.[25] Certain factors affected pensions, including rank.[26] A contemporary American study noted that 'the British policy of complete restoration is rather less democratic than our own, since it recognises social status'.[27] Although the State assumed responsibility for provision for its war disabled, administration was undertaken by regional committees. The government did not stifle individual enterprise. One handbook noted: 'It means that a department of governance with a Cabinet Minister is charged with seeing that the state's responsibility is carried out, but that this department is expected to fulfil its function largely by stimulating local and private effort.'[28]

In addition to its main function of awarding and controlling pensions, the Ministry of Pensions provided opportunities for disabled men to retrain: 'It is our duty to put him back, to restore him, in fact, to society, healed and mended in body and mind as far as possible.'[29] Centres were set up by State and voluntary agencies on their own premises. The system of curative workshops, established at crippled children's institutions, provided a template to training ex-servicemen after 1918.[30] The Lord Roberts Memorial Workshops had been set up by the Soldiers' and Sailors' Help Society in 1904 and trained disabled ex-servicemen in handicrafts.[31] Other charities' remit was broad and less centred on training disabled ex-servicemen. From 1920, the 'Not Forgotten' and 'Lest We Forget' Associations were created to take disabled ex-servicemen on outings.[32]

Initially, the Ministry of Pensions was responsible for training disabled ex-servicemen, but in 1919 this responsibility was transferred to the Ministry of Labour. Between 1919 and 1924, 88,000 men were retrained under the Ministry of Labour's Industrial Training Schemes.[33] Programmes were established to provide preferential employment for those who had been disabled. Schemes such as the King's National Roll, which provided protected employment for war disabled, ensured it was financially beneficial for companies to employ them.[34] Established in 1919 by Royal Proclamation, the Roll required companies to fulfil specific criteria before they were able to use a special seal, which identified their participation. To be a member meant employing 5% of pensioned ex-servicemen, which meant that preference was shown for government contracts.[35] The problem for disabled ex-servicemen was that 20% disability was given equal weight to 100% rating, so employers took on those less disabled and were still able to fulfil the criteria.[36] Although well intentioned, the scheme rapidly lost favour with employers, so that in 1922 only 39% of firms renewed their membership.[37] As a number of disabled ex-servicemen were still unemployed, a Committee was established 'On Training and Employment in Disabled Men', which reported its findings in August 1922, after a visit to Germany to examine a scheme that compelled employers to employ 2–3% of war disabled.[38]

Employment opportunities for more severely disabled ex-servicemen were problematic, and these special cases tended to become the responsibility of ex-servicemen's associations, which tried to find jobs for them. Charitable societies were established alongside official State programmes and supported disabled ex-servicemen in getting retrained. They also provided assistance for specific conditions. The Disabled Society was established in 1916 and registered under the War Charities Act.[39] Its main function was providing information on artificial limbs, arranging for training and disseminating information on caring for amputated limbs; 'a healthy body and a healthy stump' were considered vitally important to a limbless man.[40] The Society also agitated for provision of lighter limbs, made from aluminium, which replaced the heavy wooden ones initially provided.[41] In 1921, the Disabled Society had amalgamated with the British Legion, and asked it to provide funds to set up a sheltered workshop for men who had difficulty gaining work. The Legion provided £2,000 so severely disabled men found employment making poppies into floral tributes for Remembrance Day.[42]

Although assistance with training was offered, many disabled ex-servicemen did not take it up, although it was clearly in their best interests as 'the man is not compelled to take training or treatment, but if he refuses to take the treatment recommended, half his pension may be withheld'.[43] In 1917, the Secretary to the Ministry of Pensions lamented that less than 15% of disabled men took up training, despite benefits such as allowances and travel expenses if training was over two miles from home.[44] The reason for a lack of interest may have been because unskilled workers' wages continued to increase two years after the war.[45] During this period, jobs were available, and war veterans threw themselves back into the melée of civilian life.

The British Legion

The British Legion became a staunch and protective ally of disabled ex-servicemen.[46] A disparate number of groups represented disabled ex-servicemen immediately following the war, but in 1921 many amalgamated to form the British Legion, which had a more influential voice.[47] After its formation, the Legion took steps to ensure that the war disabled were well supported.[48] It agitated for preferential treatment for employment for disabled ex-servicemen and sought to abolish Ministry of Pension rules that claims for pensions for war-related disability must be made within seven years of the war's end. Initially, the Legion funded itself mainly from subscriptions and appeals; later, it financed its operations with profits from the British Legion Disabled Men's Industries and receipts from Poppy Day.[49]

British ex-servicemen had less support from large-scale centralised assistance and benefits than their German counterparts, as Deborah Cohen has detailed in her comparative study of Germany and Britain.[50] Comparatively, British disabled ex-servicemen were provided with a less centralised service than in Germany. Nonetheless, German ex-servicemen were better provided for than their contemporaries in Britain, as the State assumed unprecedented responsibility for disabled ex-servicemen.[51] In Britain a separate Ministry was established, aids such as prostheses were provided free, and training for work, however unsuccessful, was made available. Should the State system fail them, the war disabled had an influential organised association in the British Legion to represent them. When complaints were levelled at Appeals Tribunals, which handled pension disputes, the British Legion announced in 1922 that it would carefully watch the tribunals' activities to ensure that members were treated fairly.[52]

> Whenever, therefore, a country is considering the making of provision for the handicapped and their rehabilitation, the veterans come first . . . In even very advanced countries it is possible for the State's resources to provide

> only for the veteran and for the handicapped child and adults disabled in civil life to be left to the more or less generous mercy of private or semi-private charity.[53]

Disabled ex-servicemen were given preferential treatment and rules governing standards of behaviour were relaxed. When patients at the limb-fitting hospital, Roehampton, went on strike because their weekend leave was stopped, the Minister of Pensions merely warned recalcitrant patients to obey rules. He added, 'I may point out that the facilities granted are considerably in excess of those allowed by civil hospitals'.[54]

Ex-servicemen were provided with better facilities and more institutions for support long after the war ended. Indeed, additional organisations for disabled ex-servicemen were created in the 1930s. The British Ex-Servicemen's Limbless Association was set up in 1932 and worked to promote specific issues, such as the improvement of prosthetics for those who had lost limbs during service.[55] Concessions were of vital importance, and gave war wounded space to reconstruct new lives for themselves, as just reward for their suffering.

St Dunstan's

The original St Dunstan's opened in 1914 in a house in Bayswater. It was moved about a year later to a property in Regent's Park London, funded by donations from a private financier from the United States, and catered for blind and sight damaged ex-servicemen, both officers and regulars, exclusively. It was established by the National Institute of the Blind, the British Red Cross Society and the Order of St John of Jerusalem. This was not a small venture, but occupied some 15 acres of prime real estate in Regent's Park with several houses and annexes. St Dunstan's was the best home available for the most heroic disabled men of the First World War. During the war, approximately 1,833 servicemen were blinded in various ways as a result of the conflict and 95% of them were at one time living or being trained by St Dunstan's. In addition, 103 colonial ex-servicemen were trained at St Dunstan's and they often went back to their own countries to establish charitable enterprises based on the St Dunstan's model. Members were taught a wide range of new skills at St Dunstan's including Braille, typing, telephony, poultry keeping, vegetable gardening and basket making. After their period of training was over they returned home, only continuing at St Dunstan's if they did not have anywhere else to go. Assistance provided by St Dunstan's did not end with the conclusion of a training course. Blind ex-servicemen were also given help in finding jobs, financial advice was provided, loans granted and both legal and medical advice was available.[56] Arthur Pearson, the Chairman of St Dunstan's who had been blinded in the war, and his successor from 1921, Ian Fraser, a Member of Parliament from 1924, tirelessly promoted their institution and the 'plight' of blind ex-servicemen.[57]

The ultimate aim of St Dunstan's was to retrain blind ex-servicemen into useful citizens. As *The Times* reminded its readers in 1923,

> The aim of St Dunstan's . . . is to assist its men to become useful and productive citizens rather than idle and unhappy pensioners, the basic view being that true happiness can only be enjoyed by those who contribute in some way to the work of the world.

Prior to the appearance of the numbers of war blinded, there were two major cultural constructions of blind people. The blinded beggar was viewed with a combination of derision, scorn, guilt and embarrassment. Blind beggars were not honourable, as they stood on street corners, usually with dogs, begging for money from passers-by. The association between blindness, dogs and begging was well established by the nineteenth century, and institutions such as St Dunstan's, with its emphasis on self-help and heroism in the face of adversity, did not allow their members to beg, knowing that it would undermine their charitable work and their attempts to make blind ex-servicemen independent.[58] Additionally civilian blind, who sometimes had jobs in workshops although more respected than the blind beggar as they were gainfully occupied, were still objects of pity and charitable onus. Riding above both other types of blind people, honourable unlike the beggar and more heroic than the blind civilian worker, were the men of St Dunstan's. They allowed society to embrace the blind ex-servicemen; the institution of St Dunstan's and its leadership as cultural signifiers of heroism, triumph over adversity and the embodiment of restored masculinity. The role of St Dunstan's was to ensure that these men did not beg on the streets and continue the long history of the blind beggar. St Dunstan's men were blind men with dignity conferred not only by their status as war heroes. They proudly displayed their gold and red flaming torch, the St Dunstan's badge on their coats, as they walked arm in arm around Regent's Park. Their place in the Remembrance Day ceremony on 11 November was assured, reports in the newspapers made constant reference to the dignity in those unseeing eyes – the notion that their last 'vision' had been one of death, putrefaction and destruction gave them a moral authority that was not evident among other war disabled. Indeed, the heroic blind ex-serviceman had 'given' his sight for his country and therefore was entitled to special consideration. The blind war disabled benefited from the immediate post-war philanthropy and, with their enhanced 'war hero' status, were the objects of goodwill. The men of St Dunstan's were acceptable as they took the air in Regent's Park because they could still communicate within the constructs of normal society; their blindness did not terrify or repulse. Usually, blind men were not frightening to look at; many of them had artificial eyes, wore dark glasses or had their eyes sewn shut, so they were not as unpleasant to look they did not possess the altered gait of the one legged; nor did an empty sleeve or pinned up trouser leg highlight a missing limb. Therefore, maiden aunts, Edwardian stockbrokers or small children walking to London Zoo were not offended by these groups of men confidently striding around the Park. By comparison, some of the pathetic mangled remains of shattered humanity that had returned from the trenches were not easy to look at.

Since such positive associations were made with the heroic blind of St Dunstan's, society was keen to embrace, support and identify with the cultural resonance and significance of the St Dunstaners' triumph over adversity. Products were sold to help to meet the charitable goals set by St Dunstan's that allowed people to 'consume' the spirit of heroic blindness. Contributing in no small way to the cultural awareness of St Dunstan's in the mind of the nation were regular features in the national press: the product of inspired leadership who became the embodiment of St Dunstan's. Of all charities for disabled war veterans, St Dunstan's got the most coverage in British newspapers. One of the most important contributors to the popularity of St Dunstan's in the press was the role of its Chairman. Arthur Pearson became blind around 1910 and was made President of the National Institute for the Blind in 1912. One of the reasons that St Dunstan's became a regular feature in the dailies was the influence of Arthur Pearson, who had been a newspaper proprietor. He had established his own light entertainment magazine, *Pearson's Weekly* in 1890, the newspaper the *Daily Express* and at one time owned both the *Evening Standard* and the *Standard*. As a newspaper proprietor he knew what would sell and certainly 'sold' the narrative of St Dunstan's to the general public. Very few accounts or books were published by individuals who were at St Dunstan's. As well as narrating their stories, Pearson was the face behind St Dunstan's, his class and well-known face providing an overall identity for St Dunstan's. He wrote his own account of his blindness and his work at St Dunstan's called

Victory Over Blindness.[59] He was mourned openly and publicly as the 'Blind leader of the blind' by those from St Dunstan's when he died from complications as a result of a fall in the bath in 1921. His successor was Ian Fraser, blinded on the Somme in 1916 and originally an inmate of St Dunstan's. As a parliamentarian, he was very influential, and devoted much of his life to his work at St Dunstan's. He was also a founder member and a tireless supporter of the British Legion. These two men imbued many of the qualities admired at the time, one wealthy and well respected, and the other cutting a handsome dashing figure despite his blindness. They were responsible for many of the changing attitudes, if not toward all blind people, then certainly toward the blind ex-servicemen of St Dunstan's. At the many balls and events held by the well-to-do in their honour, including sporting events, the men of St Dunstan's rarely, if ever, appeared, but it was enough that they were embodied in these two men: Pearson and then Fraser. These two men represented to the nation, St Dunstan's as a living commemoration of the sacrifice of the blinded ex-servicemen; better to support the endeavours of the blinded than to mourn the dead by standing around expensive stone memorials. Their charity was not simply their commemoration of the war blinded, but through their own work they also memorialised, celebrated and utilised their own personal blindness.

Within the confines of St Dunstan's two significant factors were related to the well-being of the men. First to keep them fit and active, and second was the general issue of their health. St Dunstan's was set up along familiar lines to a man like Arthur Pearson, who had attended Winchester Public School. Officers and men lived separately, so class and military divisions were upheld by the institution. While the regime was not quite as brutal as the Victorian public schools, as detailed by J.A. Mangan, as the men from St Dunstan's had already paid a heavy price with the loss of their sight, Spartan living with its emphasis on stoicism and endurance was part of the daily routine.[60] Self-reliance was another principle of St Dunstan's and the phrase 'walking alone' was used to epitomise the ability of the man from St Dunstan's to live an independent life.[61] Much of the appeal of St Dunstan's, like many other institutions that managed disabled people's lives, was meshed in what historian Paul Longmore calls sympathetic spectatorship.[62] In a similar vein to the invitations offered to those who had made charitable donations to war supply hospitals, the public was encouraged to visit the ex-servicemen in their institutions. Overcoming lost youth and melancholy were not the only emotions that surrounded the blind men of St Dunstan's. There was also a lot of curiosity, and a certain amount of selection made by the public as to the type of blind ex-serviceman they felt represented St Dunstan's and who reflected their personal notions of a blind war hero. One man at St Dunstan's said in conversation with a Voluntary Aid Detachment:

> But, in general, why do people make such a fuss of us? Take us to theatres, and concerts, and drives? . . . Day after day, as I've sat in the lounge, I've observed your 'disinterested, grateful people' . . . Down the room they come, staring at us as though we were animals at the Zoo. Then stopping in front of a particular man, they decide he'll do; they won't be ashamed to take him out; they'll even enjoy parading him before their friends . . . being fairly passable in my uniform with my Military Cross, I'm in great demand . . . whereas old Podds, who's in mufti, and Jimmy, who's disfigured . . . they never get a chance . . . Now we're the 'fashion'; we're 'those dear brave lads who have sacrificed so much' . . . but how long will it last?[63]

The Star and Garter Home

Similarly to St Dunstan's, the Star and Garter Home for Disabled Soldiers and Sailors opened in 1916 and was the first institution to provide homes for disabled ex-servicemen. Unlike St Dunstan's, however, the Star and Garter catered for a range of disabilities, and provided approximately 200 disabled ex-servicemen a home on a more permanent basis, as its emphasis was less on training and more on accommodation. The Auctioneers' and Estate Agents' Institute bought the property, which was an old hotel, in Richmond, just outside London, for £21,000, and offered it to Queen Mary, who had expressed concern that men disabled in the war would not have homes to return to.[64] The Home was administered by the Red Cross, which had initiated the appeal for assistance with funding a home of this type. Much of the funding for the new building, which replaced the old hotel and was finished in 1924, was provided by the British Women's Hospital Committee, which made a world-wide appeal for funding, including from Commonwealth countries. In an appeal for donations, an advertisement declared that this new building was the Women's Memorial of the war.[65]

The Star and Garter also provided a therapeutic space for the men, with a number of sports, agricultural work and outings at its two locations in Richmond and Sandgate. Some patients were moved to Sandgate in 1920, when the old hotel was demolished, and at Sandgate, which stayed open until 1940, the men took up agriculture. As we have seen, agricultural work was seen as beneficial for men who had been physically and mentally traumatised by war. A Poultry Farm was set up in 1924, which was called 'No Man's Land', where the men bred poultry.[66] A pigeon loft was set up in 1924, and the men participated in pigeon-racing competitions.[67]

Some of the men from the Star and Garter became well known for their outings in their motorised wheeled chairs. Motorised invalid chairs had become available after the war and replaced some of the self-propelled chairs that many of the disabled ex-servicemen used. Travelling at 15 miles an hour, in their Argson tricycles manufactured by the Stanley Engineering Company, a group of men from the Star and Garter became well known for their independent tours around the countryside to various events. The men were known as the 'Star and Garter Flying Squad' and in an article in 1931 in the *Evening Standard*, one of the men said, 'We had a splendid day at Ascot . . . if we had been in a motor-coach we should have had to have stayed where we were put; as it was we could go where we liked on the course.'[68] A number of different types of chairs were manufactured, and some of the men at the Star and Garter assisted in designing self-propelling wheelchairs; one was designed by a man who could not walk and who had the use of one arm.[69] The men became adept at fixing their motorised tricycles, which often broke down. These men represented a return to an independent life, despite their disabilities, which appealed to the public's imagination.

Although life for many of the men was full of activities, attendance at sporting events and support from charities so that their lives were of relative ease, many of the men were bitter that they were forced to live at the Star and Garter. One man wrote in the *Star and Garter Magazine*, 'some of us are pensioned for our disability, but the amount we receive practically forces us to live in an institution'.[70] While the men were grateful for the assistance offered to them by way of accommodation, it appeared that life in an institution was all that they could expect. As Seth Koven reminds us, 'the experience of war bitterly reimposes on wounded male soldiers the dependence, but not the innocence, of childhood'.[71] For the men of the Star and Garter, independence could only be found on fleeting journeys in a motorised wheelchair.

The Star and Garter was the recipient of much public charitable giving; a television set was bought for the home by donations to a fund set up by the *Daily Mirror*, through its column 'Sanctuary' in 1938.[72] The Star and Garter did not achieve the popularity of St Dunstan's, which is probably because St Dunstan's relegated itself to supporting one type of disability, and the public had a natural sympathy for blind people. In addition, the Star and Garter did not have a Chairman with the expertise in newspaper proprietorship or the high public profile that St Dunstan's did with Arthur Pearson. However, the Star and Garter was a relatively well-known institution, and while it forced disabled ex-servicemen to live in an institutionalised environment, it ensured that the men there were well supported.

Sport and disabled ex-servicemen

Sport was a part of service life. It enforced discipline, helped maintain fitness and enforced notions of team membership as well as maintaining normative forms of competitive masculinity. The professionalisation of the military and realisation that the strength of the nation was not embodied in the nature of the men available to protect it, in the early part of the twentieth century, had led to a growing concentration by the military on fitness. The developing interest in fitness and body culture after the war – exemplified by activities such as the increase in popularity of body building for men in the 1920s detailed by Ana Carden-Coyne, and the fashion for participation in the Women's League of Health and Beauty in the 1930s discussed by Jill Matthews – reflects the growing awareness surrounding bodily fitness.[73] This concentration on creating fitter bodies, in line with this aesthetic dimension, was a notion that had promulgated since the Enlightenment. George Mosse reminds us that bodily fitness was associated with both health and morality.[74] During the war, attempts to improve the function of the men in lower categories of fitness were made, for their physical and mental well-being. 'Lower category' men were trained at Recruits 'Distribution Battalions, where they were provided with three months', physical training.[75] The Army Physical Training Staff were lauded for their attempts to train the less fit:

> It was the red-and-black jersied men of the Army Physical Training Staff who achieved the miracle of turning a vast host of C3 Civilians into A1 soldiers incredibly quickly, because these men had been taught how to teach sport and knew all the tricks for getting people interested in physical fitness and physical training.[76]

Sport gave disabled ex-servicemen a space to renegotiate their position, restoring their masculine identity. Masculine identity was a bodily construct – George Mosse has argued that masculinity was rooted in embodiment. Furthermore, Graham Dawson noted that 'masculinities are lived out in the flesh, but fashioned in the imagination'.[77] The nature of masculinity has been an area for much interesting historical debate across a range of historical sub-disciplines, including sport history and historians who work in disability history. Moreover, the perception of the disabled male body is that it is essentially less masculine: injured more easily, moving differently and sometimes requiring specific aids to facilitate function. Bodies can be culturally constructed as masculine without possessing all of the traits that would be perceived as essentially male. Two ways that disabled ex-servicemen demonstrated their masculinity were by working toward economic normalcy and through sport. Much of the literature on war, masculine identity and disability focuses on the First World War.[78] Joanna Bourke, and more recently Ana Carden-Coyne and Wendy Jane Gagen, have highlighted the conflict between masculinity and disability, and put forward arguments for the ways in which status was renegotiated.[79] Many of the arguments centre on the seminal work of R.W. Connell on hegemonic masculinity.[80] Gagen uses the theory of hegemonic masculinity in her study of severely disabled men in the First World War, arguing that it was possible for them to renegotiate a masculine identity.[81] Carden-Coyne goes beyond the notion of hegemonic masculinity to suggest that several competing forms of masculinity ensure that the nature of masculinity is fluid, and moves within several realms. Disabled ex-servicemen renegotiated their masculinity through a number of ways; sport and work were the routes toward a specific type of masculinity, but one that could be easily understood and accepted by wider society.

Efforts were made to provide disabled ex-servicemen a similar opportunity to revisit their full corporeality to play sport. Endeavours to organise sporting events in which war disabled featured, and publicity surrounding them, were widespread during and after the war. *Country Life* reported on 'the glorious pluck and cheerfulness' of amputee patients at Roehampton Hospital as they played variations of football and tennis in the grounds.[82] Sporting competitions were held partly to raise money for institutions, and also to provide opportunities for disabled ex-servicemen to demonstrate their sporting ability to an often curious public. In addition to disabled men playing together, matches were organised against able-bodied teams. For example, in August 1917 a cricket match was held between the 'Arms and Legs', a team of amputee ex-servicemen, and an able-bodied team. The local schoolmaster reported in his diary:

> I stood and watched for a time but it was too worrying to me to see a man on one leg trying to bat though our captain told the bowlers to bowl easy balls. Some of the women cried to see them but they were as cheerful as Crickets and hopped on one leg from the Pavilion with their one leg and without crutches.[83]

Many men were patients in hospital for an extended period of time, and games provided a diversion from monotonous hospital life. Sports days held at hospitals like Roehampton, which held its first in 1916, were attended by crowds of visitors, who were reportedly impressed by the men's prowess using their artificial limbs. Gate receipts went toward maintenance of the hospital.[84]

Why did so many disabled young men exhibit themselves by playing games in front of a curious public? There is no evidence to suggest there were particular instructions from the War Office, ordering games for disabled ex-servicemen. Sport was an accepted part of life in the Services; a resumption of games for the injured restored fitness in both body and mind. In general, as a result of medical examination and fitness testing, the fittest and strongest had fought. They played and watched sport and led fairly physically active lives. Although war had left a permanent legacy for some, the inclusion of physical recreation offered an opportunity to resume a part of their pre-war lives. The playing of sport or resumption of some type of physical activity was a way for a disabled man to re-establish his masculinity, and demonstrate that disability had not affected his interest or ability on the quintessentially masculine playing field. F.W. Heath, publisher and journalist, made special reference to the effect that sport had after his arm was amputated. He wrote, 'looking back, I realize that I was wise in concentrating on games. However indifferent some of my efforts may have been they gave me back confidence in myself, and new health and strength.'[85]

Doctors prescribed games and sport for physical and mental recovery. At the Prince of Wales Hospital in Cardiff, one doctor constructed a golf course for amputees, with bunkers, bridges, stiles and gates.[86] While playing a round of golf, men with artificial limbs practised with their appliances, and became more adept at using them over rougher terrain, and a golf course was a more stimulating training ground than a hospital gymnasium. Other games provided entertaining ways to become active; the ancient sport of stoolball was revived in 1917 as a game for wounded soldiers.[87] At hospitals, nurses and visitors played stoolball with patients. A tournament was organised which was held annually at Lords until 1927.[88]

Not all sports events featuring disabled ex-servicemen were appealing to the public. On 14 July 1923, the British Legion held an Imperial Sports Rally for ex-servicemen at the newly opened Wembley Stadium.[89] There were events for disabled ex-servicemen, including a mile walk and 100 yard race for blind ex-servicemen, and a 250 yard race for single leg amputees, which was an individual and team event.[90] The turnout was relatively small and photographs of stands appear sparsely filled with competitors, ex-servicemen and a few members of the public.[91] An appearance by the Prince of Wales to hand out prizes failed to have an impact on public attendance.[92] The British Legion continued to support sports clubs and endeavours of its membership, but did not organise a similar competition again.[93]

While military sports rallies were not well attended after the war, officers continued to resume activities such as hunting and shooting, so special equipment was designed and produced. While not requiring specialised equipment, except assistance from sighted guides, blind ex-officers managed to follow hounds, including Arthur Pearson, first Chairman of St Dunstan's, who continued his pre-war passion for hunting.[94] Participation in activities for upper-class disabled ex-servicemen was simpler for amputees because of developments in specialised equipment, including bridles for amputees and saddles for those with artificial lower limbs. Unique guns were designed so one-armed ex-soldiers could resume shooting game.[95]

Sport at St Dunstan's

Homes that provided disabled ex-servicemen a place to live and retrain also organised sport. St Dunstan's promoted itself among the public to pay for high levels of service for its blind patients, and much of this publicity had a sporting aspect. The men took up sport, not only for their health, but to promote the home's interests. In March 1920, blind athletes at St Dunstan's gave a half hour display to a group of journalists of rowing, putting the shot, throwing a cricket ball, 100 yard sprint, football kicking, rope climbing and tug of war.[96] Special events were staged for distinguished and royal guests. Prince Albert went to St Dunstan's in 1920 and saw a demonstration similar to the journalists'.[97]

St Dunstan's used sport partly to restore a sense of masculinity to blind ex-servicemen. When it first opened, rambles 'beneficial to the health of the boys' were organised.[98] Swedish exercises, which had been introduced to Britain in the nineteenth century, were also practised. Rambles and

Swedish gymnastics were soon eclipsed in popularity by more masculine pursuits in the sporting arena. Competitive rowing became popular among blind ex-servicemen, and by May 1918 48 boats were moored on Regent's Park Lake.[99] Sport and training were taken seriously; rowers were on Regent's Park Lake at six o'clock in the morning. The first Annual Regatta was held at Putney in 1918 and continued until 1940.[100] Enthusiastic crowds who attended these events were especially keen on races between one-armed blind men.[101] The sporting competitions also proved to be attractive to the curious. It must also be remembered that the numbers of people attending freak shows grew after the war.[102] The physical drill displays carried out in winter months, it was reported, also attracted crowds of 'interested onlookers'.[103]

Many of the physical activities had a highly competitive edge. St Dunstan's was one of the earliest examples of what is referred to in the more formalised language of rehabilitation in the 1940s, as competitive recovery. As we will see, this system was more organised in the Second World War, particularly in the RAF. This regime harnessed the men's natural competitive feelings to assist in the acceptance of disability and to return to a sense of identity, either renegotiated or taken up once more. A house system of teams was established, very similar to the public schools that many men who were responsible for administering St Dunstan's had attended before the war. St Dunstan's had an official system of awards. For participation in a race, men were entitled to a St Dunstan's Athletic Club badge.[104] Athletic competitions, called 'Saturday Sports', were held; competitions included running races where a rope fixed to a competitor's wrist was attached to a wire stretched along a track. Participants were warned of the finish by a bell. Other sports included tug of war, putting a weight, skipping races and rope climbing.[105] Physical training was held every morning at seven.[106] When a Sports Day was imminent, one ex-serviceman recalled the additional preparations made, including 'much extra physical effort, and much extra training, cold showers and massage'.[107] Tug of war assumed a special importance at St Dunstan's as the Pearson Challenge Cup was awarded every year to the winner of the intra-house competition. The strenuous efforts of inter-blind competition contrasted with the 'Rag-Time' sports often held for the members where the men invited their wives and children and enjoyed a day of games, including wheelbarrow races and a cigarette race. Members were exhorted to continue with their exercises when they left St Dunstan's as 'bodily fitness' was 'a most essential asset to happiness'.[108]

There was also a football competition which was similar to a penalty shoot out. Teams consisted of three semi-sighted, three totally blind and a sighted goalkeeper.[109] The game was played in two halves and players had two attempts to kick a goal. During the final, the usual sighted goalkeepers were replaced by a sporting celebrity; usually a famous footballer was invited.[110] Reports and photographs of the competition appeared in national newspapers, which kept the work of St Dunstan's uppermost in the public's mind. *The Times* reported in 1920:

> A soldier who played football while in the Army cannot get away from the desire to have a kick at the ball, even though he is sightless . . . goal kicking by the blind has been developed there into a popular and even exciting sport.[111]

More of these associations between St Dunstan's and the highly thought of world of football players cemented its work in the public consciousness. In 1920, Arsenal Football Club were blindfolded and played a game of St Dunstan's football.[112] St Dunstan's used games as public events to promote itself, and coupled with support for disabled soldiers and sympathy that sighted people felt toward blind people, it was highly successful.

Blind ex-servicemen participated in an increasing range of activities. The first walking race for St Dunstaners was held in December 1920 when men walked three miles around the outer circle of Regent's Park.[113] This was followed by a walk to Brighton in October 1922 which paved the way for increased distances and competitive events.[114] With this achievement behind them, St Dunstaners were among the first to compete with sighted people. In 1924, it was suggested to the Amateur Athletics Association (AAA) that blind athletes participate in open walking events.[115] There was initial resistance from the AAA because blind walkers required an escort, which was against the rules of able-bodied competition. Longer-distance running races were experimented with in 1925, but were never as popular as the walking competitions.[116]

Even after war had faded from the public's mind, St Dunstan's continued its work, which was often recognised in newspapers. Their sporting exploits were publicised as they joined the ranks of the sighted in walking competitions. By the 1930s problems with the AAA had been overcome and St Dunstaners were allowed to participate in able-bodied Stock Exchange races. From December 1931 to May 1932 there were six official walking events, including a six mile outer circle walk, a three mile novice walk, a nine mile outer circle walk, a fifteen mile outer walk and an annual walk in Birmingham. Sighted escorts, from officers in the Metropolitan Police to members of the Stock Exchange, were provided.[117]

Sporting facilities were offered to the men at St Dunstan's. The Marylebone Baths was open for ex-servicemen at St Dunstan's and swimming competitions were held throughout the 1930s. Ian Fraser commented on its benefits: 'There's something about swimming which is quite unique when you're blind – it is the fact that you can move about as vigorously and as fearlessly as you like in any direction without any fear of hitting anything.'[118]

Sports were used to raise money for blind ex-servicemen. In 1920, an August bank holiday athletics competition was held to benefit those at St Dunstan's. The advertisement in *The Athletic News* exhorted all potential athletes to 'enter at once and support our Blind Heroes'.[119] While events such as these were well intentioned, there were complaints that such charity games were not benefiting good causes as much as they might, as charges for refreshments, the watchman and tax were eating into the receipts.[120] In 1920, the first of a long-standing series of competitions, the Stable Lads Boxing Tournament, was held to raise money for St Dunstan's. Trainers held local competitions and the winners from these went to London to participate in the final.[121] St Dunstan's was a worthwhile charity to support and the wholesome activity of sport reflected the heroic status of the St Dunstan's blind.

Blind veterans also obtained preferential attendance at major sporting events. St Dunstan's members received free admission to football matches. The first time that the men of St Dunstan's were taken to a football match was in January 1920, when a group went to the game between Chelsea and Manchester United.[122] By 1929, although still attending matches held at Chelsea, Fulham and Arsenal, the *St Dunstan's Review* warned its readers not to take advantage of their invitation:

> They have been more than generous in the past and we must see to it that we do not transgress upon their generosity and feel that we have a right to demand admission and create a scene if this is found impossible.[123]

St Dunstaners were reminded that at Chelsea and Fulham, each man was only allowed one escort into the ground with him.[124] Obviously the St Dunstan's men had been trying to share their good fortune with their sighted friends. Football was not the only sport where disabled ex-servicemen could be admitted for free. Tickets were made available from Twickenham for rugby and the Oval for cricket matches. Another favourite venue among disabled ex-servicemen was horse races, where they were able to have a bet, gambling still being one of the most popular activities at the time.

Sport at the Star and Garter Home

The men at the Star and Garter Home in Richmond also played sport. However, unlike St Dunstan's, men at the Star and Garter had a range of different disabilities, including paraplegia and multiple amputations. For amputees, prostheses were cumbersome and did not allow ease of movement. One amputee ex-serviceman remarked:

> The loss of a leg on the Western Front in 1918 was a considerable loss to me whose chief recreations were swimming and walking. I could still swim, but walking is no fun to a man with an artificial leg which feels, when he is tired, as if it were a ton in weight.[125]

Despite these difficulties, Star and Garter residents enthusiastically took up exercise. On 11 November 1920, they formed their own Star and Garter Sports Club, the main objective of which was to 'enable both Staff and patients to join in all games that are possible, thereby encouraging a feeling of comradeship between them'.[126] Games were fun and helped pass the time.[127] For those who could move around with a prosthesis or wheelchair, games were diverse and included tennis, bowls and croquet.[128] One writer in the *Star and Garter Magazine* noted:

> I do not see why croquet should not be played by the Patients as well as the Staff, certainly those boys who can walk could play, and I have known croquet to be played from a wheelchair; it may not be good for the lawn, but that does not matter as long as it gives pleasure.[129]

As with St Dunstan's, and to a lesser extent Roehampton Hospital, the Star and Garter put patients and their sporting achievements on public display. As an answer to the patient's boredom, while ensuring that the public were aware of the Home's responsibility to its disabled, sports days were held. Many people, partly out of concern and partly out of a voyeuristic sense to see disabled ex-servicemen, came to see these institutionalised men practise sport and demonstrate their prowess at games and activities. A sports day for residents was held in 1923 when patients took part in races, including obstacle zigzag in wheelchairs.[130]

During the 1930s, the fashion for physical exercises was followed at the Star and Garter Home, as a gymnasium full of equipment was provided for daily exercise. As noted by Robert Graves and Alan Hodge, early morning physical jerks became part of many men's daily routine in the 1920s and 1930s.[131] The men subscribed to ideas that exercise might reduce the effects of disability. The Home's magazine reported:

> The faithful band of those who are hoping for improvement, and those who at least believe that the regular exercise keeps them from any further deterioration in their limbs, begin to line up outside the door of the gym.[132]

Sporting teams gave demonstrations and visited ex-servicemen's Homes. Some Homes would stage sporting exhibitions by local teams; residents at the Star and Garter saw fencing, boxing and bowling exhibitions by teams from Richmond. Competitions with disabled ex-servicemen were a charitable duty. In 1925 the Star and Garter played billiards against a local Belmont Working Men's Club.[133] These meetings were important because they re-established forms of social normality to the institutionalised war disabled. The Conservative Club played a long-running series of games with patients: 'the idea of the contests was not a matter of points to their members, but a means of keeping in touch with and helping to entertain their less fortunate comrades of the war'.[134] Indeed, games formed part of disabled soldiers' visits to Buckingham Palace. Garden parties were held regularly by the King and Queen for wounded ex-servicemen. One function of the Not Forgotten Association was arranging these events; there was competition to be chosen to represent the Home. Cricket, stoolball or football was played at these parties and, for the less energetic, punting around the lake.[135]

Sporting Life announced in 1934 that one of the races at the January Meeting at Hurst Park would be known as the Star and Garter Handicap Steeplechase.[136] A group of disabled veterans from the Star and Garter Home attended a number of football matches, cricket matches and other sporting events. One resident reminisced in the *Star and Garter Magazine* in 1939:

> Self-propelling and motor chairs are a common sight in London and a few years ago, before the ground was altered, as many as a hundred disabled men could be seen lined up in their chairs watching Chelsea at Stamford Bridge.[137]

These were generally organised outings in coaches, and the 'Flying Squad' usually made their own way in their motor tricycles. While there were criticisms that the war disabled were neglected by the public, there is evidence that these men disabled in service for their country continued to be supported by donations, and were not entirely absent from the public's consciousness.

Opportunities for sporting competitions that pitted disabled ex-servicemen against able-bodied people were often sought. As we have seen, blind men of St Dunstan's took part in walking competitions with able-bodied people. Able-bodied men were asked to play at less aggressive levels, however, so as not to highlight the disabled team's reduced ability. Indeed, there were more suitable competitors. Women formed teams and played against disabled ex-servicemen, and were found to be suitable competitors for disabled men. Sometimes nurses formed the opposition; other women took up sport against disabled ex-servicemen as part of their charitable work. From 1928 an annual cricket match was held between the Star and Garter Home and Folkestone Ladies teams. The game was altered slightly, with no running between wickets 'to prevent the patients overtaxing their strength'.[138] These games had physical and social benefits, allowing disabled men to maintain their sense of masculinity, yet also enjoy the company of women.

Conclusions

The First World War put disability on display as the bodies of many young, strong men returned to Britain severely damaged. Doctors repaired these bodies to the best of their ability, but after 1918 numbers of disabled ex-servicemen were on the streets, in pubs and, in some cases, employment, gnawing at people's sensibilities. The State faced up to the problem of these broken bodies with the provision of pensions; albeit not always adequate, the worthy disabled from the war were still better provided for than those civilians with a disability. As noted by Kershaw:

> It is almost universally accepted that they have 'given' their sight, their hearing or their limbs to save their fellow countrymen from nameless horrors, and whether they were volunteers or conscripts, brave men or cowards the sacrifice sanctifies them.[139]

Disabled ex-servicemen also had advocates such as the British Legion and a number of charities that looked after men's needs, as State support only went so far. Two charities that supported disabled ex-servicemen, the Star and Garter Home and St Dunstan's, were part of the complex web of assistance offered to disabled ex-servicemen. Albeit St Dunstan's only supported blind ex-servicemen, but both institutions are worthy of discussion as they were both large, well known and epitomised the therapy and support offered to some ex-servicemen after the war.

There is no doubt that, owing to the influential figures of Arthur Pearson and Ian Fraser, St Dunstan's was the most promoted and well-recognised war charity, amidst some of the best-known and well-promoted charities following such an appalling and wasteful war. St Dunstan's gave its members a sense of masculinity with its provision of sport and games; a sense of independence with training regimes and efforts to find blind ex-servicemen employment; and a sense of pride and dignity in their association with an establishment that commanded the interest of the very influential in society. The values epitomised by the public schools on which St Dunstan's was based, including hardiness and endurance, were recognisable across a range of classes and so St Dunstan's' appeal was broad. The Star and Garter's men, driving around the country independently in their motorised wheeled chairs, also appealed to the public's need to feel that these men had not been deserted and they participated in social and cultural life.

One of the reasons why sport was taken up by blind ex-servicemen with such alacrity and dedication at St Dunstan's and the Star and Garter was partly the men's need to recapture their youth and fitness and to assert themselves as men. Additionally, their participation demonstrated to the public that disability did not diminish sporting prowess or enjoyment. Sport at St Dunstan's and the Star and Garter relocated disabled ex-servicemen, potentially emasculated by their disability, removing them from the margins of masculinity to return to a recognisable masculine identity. Nevertheless, what raised a man from St Dunstan's or the Star and Garter to heroic status was not his prowess rowing on the lake or driving around the countryside on a motorised wheelchair. Representations of overcoming disabilities and living a useful life cemented the men's position as heroes in the public's mind.

Notes

1 Bourke, *Dismembering the Male*, 31.

2 Although neurasthenia, referred to more commonly as shell shock, affected large numbers of men during the First World War, it is not within the scope of this book to cover the subject. See Martin Stone, 'Shellshock and the Psychologists' in W.F. Bynum, Roy Porter and Michael Shepherd (eds), *The Anatomy of Madness* (London, 1985) and the special edition on shell shock of the *Journal of Contemporary History*, Vol. 35, No. 1 (2000); Peter Leese, *Shell Shock: Traumatic Neurosis and the British Soldiers of the First World*

War (Basingstoke, 2002); Ben Shepherd, *A War of Nerves: Soldiers and Psychiatrists in the Twentieth Century* (Cambridge, MA, 2001).

3 In total 1.2 million ex-servicemen were sufficiently disabled to receive a pension; 40,000 of them were seriously disabled. J.M. Winter, *The Great War and the British People* (London, 1985), 273.

4 Jeffrey S. Reznick, *Healing the Nation: Soldiers and the Culture of Caregiving in Britain During the Great War* (Manchester, 2004), 116–36.

5 There were over 41,000 amputations during the war. Bourke, *Dismembering the Male*, 33.

6 In one example, it took two years before one soldier's thigh wound had healed enough to be operated on. *British Legion Journal*, Vol. 1, No. 4 (October 1921), 81.

7 See Frederick Brereton, *The Great War and the R.A.M.C.* (London, 1919), 48.

8 Percy O. Douglas, 'Aboard an Ambulance Train 1915–1918', in Pauline Samuelson (ed.), *I Owe My Life* (London, 1995), 25.

9 'The Surgeon's Eye', *The Times*, 19 January 1915.

10 S. Alan and S. Malkin, 'The Conquest of Disability', *Annals of the Royal College of Surgeons of England*, Vol. 20 (1957), 106.

11 Porter, *The Greatest Benefit to Mankind*, 618.

12 Sandy Callister, '"Broken Gargoyles": The Photographic Representation of Severely Wounded New Zealand Soldiers', *Social History of Medicine*, Vol. 20, No. 1 (2007), 118.

13 The First World War was the first war in which deaths from wounds exceeded deaths from disease.

14 Queen Mary's fitted 26,262 of the 41,050 who lost limbs during the war. Commemorative leaflet, *Queen Mary's (Roehampton) Hospital 1915–1943.*

15 The hospital opened with 25 beds, which rapidly grew to 900 at the end of the war. Ian Fletcher, *Queen Mary's Hospital Roehampton 1915–1965* (Roehampton, 1965), 1.

16 Workshops for different manufacturers were on site. Roehampton recovered much of its costs from renting out space to limb manufacturers. Helen Alper (ed.), *A History of Queen Mary's University Hospital Roehampton* (Roehampton, 1997), 15–16.

17 Up to 25 trades and crafts were offered at different times. Ibid., 15–16.

18 Koven, 'Remembering and Dismemberment', 1188.

19 Rules for the awarding of pensions were very complex. For example, a soldier from a previous war would only receive a First World War disability pension if he had 14 years' service previous to his disablement and served again during the war, but he did not have to be disabled in the fighting to get the First World War pension rate. *British Legion Journal*, Vol. 1, No. 1 (July 1921), 17.

20 *The Disabled Soldiers' Handbook*, 1918. The lowest percentage was fixed at 20% and was for the loss of two fingers on either hand. Ministry of Pensions leaflet quoted in Bourke, *Dismembering the Male*, 66.

21 The Constant Attendance Allowance was mainly provided to double arm amputations. The maximum payment was 20 shillings, which was given to one amputation to the shoulder and the other to the elbow. There were only 50 double arm amputees in Britain. Some blind and double short thigh amputations also received some assistance. G. Howson, *Handbook for the Limbless* (London, 1922), 147, xii.

22 *The Disabled Soldiers' Handbook*, 7.

23 G. Harris, *The Redemption of the Disabled* (New York, 1919), 98.

24 Any children born to a disabled soldier after the war were excluded. Koven, 'Remembering and Dismemberment', 1191.

25 *British Legion Journal*, Vol. 1, No. 11 (May 1922), 247.

26 It has been argued that, for those working- or lower-middle-class men not possessed of a private income, promotion to the rank of officer was actually a burden when it came to demobilisation. M. Petter, '"Temporary Gentlemen" in the Aftermath of the Great War: Rank, Status and the Ex-Officer Problem', *Historical Journal*, No. 37 (1994). See also Antony Brown, *Red for Remembrance: The British Legion 1921–1971* (London, 1971), 8–10.

27 Harris, *Redemption of the Disabled*, 92. A 100% pension in 1919 was from 27s 6d for a private and 42s 6d for a Warrant Officer Class 1. Edward T. Devine, *Disabled Soldiers' and Sailors' Pensions and Training* (New York, 1919), 168.

28 Devine, *Disabled Soldiers' and Sailors'*, 183.

29 Article by Sir Arthur Griffith-Boscowen, Parliamentary Secretary to the Ministry of Pensions in the *War Pensions Gazette*, October 1917. Quoted in Devine, *Disabled Soldiers' and Sailors'*, 177.

30 Watson, *Civilisation and the Cripple*, 30.

31 Howson, *Handbook for the Limbless*, 108.

32 S. McGrah, 'Not Forgotten', *The Cord*, Vol. 4, No. 2 (Spring 1951), 15.

33 T.F. Lister, 'Servicemen Must Know What To Expect', *British Legion Journal* (November 1943), 211.

34 For a detailed discussion of the King's National Roll see Meaghan Kowalsky, 'This Honourable Obligation: The King's National Roll Scheme for Disabled Ex-Servicemen, 1915–1944', *European Review of History*, Vol. 14, No. 4 (December 2007), 567–84.

35 This excluded members of the Merchant Navy and Civil Defence. George Tomlinson, *Report of the Inter-departmental Committee on the Rehabilitation and Resettlement of Disabled Persons* (January 1943), CAB 117/145, National Archives, London, 22. See also CMA SA/RBC C 8.9, Tomlinson's address to the Association of the Royal Empire Society, 'Rehabilitation in Industry of Disabled Servicemen', 23 March 1944, Wellcome Trust Archives, London.

36 By February 1920 10,867 employers were using the seal and employing 102,011 disabled ex-servicemen. Howson, *Handbook for the Limbless*, 69.

37 *British Legion Journal*, Vol. 2, No. 1 (July 1922), 14.

38 Ian Fraser, 'Employment of the Disabled', *Occupational Therapy and Rehabilitation*, Vol. 22 (December 1943), 281.

39 The Disabled Society experienced financial difficulty and was absorbed by the British Legion in 1921. Graham Wootton, *The Official History of the British Legion* (London, 1956), 40.

40 Howson, *Handbook for the Limbless*, 55.

41 Ibid., x.

42 Account in Brown, *Red for Remembrance*, 80–5.

43 Harris, *Redemption of the Disabled*, 99.

44 Devine, *Disabled Soldiers' and Sailors'*, 185; Howson, *Handbook for the Limbless*, 82.

45 Ross McKibbin, *Classes and Cultures: England 1918–1951* (London, 1998), 112.

46 The British Legion represented the interests of all ex-servicemen who joined. It had a Women's Section comprised mainly of war widows. In 1922 membership stood at 122,986 and reached its highest level of pre- Second World War membership of 526,413 in 1939. Wootton, *History of the British Legion*, 305.

47 They included The Blackburn (later National) Association (1916), the National Federation (1917), the Comrades of the Great War (1917) and the Disabled Society (1916), which amalgamated in 1921 to form the British Legion. Graham Wootton, *The Politics of Influence: British Ex-Servicemen, Cabinet Decisions and Cultural Change 1917–1957* (London, 1963), 63.

48 R. Heaf, 'The British Legion and Rehabilitation', *Rehabilitation*, No. 54 (July–September 1965), 53.

49 The first appeal was Warriors' Day, which was held in March 1921, but this was replaced by Poppy Day in November of that same year. Wootton, *History of the British Legion*, 38.

50 Cohen, *The War Come Home*.

51 Ibid.

52 *British Legion*, Vol. 1, No. 11 (May 1922), 247.

53 John D. Kershaw, *Handicapped Children* (London, 1961), 13.

54 Weekend leave at Roehampton was cancelled because the patients took it whether or not it had been granted. *The Lancet* (16 May 1925), 1058.

55 For further detail, see the British Limbless Ex-Servicemen's Association's official history. Peter Ryde, *Out On a Limb: A Celebration of the British Limbless Ex-Servicemen's Association Golden Jubilee 1932–1982* (London, 1982).

56 *The Lancet* (6 April 1935), 819.

57 Ian Fraser was a blind Conservative Member of Parliament from 1924–29 and 1931–39. See Fraser, *Whereas I Was Blind*.

58 For a discussion on the reluctance toward the use of guide dogs in Britain see Julie Anderson and Neil Pemberton, 'Walking Alone: Aiding the War and Civilian Blind in the Inter-war Period', *European Review of History*, Vol. 14, No. 4 (December 2007), 459–79.

59 Arthur Pearson, *Victory over Blindness* (London, n.d. but c. 1919).

60 See J.A. Mangan, *Athleticism in the Victorian and Edwardian Public School: The Emergence and Consolidation of an Educational Ideology* (Cambridge, 1981).

61 For a discussion of this in relation to guide dogs see Anderson and Pemberton, 'Walking Alone'.

62 Paul Longmore, 'Sentimentality and the Framing of Disability in American Charity Fundraising. Not the Medical Model. Not the Social Model', paper presented at 'Reassessing Disability: New Approaches to Disability History' Conference, Truro, UK, 28 June 2007.

63 V.M. Duché, *The Spirit of St Dunstan's* (London, 1938), 44–5.

64 Simon Weston, 'The Royal Star and Garter Home', in Pautine Samuelson (ed.), *I Owe My Life: British Red Cross Celebrating 125 Years* (London, 1995), 34.

65 *Star and Garter Magazine*, Vol. 30, No. 4 (October 1950), 19.

66 Ibid., Vol. 2, No. 4 (October 1922), 15.

67 Ibid., Vol. 1, No. 3 (July 1921), 25.

68 'The Star and Garter Flying Squad', *Evening Standard* (5 August 1931).

69 *Star and Garter Magazine*, Vol. 19, No. 4 (October 1939), 12.

70 Ibid., Vol. 18, No. 4 (October 1938), 29.

71 Koven, 'Remembering and Dismemberment', 1171.

72 *Star and Garter Magazine*, Vol. 18, No. 4 (Otober 1938), 29.

73 Ana Carden-Coyne 'From Pieces to Whole: the Sexualisation of Muscles in Post-War Body Building' in Forth, Christopher E. and Crozier, Ivan (eds.) *Body Parts: Critical Explorations in Corporality* (Lexington, 2005) pp. 207–8 and Jill Julius Matthews, 'They Had Such A Lot of Fun: The Women's League of Health and Beauty between the Wars', *History Workshop*, No. 30 (Autumn 1990), 22–54.

74 George L. Mosse, *The Image of Man: The Creation of Modern Masculinity* (New York, 1996), 24–50.

75 Editorial, 'Physical Development Centres', *Journal of the Royal Army Medical Corps*, Vol. LXXXI, No. 4 (October 1943), 183.

76 Captain F.A.M. Webster, 'Real Welfare Supervision Is Wanted', *Sport in Industry*, Vol. 2, No. 4 (March 1939), 9.

77 Graham Dawson, *Soldier Heroes: British Adventure, Empire and the Imagining of Masculinities* (London, 1994), 1.

78 Other works have examined a number of wars in relation to cultural production, such as literature in wars other than the First. See K.J. Phillips, *Manipulating Masculinity: War and Gender in Modern British and American Literature* (New York, 2006) and Paul R. Higate (ed.), *Military Masculinities: Identity and the State* (New York, 2003).

79 See Bourke, *Dismembering the Male*; Carden-Coyne, *Reconstructing the Body*; Gagen, 'Remastering the Body, Renegotiating Gender', 525–41.

80 See R.W. Connell, *Masculinities* (Cambridge, 1995).

81 See Gagen, 'Remastering the Body, Renegotiating Gender', 525–41.

82 *Country Life* (14 August 1915), 241.
83 IWM Document Archives 79/15/1, Diary of R. Saunders.
84 Alper, *A History of Queen Mary's University Hospital Roehampton*, 11.
85 F.W. Heath, 'One of the Lucky Ones', in Ian Fraser (ed.), *Conquest of Disability* (London, 1956), 196.
86 Robert Tait MacKenzie, *Reclaiming the Maimed: A Handbook of Physical Therapy* (New York, 1918), 91.
87 The game closely resembled a less formal form of cricket; the ball was bowled underarm and the wicket was stylised, about 1.4 metres high and had a board attached to it.
88 John Lowerson, 'Stoolball and the Manufacture of "Englishness"', in Gertrud Pfister, Toni Neiwerth and Gerd Steins (eds), *Games of the World: Between Tradition and Modernity* (Sankt Augustin, 1993), 411.
89 *The Times* referred to the event as the Empire Sports and the British Legion named it the Imperial Sports Rally. This was the second time that Wembley Stadium had been used for a major event. The first had been the Cup Final in April. *The Times* (16 July 1923).
90 Ibid. (14 July 1923).
91 Photographic plates at Queen Mary's University Hospital, Roehampton.
92 Businesses provided donations to pay for the entry fee of disabled ex-servicemen and unemployed officers. They included companies such as Kodak, Boots and Eyre and Spottiswoode. *British Legion Journal*, Vol. 2, No. 14 (August 1923), 53.
93 The Legion continued to support the various sporting clubs formed by its members, including football, billiards, cricket and tennis, although there is no specific mention of sporting clubs for disabled ex-servicemen. *British Legion Journal*, Vol. 10, No. 3 (September 1930), 71.
94 *The Beacon*, Vol. 5, No. 50 (February 1921), 16.
95 Advertising pages in Howson, *Handbook for the Limbless*, 199.
96 *St Dunstan's Review*, Vol. 4, No. 43 (April 1920), 11.
97 Ibid., Vol. 4, No. 45 (June 1920), 10.
98 Ibid., Vol. 2, No. 18 (January 1918), 23.
99 Ibid., Vol. 22, No. 2 (May 1918), 11.
100 Ibid., Vol. 25, No. 265 (July 1940), 6.
101 *The Beacon*, Vol. 4, No. 44 (August 1920), 9.
102 Nadja Durbach, *Spectacle of Deformity: Freak Shows and Modern British Culture* (Berkeley, CA, 2010), 177.
103 *Report of St Dunstan's Hostel for Blinded Soldiers and Sailors* (31 March 1917), 10.
104 *St Dunstan's Review*, Vol. 2, No. 21 (April 1918), 25.
105 The rope climbs were of varying heights, but included one of 90 feet. James Tindal Scrymgeour, *Reminiscences of St Dunstan's* (Devon, 1920), 70.
106 *St Dunstan's Review*, Vol. 3, No. 29 (January 1919), 14.

107 Scrymgeour, *Reminiscences of St Dunstan's*, 68.
108 *St Dunstan's Review*, Vol. 2, No. 18 (January 1918), 23.
109 Ibid., Vol. 4, No. 39 (December 1919), 14.
110 In 1920, the goalkeeper was Chelsea Football Club's Molyneux. In 1921, both Arsenal's goalkeeper, Williamson and the English international referee, Rutherford were in attendance. Ibid., Vol. 5, No. 53 (March 1921), 15.
111 *The Times* (26 February 1920).
112 Ibid.
113 *The Beacon*, Vol. 5, No. 49 (January 1921), 13.
114 *St Dunstan's Review*, Vol. 7, No. 70 (November 1922), 7.
115 Ibid., Vol. 10, No. 104 (December 1924), 28.
116 Ibid., Vol. 9, No. 99 (June 1925), 16.
117 Ibid., Vol. 17, No. 182 (January 1933), 8.
118 Fraser, *Whereas I Was Blind*, 38.
119 *The Athletic News* (Monday, 26 July 1920), 5.
120 Ibid. (Monday, 10 May 1920), 4.
121 *St Dunstan's Review*, Vol. 18, No. 193 (January 1934), 2.
122 Arsenal also gave free tickets to the blind in 1921. Ibid., Vol. 4, No. 41 (February 1920), 9.
123 Ibid., Vol. 14, No. 145 (September 1929), 8.
124 Ibid., Vol. 15, No. 157 (October 1930), 8.
125 John Ervine, 'We Must Grin and Bear It', in Fraser, *Conquest of Disability*, 82.
126 *Star and Garter Magazine*, Vol. 1, No. 1 (January 1921), 27.
127 For those that were bedridden, games such as whist, bridge and chess were played.
128 The first time croquet had been played in wheelchairs was probably in 1920 when a group of disabled Ex-servicemen from the Queen Alexandra Hospital Home played their first tournament. David Farrant, *The Queen Alexandra Hospital Home for Disabled Ex-Servicemen* (Worthing, 1997). 43.
129 *Star and Garter Magazine*, Vol. 1, No. 1 (January 1921), 28.
130 Ibid., Vol. 3, No. 4 (October 1923), 192.
131 Robert Graves and Alan Hodge, *The Long Weekend: A Social History of Great Britain 1918–1939* (London, 1985), 381.
132 *Star and Garter Magazine*, Vol. 14, No. 1 (January 1934), 20.
133 Ibid., Vol. 5, No. 4 (October 1925), 154.
134 Ibid., Vol. 9, No. 2 (April 1929), 67.
135 *The Red Cross* (October 1925).
136 *Star and Garter Magazine*, Vol. 14, No. 1 (January 1934), 23.
137 Ibid., Vol. 19, No. 4 (October 1939), 14.
138 Ibid., Vol. 8, No. 3 (July 1928), 119.
139 Kershaw, *Handicapped Children*, 13.

3

Soul: rehabilitation in the Second World War

> After all, in a war it is the fighting man (or woman) who should have first consideration; the more so because once definitely incapacitated they become a social burden till the end of their lives.[1]

While popular memory observes the First World War as a more bloody and pointless conflict than that of 1939–45, nevertheless the Second World War resulted in significant injuries and deaths. However, medicine had made some significant advances. These led to a growth in the numbers of people with residual disabilities; many of whom would not have lived through such wounding if it had been received during the First World War. These simple numerical facts meant that the medical establishment, the Forces, the State and society had to reassess the position in regard to large numbers of injured people requiring care.

Rehabilitation forms the central focus of this study, and the chapter will demonstrate how it operated on a practical level and its theoretical basis. The chapter contends that war was a necessary environment for the development of large-scale rehabilitation and its successful operation. Rehabilitation became an all-encompassing technique and man management system that ensured that injured people were restored to the highest level of function possible after injury. Bodies were not wasted. Rehabilitation, similar to many other systems of management, had its roots in the Efficiency Movement, which had been introduced to Britain by Herbert Cassell in the 1910s.

This chapter will demonstrate how rehabilitative methods were used to create fitter servicemen and women before the war even started, which added to their successful adoption into an injured person's treatment regime during the war. It will become clear that retaining injured servicemen in the Forces during their rehabilitation was central to their success, as morale was maintained, which was deemed crucial to recovery. Rehabilitation also produced a system increasingly based around hospitals, the Ministry of Pensions and the Ministry of Labour and National Service. The development of a more centralised administrative system of caring for the injured operated under the auspices of the Emergency Medical Service, which was set up in 1939, and this environment secured rehabilitation's successful adoption, medically and organisationally. In addition, new centres were set up to treat specific types of injury and conditions and, together with old established institutions such as St Dunstan's and the Star and Garter Home, continued to provide levels of care and rehabilitation regimes. The chapter argues that the impact of rehabilitation was reinforced by the establishment of government committees, such as the Tomlinson Committee, which produced much of the basis for the legislation that was adopted during the war and characterised rehabilitation in the post-war period.

Medical care was only the first step in rehabilitation, and the chapter will focus on the centrality of work as a way to complete the rehabilitation process. The notion that hard work was a panacea and enforced notions of masculinity throughout the First World War has been discussed by historians such as Joanna Bourke and Ana Carden-Coyne.[2] However, the overarching system that involved a number of different agencies was not evident in the First World War, despite the emphasis on work. Employment was a central component to an individual's rehabilitation, and it was also important to the wider aims of the State. The chapter will discuss the State's interest in providing work, mainly to ensure that the effort provided by bodies, whether disabled or not, would feed the wartime economy. In turn, attitudes toward the productivity of disabled bodies changed, and with that some rethinking of attitudes previously held toward disabled people.

Finally, while the war injured occupy a central role in this chapter, in addition to disabled people who were employed under rehabilitation schemes, discussion will move to the wartime experience of people with disabilities. How disabled people functioned within the constraints of a wartime environment will provide an overview of the changing nature of their lives during war, the impact of State-sponsored schemes and changing attitudes surrounding people with disabilities.

Medical treatment during the war

There have been a number of works that detail medical treatment during the Second World War, and the focus of this section will be on specific aspects of medical developments that relate more specifically to rehabilitation. Clearly, wartime offered medicine new opportunities for developing new systems and regimes of treatment. As has been noted elsewhere, 'the ill winds of war have a habit to blow good to surgeons and through them to surgery'.[3] While there has been much historical debate surrounding the relationship and the impact of war on medicine, and whether or not it was beneficial, it can be argued that the sheer volume of patients requiring treatment during war impacts on regimes of care and medical practice.[4] In the Second World War, innovations in pharmaceuticals, surgery and technology functioned to reduce the effect of advances in weaponry that caused terrible damage to bodies. The Second World War saw the development of powerful destructive weaponry, as advances in technology had improved weapons of war such as bombs, missiles and bullets. In addition, motorised technology caused high numbers of injuries, many due to an increase in the numbers of servicemen who had traffic accidents, particularly while riding motorcycles.[5]

The mechanisation of war with its increased ability to cause widespread damage to buildings and bodies was matched by the ingenuity of scientific discoveries. This was particularly evident and fortuitous in medicine. Pharmaceuticals and techniques were developed which meant that people who might previously have died were more likely to survive serious injury. It is generally accepted that there were significant advances in medicine that reduced the death rate during the war, and war was responsible in some way for their accelerated development.[6] These new drugs were developed before the war, and their use became more widespread as a result of the conflict. In 1935 sulphanilamide was discovered, a drug whose strength was its ability to control widespread infection.[7] This was a real breakthrough, as sulpha drugs' ability to eliminate infection made them a powerful weapon against secondary infection, which had previously caused many deaths.

Similarly to sulpha drugs, penicillin had been the subject of pre-war research. French scientists had experimented with it in the late 1920s, and Fleming had accidentally grown some in 1928; however, there was still no way to purify it.[8] Howard Florey and Ernst Chain developed Fleming's early research in Oxford in 1939, and it was not until the war had been underway for about two years that penicillin became more easily available.[9] A crude variety of the drug was manufactured in small quantities in 1941, with increasing capacity by 1943.[10] Penicillin eradicated infection and was particularly useful in some medical conditions, including sexually transmitted diseases. Amputation became less likely with penicillin available, and the danger of gas gangrene was reduced. The problem with penicillin was that it was unavailable in large quantities, so only servicemen fighting on front lines were given it.[11] Since the effects of penicillin on infection were so great, every effort was made by the military authorities to produce sufficient quantities for the Forces.[12] At crucial stages of the war, penicillin was credited with having a significant impact on recovery rates; during the D-Day landings in Normandy in 1944 the Army had an organised agenda for administering penicillin. The 21st Army Group's programme ensured that most wounded had a penicillin injection within a few hours of injury.[13] Penicillin and its rapid and widespread administration were given as one of the reasons for high rates of survival after injury compared with the First World War.[14]

In addition to drugs to fight infection, other innovations, such as blood transfusion, were developed, which improved servicemen's chance of recovery. The technique was not new, and had been used on a limited scale during the First World War; however, blood transfusion was perfected between the wars. The introduction of blood and plasma to casualties lessened the body's shock reaction and reduced death rates from injury. The major problem with this technique in the past had been the scale and location of provision, as blood had to be transfused directly from one patient to another, since there was no knowledge of how it could be stored, and it was difficult to provide a willing group of donors when blood was required. This problem was solved during the Second World War when it became possible to refrigerate blood and plasma, which meant that there were usually supplies on hand.[15] Britain had a central blood bank prior to the war with 5,000 donors who provided a regular supply of blood; numbers increased to 350,000 by 1944.[16] It was noted that, 'Supplies were so abundant that at one phase of the war a wounded man was almost lucky if he escaped a transfusion'.[17]

In addition to new drugs and techniques, specialist centres reflecting medical advances and treating new types of war injuries were established. One of these centres specialised in treatment and reconstructive surgery for pilots who had received burns when they crashed. As we will see later in the book, the Royal Air Force had its own specialist facility in East Grinstead where surgeon Archibald McIndoe performed numbers of highly successful surgical procedures on pilots with burns.[18] Owing to sheer weight of numbers and the place that airmen held in the popular imagination, plastic surgeon and burns specialist McIndoe was able to improve his technique and provide some relief from permanent disfigurement.[19] Another important aspect of treatment, which was not strictly medical, was improved speed of transport which ensured that casualties moved to field hospitals more quickly and with reasonable levels of comfort. When the wounded arrived at these stations, more complicated injuries could be treated in the field, increasing the chances of recovery. Field hospitals were moved more regularly; often with little notice.[20] Other medical treatment was made portable; in the Middle East neurosurgery units were mobile and offered immediate care to the injured. Effective methods were employed so servicemen returned to Britain relatively quickly should serious injury have been sustained or a long period of treatment and recovery be required. The increased use of aircraft to transport the wounded shortened the time getting back to expert care in Britain. As rehabilitation relied on early intervention, getting back to a location where the regime could start was a vital stage of the whole process.

While innovations in drugs, medical techniques and even more effective transport saved lives, there is little doubt that as many survived extensive injury, there were other considerations that had to be made in regard to them. Innovations in medical treatment that owed more to a range of therapies than to drugs were also developed, and it is to this that the chapter now turns. During the Second World War, physical medicine developed new techniques and regimes, thus enlarging on concepts of rehabilitation that had begun in the First World War and had largely been forgotten.

Physiotherapy was one such area. While not a new form of treatment, the growth of physiotherapy, as an active as opposed to a passive treatment, throughout the 1920s and 1930s and its expansion during the Second World War had lasting implications for many injured people. In 1938, a Massage Corps was established in preparation for hostilities.[21] Although the establishment of a Massage Corps showed that physiotherapy was gaining in acceptance as a form of treatment, medical practitioners were not completely convinced as to its value. Even in 1939, the medical profession had not been certain of the impact of physiotherapy, the *British Medical Journal* suggesting that in restoring function to fracture cases, occupational therapy was 'more important'.[22] Despite the British Medical Association's (BMA's) scepticism, by 1942 there were 6,000 members of the Massage Corps working in various locations around the world.[23] Methods became more scientifically based and benefits of this type of treatment were becoming more evident to the medical profession. Even the name changed in 1943 when the Massage Corps became the Physiotherapy Service. The war interfered with some treatment, for instance short wave therapy and diathermy had to be stopped as they affected with aircraft radio waves, but physiotherapy became an important therapeutic practice toward the rebuilding of the injured.

Medical technologies were also advanced by the war, including improvement in the development and provision of artificial limbs. By 1940, those who had lost limbs in the Blitz were issued with a free prosthesis and spare limbs were available to them from 1943.[24] Innovations in techniques and materials in the fitting and production of artificial limbs were also developed, including cineplasty, an operation where the muscles of the remaining stump were used to assist in the activation of a prosthesis.[25] Like physiotherapy and drug developments, these specific therapies advanced more rapidly due both to the necessity of recovery to feed the war machine with the requisite number of bodies, and greater numbers of injured people with which the medical profession had to deal. The lines between Service and civilian hospitals were blurred with the establishment of the Emergency Medical Service in 1937, and as the war progressed EMS hospitals adopted the Service method of keeping patient records. In order to solve some of the logistical problems that were associated with this mammoth task of injured people, the process of rehabilitation was developed and perfected during the Second World War.

Bodily 'making do'

One of the slogans from the war, 'make do and mend', could have been applied to the efforts of the Services to make healthy bodies to participate in the war. The Services required substantial numbers of fit men, and what could not be found was created. For some recruits between the wars, rehabilitation began before they were able to participate in Service life. Damage to bodies as a direct result of low standards of living had to be ameliorated to provide a fighting force. The emphasis on programmes for good health, diet and exercise had a direct impact on the Army, so physical training was employed to reduce the effect of poor health, nutrition and lack of exercise. In the inter-war period, the Army devised a system so fit men could be 'made' from the poor standard of recruits. Sub-standard Recruits Physical Development Depots were opened after the First World War and operated until 1939. Their purpose was to make strong fit men out of the groups of undernourished and unfit men who offered their bodies to the State. The State, in its efforts to create a fit fighting force, did not fail them. Instead of rejecting unfit men immediately, the Army provided good food and physical training for men at these depots.[26] In 1937, the Secretary of State for War, Oliver Hore-Belisha, declared that these depots were 'one of the finest services that the Army had rendered to the community.'[27] The efforts on behalf of the recruits brought them up to acceptable standards for military service, a necessity as Britain prepared itself, however reluctantly, for war. A report on Sub-standard Recruits Depots in 1943 detailed, 'thereby was inaugurated an experiment in social medicine of vast importance, and few were aware at that time of its implications'.[28] As we will see, this 'experiment' was already being carried out within a number of schools and industry. Although the Depots were closed in 1939, the War Office re-opened them during the war when those conscripted under the National Service Acts were found to be in relatively poor physical shape. This was despite the more concerted efforts of the national fitness campaign of the 1930s, as large numbers were required to maintain military strength in a total war.[29] Two Depots specialised in defects such as scoliosis, poor posture and flat feet; conditions that would have previously barred anyone from being accepted into the Forces. The first Depot was re-opened in 1941, and in two years 12,000 men had undergone an eight week course of remedial training and physiotherapy, as well as drill, games and recreation.[30] One of the Depots upgraded 80% of its recruits to A1 fitness.[31] A few officers wounded in the fighting and in need of 'restoration' were also included in the regime at the Physical Development Depots.[32] This application of therapy to raise standards was also applied to women who were conscripted or who enlisted in the Auxiliary Territorial Service (ATS); they were sent to Reconditioning Depots to have 'postural or foot defects' cured and overall fitness levels raised to a higher standard.[33]

In addition to bodily fitness, emphasis was also placed on mental health and strength. The association of fitness of body and mind, established medical opinion, was strongly reinforced by the nature of military service. The process of emasculation was played out on the body. Men who 'broke down' during battle were judged 'feminine' and unsuitable for military life.

Throughout the early decades of the twentieth century, recruits' bodies had been examined and graded for their ability to serve the needs of the military, whose demands altered as the century progressed and the nature of warfare changed. In the early part of the century, medical examinations of potential recruits were conducted in a cursory way; a visual examination of their physique and mouth was the standard check.[34] Between the wars, physical examination was conducted in a more in-depth way, and emphasis was placed on volunteers' mental capacity for coping with the strains of battle. Throughout their military service men were tested, categorised and graded. Even when recovering from injury, servicemen were graded, and specific tasks were assigned to the grade in which they were placed. In Convalescent Depots, men were graded according to their fitness levels, usually on a weekly basis. They underwent different levels of tests, usually on an assault course, and if they were able to manage particular tasks, were moved to the next level.[35] As we will see, grading was particularly important for those undergoing rehabilitation.

The growth of rehabilitation

While advances in medical science improved survival rates from wounds, and there were better prognoses for a full recovery, there remained the problem of restoring a patient to full function. As we have seen, concerns were expressed surrounding permanent debility which could result from a broken leg in the 1930s. As the war progressed, the need for an effective system of treatment to return the many injured of the war back to health became even more vital. A regime that ensured that full function was restored to patients after injury was of paramount importance to a nation requiring enormous manpower. One of the most important developments in physical medicine during the war was rehabilitation. Richard Titmuss noted: 'The creation of a framework for a national rehabilitation scheme may thus be recorded as one of the chief successes of the Government's Emergency Medical Service.'[36]

By 1941, 'rehabilitation [had become] the most fashionable word in medicine'.[37] As the nature of its application widened, increasingly diverse terms of reference developed around the word rehabilitation: 'resettlement', 'habilitation' or 'reablement' all referred to the process of becoming fit again after damage.[38] But what was rehabilitation? The Tomlinson Committee, formed principally to institutionalise rehabilitation, as we will see, defined rehabilitation thus: 'In its strictly medical sense, [rehabilitation] means the process of preventing or restoring the loss of muscle tone, restoring the full fluctions of the limbs, and maintaining the patient's general health and strength.'[39] From reports in medical journals such as *The Lancet* and the *British Medical Journal*, and government reports and newspapers such as *The Times*, rehabilitation was an innovative development that had been born out of a need to return the war wounded to their duties with all possible speed. Time was a luxury that the Services could ill afford; a report from one rehabilitation centre noted, 'as many as possible of the patients are discharged to duty without being given sick leave'.[40] According to the *British Medical Journal*, until the British Medical Association's committee on fractures in 1935, organised medicine in Britain had not considered programmes for rehabilitation and resettlement.[41] However, orthopaedic surgeons such as Sir Robert Jones, who treated wounded soldiers during the First World War, provided an important basis for the contemporary rehabilitation model.[42] Credit was given to early pioneers of what became known as rehabilitation in an article in the *British Medical Journal* of 1942: 'Rehabilitation is not a new method of treatment at all. It is the application to all types of recent disability of those varied methods of supervised exercise which exponents of physical medicine have advocated for years.'[43]

Generally, rehabilitation consisted of the process of restoring people to a level of fitness and function. Initially, the regime was prescriptive, concentrated on medical treatment to improve function, working on a system of trial and error.[44] It became virtually impossible for patients to avoid rehabilitation as it was provided for all military and civilian casualties, and those injured working in industry.[45] It was argued successfully that all those involved in the war effort should be provided with access to rehabilitation schemes as it was imperative that important civil defence and industrial work continue.

Early rehabilitation focused on medical treatment after the initial recovery period in hospital and included physiotherapy including different light and heat treatments, galvanism and massage. Rehabilitation became a fundamental part of a hospital stay, and patients were included in the regimes to hasten their recovery. As noted in one report from 1943: 'Instead of being regarded as an ancillary department of a hospital, confined to a limited group of selected patients, it is now becoming recognised as a form of therapy applicable to almost every type of illness or injury.'[46] The hospital became the locus of early rehabilitation, and medical practitioners established programmes that cemented rehabilitation as part of physical medicine. Medical practitioners were educated about the importance of rehabilitation, and practical training was offered including weekend training courses for doctors, fortnightly courses for masseuses and longer courses in occupational therapy.[47]

As patients recovered in hospital, more activity was entered into; remedial exercises were prescribed by physiotherapists and surgeons. As patients responded to the exercise regime, they progressed to more difficult exercises and finally sport and games. How did rehabilitation work on a practical level? Although treatment varied according to the type of injury sustained, a similar method was adopted by most hospitals when a patient was admitted. As soon as possible, patients were busied with occupational therapy; two examples of bedridden types were basket making and rug weaving. The other important aspect of rehabilitation was exercise, and patients were given remedial exercises to perform while still in bed. They were also given different types of physiotherapy, consisting of repetitive exercises usually assisted with strings and pulleys, refined from the earlier designs of the First World War. More active types of physiotherapy were used in hospitals. According to Olive Guthrie-Smith, the developer of the suspension apparatus that bears her name,[48] 'Suspension exercises are varied and interesting to perform owing to the rhythm and freedom of movement.'[49] Other contemporary physiotherapists agreed that 'weightless exercise is almost as good as a swimming pool . . . with the added advantage that it is dry so a chill can be avoided'.[50] Unfortunately those having to practise remedial exercises did not agree they were 'varied and interesting'. Most patients considered them boring and repetitive, but still a necessary part of therapy. After a period of hospitalisation and rehabilitative training, patients were usually transferred to a nation-wide network of Convalescent Homes where further rehabilitation would continue, often in a less formal setting than a hospital. Administration and grading systems were a vital method in this war and rehabilitation was no different, as hospitals and rehabilitation centres placed patients into one of several grades to ensure they received levels of training associated with their standard of fitness. Ostensibly, the foremost purpose of rehabilitation was to restore the same level of health that the injured person had enjoyed prior to their illness or injury. But physical health was not considered the only important factor for full rehabilitation. A report from 1944 noted: 'The importance of the morale factor cannot be over-stressed. It is essential to remove the inertia and despondency of hospitalisation and to restore this "will to get well".'[51]

As we have seen, sport and games had provided entertainment and a restoration of notions of masculinity for men in institutions such as the Star and Garter and St Dunstan's after the First World War, and these activities were more formalised in rehabilitation regimes. Organised sport specifically geared toward regaining fitness became more important in the overall recovery of wounded servicemen. As we will see in the

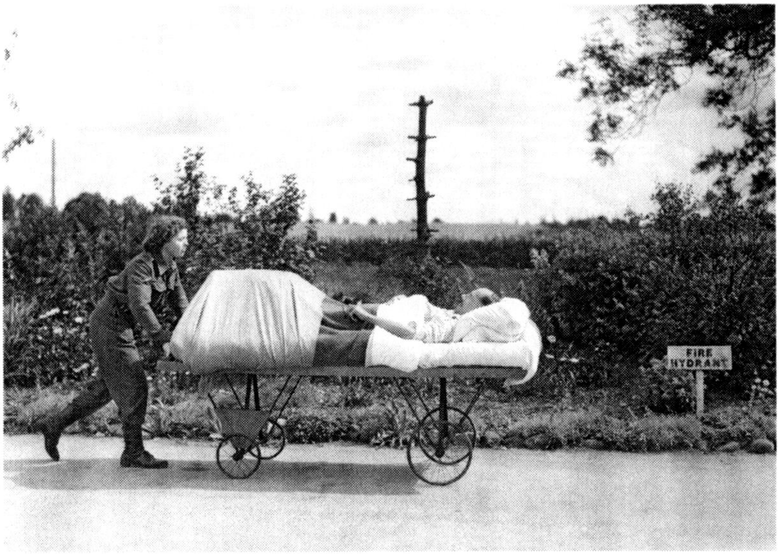

Figure 3.1 Rehabilitation of soldiers from Normandy, 1944, at the Robert Jones and Dame Agnes Hunt Orthopaedic Hospital, Oswestry, Shropshire. This soldier is being walked outside in the open air, which was part of the early stages of rehabilitative therapy (reproduced with permission of the Imperial War Museum)

case studies of the RAF and Stoke Mandeville, many centres established by the Services used sport for rehabilitation; it was considered fun and it was felt that, as enjoyable recreation, it would keep up the spirits of those in the treatment centres while occupying their time. Although the medical profession considered remedial exercises and physiotherapy more important components of the rehabilitative process, sport was imbued with additional benefits that included the psychological. It was also felt that sport would re-create the sense of ordinary human association, particularly for those permanently disabled.[52] Recreational games and sport became important for the physical health and mental well-being of those recovering from injury.

Some patients did not regain full function, yet rehabilitation, as an all-encompassing therapy, was practised to lessen the impact of residual disability. It was for people with disabilities that rehabilitation demonstrated its flexibility as a type of therapy. For men or women in the Services, even if there was serious residual disablement, rehabilitation was provided in order to attain the highest level of fitness and mobility. Centres were established to cater for the treatment of specific types of disability and numbers of these grew as the war progressed. As we will see from the case studies, after 1944 those with paralysis would often be sent to Stoke Mandeville in Aylesbury for rehabilitation.[53] St Dunstan's continued to use its specialised knowledge and years of experience to rehabilitate and retrain blind men and women who had been in the Services. By 1943, 339 men and women who had been blinded were being rehabilitated at St Dunstan's.

As we noted earlier, a serious side effect of disablement was depression and it was important that this situation be avoided, as it interfered with recovery and, probably more importantly, productivity. While exercise and games were an vital part of Service life and also a significant part of rehabilitation programmes, each Service had a different way of dealing with its injured, and operated its individual rehabilitation centre in keeping with its own agenda. Although rehabilitation centres were different in scope to a certain point, all of them had one component in common: the desire to return the soldier, sailor or airman to the war effort as quickly as possible. For those who had suffered permanent disability, it was felt that rehabilitation would lessen that disability or at the very least curb residual impact.[54] Patients in the Services were forced to maintain military discipline while undergoing rehabilitation, and concentrate heavily on their rehabilitation regime. One article noted: 'It is considered that more improvement is made in the early stages of treatment by encouraging the patient to concentrate on overcoming his disability by working away at it all day long.'[55] Hard work was conducted in a number of environments. For those who were returning to the Forces, the emphasis was on cooperation through sport and games, which maintained the camaraderie of Service life; but for those who were civilians or returning to civilian life, rehabilitation therapy was conducted in a different context. One doctor noted: 'It is probably that the advice "get a job on a farm" represented our profession's earliest attempt to deal with the problems of settling patients with a disability.'[56] As noted in the film, *Return to Action*; 'the earth is a good doctor and a patient nurse. Close to the earth with nothing to hurry him and no appointments to keep, a man slows down.'[57] Nature was also a good physical trainer. At many of the rehabilitation centres, the gardens were the patients' first place of work. At Egham, men who had to go back to labouring jobs were kept working in the garden so they would be fit and strong enough to return to work.[58]

While the RAF had a centralised rehabilitation system, other Services did not. The Navy had its own hospital centres, but it usually discharged most of its severely wounded to civilian hospitals. Naval and Army patients were transferred to EMS hospitals, 'until a high proportion of military patients in the United Kingdom were in civil hospitals'.[59] Eventually, the Navy had its own rehabilitation centres but they were not opened until 1944.[60] The Army, however, continued to rely heavily on civilian resources of EMS hospitals for the treatment and rehabilitation of its soldiers. It ensured that discipline was maintained by placing its own physical training instructors into rehabilitation units, some of which were operated by the EMS and others by the Convalescent Department.[61]

For those employed in the Forces whose injuries resulted in permanent disability, being 'invalided out' was the only option. Although a few stayed in the Services after disablement, the majority of servicemen and women were invalided out on medical grounds. Figures for discharge from the Army differed widely from year to year. In 1943, only 46% of total discharges were a result of enemy action, whereas in 1945 this had risen to 75%.[62] Apart from enemy action, or injury as a result of being in a war zone, though not directly attributable to the fighting, servicemen were discharged for a multitude of reasons. Mental disorders accounted for 50% of all discharges on medical grounds other than physical injury.[63] High numbers of stomach ulcers, induced by stress, led to early discharge.

While in the Forces, a patient's rehabilitation was the responsibility of their Service, but should their disability be permanent, they were discharged and their final rehabilitation became the State's responsibility. All of the Services used the employment retraining provided by the Ministry of Pensions or the Ministry of Labour and National Service. It was believed that, despite serious injury or merely not being up to the rigours of fighting, the discharged serviceman could still serve his country in industry to assist the war effort. Discharge from the Services upon serious injury was normally immediate, but this practice gradually changed. Emphasis was placed instead on keeping up morale, as part of the process of rehabilitation, thereby increasing the serviceman's potential for complete recovery.[64] In view of this, members of the Forces who had suffered injury were not discharged until eight months plus 56 days of leave had elapsed.[65] How easily an ex-serviceman could move back into civilian employment was an important consideration. The level of 'degree of disablement' was an indicator of how easily this could be accomplished. If the degree of residual disability was judged to be 40% or less, then the Army deemed that ex-servicemen would have access to a more varied choice of employment than would others with a higher disability percentage.

Though unable to serve on the front lines, discharged ex-servicemen were utilised in helping the war effort. It was essential to hasten the return of injured people, whether disabled or not, back to factories, mines or fighting. The State was keenly interested in and supported rehabilitation; the Ministry of Labour and National Service controlled many of the civilian rehabilitation centres that were opened both during and after the war.[66] Disabled ex-servicemen were often sent for retraining at centres such as Egham, which opened in 1941, or Roffey Park, where they retrained to gain skills for other types of war work.[67] A pamphlet in 1943 for Egham noted: 'The object of the Centre is to restore confidence and mental and physical fitness through healthy indoor and outdoor occupation, and physical exercises.'[68]

The majority of disabled men and women attending training centres were unable to return to their former occupations, but were trained for alternative types of employment. Women were not allowed to attend any rehabilitation centres, unless they were specifically designed for them, as for the most part, sexes were segregated. It is clear that one of the main reasons for the rapid and large-scale adoption of rehabilitation by the State during and after the Second World War was that manpower was at such a premium.[69] In a report by the Minister of Labour and National Service, in 1941, Ernest Bevin noted:

> There must be any thousands of men and women in the country who, having received little more than a cash compensation for a disability are now unfitted for productive employment; this is a waste of man-power which is impossible to defend.[70]

Essentially, rehabilitation's elastic definition and its many applications ensured that many disparate interests were served by it. The medical profession achieved good outcomes for patients, and the impact of associated therapies such as physiotherapy was more apparent, which reinforced physiotherapists' association and acceptance by the medical hierarchy. For the Ministry of Labour and National Service, rehabilitation was about making good use of available manpower for industry. The War Office was able to deploy the Forces and reuse them even after they had been injured. Although physical recovery of the individual was the main aim and most desired result of rehabilitation, there were other factors that impinged on its enthusiastic adoption by the State. Was the restoration of health to the individual really the most important task of rehabilitation? As well as a return to the best possible health, notwithstanding residual disability, fundamental consideration was also given to the injured person's economic capacity as a worker or as part of the war effort. The State considered the return of those injured or with residual disability to a 'normal' life a 'national duty'.[71] The importance of rehabilitation for workers was put pithily in a letter to *The Times* from 'Horder' of the British Red Cross and Order of St John in 1943. He noted, 'we "service" our taxi-cabs and how rarely do we see one "break-down"? Is it not time that we began to "service" our workers?'[72] Co-opting medical professionals to oversee rehabilitation was also possible as it was easier for the State to harness the expertise of doctors during wartime for service to the State. Doctors enthusiastically adopted the State's aims, exemplified by surgeon Harold Balme in a book, *The Unfit Made Fit*:

> And it must not be forgotten that not only the injured man and his family, but also the nation as a whole suffers economically from a man's inability to work. Both in wartime and in the period of post-war reconstruction, this factor is of vital importance to Britain.[73]

However, there were also detractors in the medical profession who did not agree with the prioritisation of rehabilitation. As one article in *The Lancet* noted:

> Many of the more conservative members of the profession are suspicious of what they consider political boosting of 'this rehabilitation ramp'. They feel, wrongly no doubt, that their patients have got on very well in the past without all this fuss about rehabilitation and they see no reason why they should not do so in the future.[74]

In addition, some of the smaller hospitals were poorly staffed and did not have the necessary equipment for the types of therapy considered essential for rehabilitation.

Prior to the Second World War, centres for rehabilitation were small and were only used successfully in cases of particular types of disablement, like fractures. They were not a large systematised programme, where numbers of professionals from different areas of expertise worked jointly within a framework to ensure that the best medical and employment outcomes were achieved. Answering a question in the House of Commons, Ernest Brown, Minister of Health, noted the wide range of treatments, both medical and vocational, that rehabilitation encompassed. Before the war, only certain types of injury were treated and benefits were limited to a relatively small number of patients. Brown reported that basic methods had improved and become more sophisticated as the war progressed, so by 1945 over 250 hospitals in England and Wales had adopted rehabilitation methods, 'including physiotherapy, remedial exercises and handicraft'.[75]

As the war progressed, rehabilitation became even more systematised. Medicine, government, industry and voluntary services combined to assist injured and disabled people through medical rehabilitation, where the most effective contemporary medical care restored individuals to the best possible health and then moved them to industrial or vocational rehabilitation, where the individual learned to go back to work, retraining for a new job if their disability necessitated it. As we will see, rehabilitation was used in a number of ways, including socialising those with facial disfigurements and ensuring that those with residual disabilities coped with their altered status and renegotiated environment. Rehabilitation was borne out of a modern, administratively led environment; it required sophisticated administration to ensure its function, which meant cooperation between government departments, which oversaw rehabilitation and outside interests. It was popular because its successful application meant that those injured recovered quickly, with minimised impact of residual disability and could return to the war effort sooner. After the war, the term rehabilitation was still imbued with such meaning that when changes to the names of industrial and vocational training centres were mooted, it was pointed out in a memo from the Ministry of Labour and National Service that 'in the word "rehabilitation", we have something of real value which should not be lightly discarded'.[76] While this was laudable and also an obvious commitment to the war wounded, there were other factors that contributed to the government's eager adoption of methods of rehabilitation, including the potential for saving costs on supporting disabled people.

Rehabilitation centres opened and regimes for the restoration of combatants and workers continued throughout the Second World War. It was clear that the nation could not afford to service the needs of invalids, and only those that worked hard deserved the assistance the State willingly offered. The State theoretically, and in many cases materially, provided a new way of life for those that worked hard to restore their bodies to the highest levels of functionality. Rehabilitation was effectively a method of man management, adopted from contemporary modes of management that had become popular throughout the 1920s and 1930s, one of which was the maintenance of a healthy workforce and the limitation of costly time spent away from work.[77] Wartime conditions favoured these

Figure 3.2 Amputees exercising in the gymnasium, Queen Mary's Roehampton, 1944 (reproduced with permission of the Imperial War Museum)

systems of management, and they were necessary to ensure that the war machine was stoked with a requisite number of bodies. The legacy of rehabilitative therapy in the Second World War was in the scale of its use, its systems and administration, and its wide application to injuries and disabilities.

The Tomlinson Report

One of the most influential government reports of the war was produced by the Inter-departmental Committee on the Rehabilitation and Resettlement of Disabled Persons, headed by George Tomlinson, which reviewed rehabilitation services and put forward plans for supporting disabled people after the war was over. The report was published in 1942 and presented to Parliament in 1943, and was instrumental in informing government policy for disabled people after the war.[78] Its recommendations included the expansion of rehabilitation services for all patients, protected employment for disabled people, and cooperation between numbers of government departments, medical professionals and voluntary agencies to ensure that the best possible outcomes were achieved. It noted:

> a disabled person represents a double loss to the community, vis. a reduction of the total productive capacity and an increase in the cost of maintenance and remedial services, the restoration of the disabled person to productive employment will be an economic advantage.[79]

In addition to this scheme, an inter-departmental committee was established to make proposals for more permanent systems to train and employ disabled people after the war.[80] The main principle underlying the report was that the only acceptable result of rehabilitation for a disabled person was 'employment which he can take and keep on his merits as a worker in normal competition with his fellows'.[81] Ian Fraser, President of St Dunstan's and parliamentarian, noted:

> A unique feature of the Tomlinson Report is that it is perhaps the first State document which advocates that the State itself shall handle the problem of finding suitable work for disabled persons, a problem which in the past, voluntary organisations have endeavoured to solve.[82]

The Tomlinson Report also made the distinction that had been established for some time that physical and mental disabilities were not synonymous. On the contrary, it noted that the 'rehabilitation and resettlement of mental patients is a special task with peculiar difficulties'.[83] The Tomlinson Report had a long legacy; its recommendations were carried out, and the Standing Committees that oversaw the programme for disabled people that were established after the war survived changes of government until the last report was published in 1956.

Working for war

The report of the Inter-departmental Committee on the Rehabilitation and Resettlement of Disabled Persons applied mainly to those injured in the war or as a result of enemy action. As victims of bombing, civilians became a type of war wounded, therefore joining the ranks of ex-Service personnel who received a different standard of treatment and assistance. Those already disabled were initially left out of rehabilitation services, although the report did mention that the industrial disabled should be assisted under hospital schemes, which had been recommended by the Delevingne Committee in 1939.[84] Ernest Bevin, Minister of Labour and National Service, agitated for rehabilitation methods to be applied to all citizens, not just members of the Services. He wrote in a report:

> Both Committees were of the opinion that the Government's responsibility in respect of the Civil Defence Services and civilians who suffer injury through enemy action should be as complete as that in respect of ex-service casualties, but I take the view that casualties in industry should be treated on exactly that same basis.[85]

Bevin wished to remove the preferential system for disabled ex-servicemen, and wanted to see all people awarded the same consideration as war disabled.[86] He was concerned about the industrial disabled, as numbers of accidents in factories were increasing.[87] Bevin demonstrated his commitment to those injured in industry as he established special rehabilitation centres for them. In 1942, the Claremont Hotel in Manchester was opened to house a rehabilitation centre for disabled dock workers.[88] Yet there remained few centres specifically for those disabled in industry, despite the necessity of maintaining industrial production to help the war effort.[89] Many industrial rehabilitation centres were operated by their own industry; the Miners' Rehabilitation Centres and hospitals were controlled under the auspices of the Miners' Welfare Commission. As accident rates in mines were five times higher than in other industry, and as products from mines were crucial for the functioning of industry in peace as well as during wartime, these rehabilitation centres were fundamental to the maintenance of an industrial workforce.[90] As the war progressed, the government, through its different departments, set up special units to rehabilitate workers from particular industries. The Ministry of Supply established rehabilitation units in Ordnance factories to treat those injured while working in the extremely hazardous munitions industry.[91] The recognition of industrial workers as vital to the war effort was key to the establishment of these rehabilitation centres.

While the war created numbers of disabled people, what opportunities were afforded to those already disabled? Prior to the war, overall unemployment rates were very high, especially in the north east of England, central Scotland and south Wales.[92] With the onset of war, the demand for labour in industries, particularly munitions and mining, increased dramatically. Neither employing large numbers of women nor redeploying retired people could quench this thirst for industrial and administrative labour. Disabled people, who had endured extremely limited access to employment for decades, became valued workers. In October 1941, the Ministry of Labour announced an 'Interim Scheme for the Training and Settlement of Disabled Persons in Industry'.[93] The government required disabled people for work in particular jobs, especially in munitions factories.[94] In addition to the official scheme for employing disabled people, a casual system was in place where those with disabilities filled the jobs of those who had worked in hospitals and farms.[95] This scheme provided jobs for between 300,000 and 500,000 disabled people during the war.[96] Disabled women joined the Auxiliary Forces such as the Women's Land Army. Journals for deaf people reported proudly on the exploits of these women.[97] Disabled people took up positions as clerical workers in which there were no physical barriers. In 1940, Emily Porter, who had bovine tuberculosis of the spine, got a clerical job censoring mail. After the war, she progressed into a permanent job as a civil servant.[98] The war helped many disabled people into jobs and moved them away permanently from a life of unemployment and poverty. However, the Inter-departmental Committee on the Rehabilitation and Resettlement of Disabled Persons warned that this situation might be temporary:

> The real position is obscured by the prevailing shortage of labour and the ease with which disabled persons (including many who are below the normal standard of fitness) can obtain employment for which in normal times a higher standard of fitness would be required.[99]

Training for disabled ex-servicemen had to be thought out carefully. As noted in a letter from a Chairman of a machine tool maker to the Minister of Reconstruction in 1943:

> If Industry is limited to employing ex-servicemen, and particularly crippled ex-servicemen, solely in labouring jobs, it will make it much more difficult to fit in the men. This applies particularly in the case of the crippled, because labouring, except for lift operating, crane-driving and a few other such jobs, is usually heavy work.[100]

As a result of the war and the resultant labour shortage, disabled people were provided with the chance to do jobs for which they had been thought unqualified. Unlike women, disabled people were never conscripted, but filled jobs recently occupied by people who were needed for other types of work. Many disabled people were trained in munitions work, which was deemed suitable employment.[101] In a letter to *The Guardian*, Mr G.-W. Mayfield from the Hull Education Committee noted: 'Owing to the war there has not for a generation been so few unemployed deaf people in the country.'[102] In some cases, disablement, particularly deafness, was regarded as an asset in the workplace as the noise level caused during certain stages in shell construction could damage hearing, and, due to the lack of safety equipment, deaf people were best placed to perform this job.

Blind people also clamoured to be included in war work. At the National League of the Blind Conference in July 1940, blind people passed resolutions pressing the government to give them work of 'national importance'.[103] By 1942, the Ministry of Labour and National Service had authorised employment exchanges to give priority and look upon blind people 'favourably' when they made applications to work in industry.[104]

Disabled people who were unable to get paid employment, or those working who wanted to do more, helped on the home front. Many participated willingly in the 'Dig for Victory' campaign, and journals for blind and deaf people contained instructions for setting up allotments and what food to grow. In Leicester, a blind man and a single armed amputee took over an allotment as part of their contribution to the war effort.[105] Others performed emergency work, and some deaf people trained as stretcher-bearers.[106] Disabled people made important contributions to the war, and their value as workers signalled a change in perception of disabled people's abilities.

Daily life with disabilities

Beyond issues of employment, daily life in Britain proved difficult for disabled people, as they had their own unique problems. Air raids were one difficulty; how could those that could not walk get to air raid shelters? As they were unable to hear air raid sirens, deaf people used ingenious methods to be warned of approaching enemy planes. Some deaf people tied long pieces of string to their toes, and the end was dangled out of a bedroom window, so when the warning sounded the Air Raid Precautions (ARP) warden would pull heavily on the string in order to wake deaf people up.[107] Others kept pets on their beds, and when the animal jumped at the siren's sound, then its owner knew that it was time to take cover.[108]

Many disabled adults found employment and new opportunities during the war. For children with disabilities, especially those who were institutionalised, the situation was less clear cut. When it was announced that cities at risk of bombing were to be evacuated, those considered vulnerable were moved out of metropolitan centres. The groups mainly comprised able-bodied children and mothers, but 'cripples' were included in those to be evacuated.[109] It was also deemed necessary to clear hospital beds, as it was thought they would soon be filled by war casualties. The EMS estimated that 300,000 casualties would require beds, so all patients who could walk were sent home.[110] This was of especial concern for those with contagious diseases. Patients with sputum-positive tuberculosis and other diseases were 'discharged wholesale from institutions without any arrangements having been made for their alternative treatment and care'.[111] Many bed-ridden and disabled patients were sent back to their homes, despite few facilities and an uncertain welcome when they got there. Similarly to families who vacated their homes, there was little organisation for disabled people apart from the initial evacuation plan.

As children were usually those destined for evacuation, those at residential schools for disabled children were also included in the move away from major cities. However, the organisation of evacuation for disabled children was less ad hoc than for disabled people turned out of hospitals. In London, the Blanche Nevile School for the Deaf was evacuated on 1 October 1939, and relocated near Lowestoft. After that, the School was moved further away from the threat of bombs to North Wales, where it joined five other deaf schools.[112] The Liverpool School for the Blind relocated itself out of the city centre, the relatively short distance to Rhyl.[113] Not all disabled schools were evacuated. Some deaf schools, such as one in Leicester, closed while trenches were dug and air-raid shelters built, and then re-opened, the children having been taught in their homes in small groups while these safety improvements were made.[114] Leatherhead Royal School for the Blind's buildings were requisitioned by the government for the duration of the war, but those enrolled in training and in workshops were not evacuated, but boarded in a hostel close by in order that they could resume their employment.[115] Many evacuated schools and their pupils stayed where they were relocated for the duration of the war. Some schools provided spaces for wounded soldiers to recuperate, yet at the same time continued educating children. The Heritage Craft School in Chailey took in hundreds of wounded men, just as it had during the First World War.[116] Some schools closed completely when war broke out. As an alternative to school, disabled children who normally lived with their parents were sent to hospitals or disabled children's homes for educational purposes. Vera Dean, who had cerebral palsy, was sent to Queen Mary's Hospital, where she lived for the duration of the war.[117] Disabled children were not easily billeted and the lack of places to live meant some relocated day schools were forced to become residential.[118]

Conclusions

During the Second World War, advances in medicine increased survival chances for injured people. While there has been much discussion about whether or not war is good for medicine, I would argue that war was certainly instrumental in establishing the system of rehabilitation. However, rehabilitation was not merely a medical treatment, it was a holistic type of therapy that blended medical, employment and social techniques that ensured that those injured, both combatants and civilians, were provided with support to ensure that they made the best possible recovery. Rehabilitation regimes required cooperation on a large scale, and total war provided the perfect locus for ensuring that collaboration between the many potentially competing interests occurred. In addition, numbers of men trained in modern business techniques, and who understood the impact of wasted man hours, entered the Services, and used their expertise to improve levels of efficiency, in line with theories of efficiency and man management. Rehabilitation was the perfect setting for theories to be played out. Residual disability was no barrier to employment and, as we will see, did not always result in discharge from the Forces. Rehabilitation was a successful system for returning those in the Services back to the frontline defence of the nation and redeploying those with disabilities to employment in industry. Rehabilitation could not be considered complete until the State had fulfilled its 'national duty' and the rehabilitated person was employed. For those already disabled, the war presented them with some further opportunities, especially in employment. Disabled people presented themselves as willing workers both in industry and also on the home front. Disabled people's bodies were redeployed to assist in the war effort in industry; those who had been injured and discharged, or those who were disabled before the war.

Rehabilitation signified an important change in attitude; it made government, industry and medicine rethink its opinion of those with disabilities, particularly in relation to disabled people as workers. The State had also experienced the drain of large numbers of disabled ex-servicemen on the economy after the First World War. Naturally, this repositioning of disabled people from societal drain to valued workers was largely due to the demands of a wartime economy; nevertheless, disabled people did make important contributions to the war effort, as citizens and workers. Faced with a common enemy, the war integrated disabled people in society in a way not seen previously. Daily life during the war presented specific difficulties for disabled people; institutionalised children were moved great distances and the long-term sick were removed from hospitals where they had remained for numbers of years. Nonetheless, the Second World War was a catalyst in changing attitudes toward disabled people. The theories underpinning rehabilitation and its application to all disabled people from the 1940s through the efforts of the Tomlinson Committee ensured that more of them were enabled to take part in economic and social life in ways that had not been available to them previously.

Notes

1 'Correspondence', *British Medical Journal* (16 May 1942), 621.

2 See Bourke, *Dismembering the Male*; Carden-Coyne, *Reconstructing the Body*.

3 Leon Luis, 'Recent Adaptations in the Treatment of Arm Amputations, Kineplastic Surgery and Arm Prostheses', *Annals of the Royal College of Surgeons of England*, Vol. 3 (November 1948), 227.

4 Cooter, 'Medicine and the Goodness of War', 147–59.

5 It was estimated that 65,000 servicemen were admitted for traffic accidents not due to operations of war. Of these, 23,000 were aboard motorcycles. Eileen M. Brooke, 'Emergency Medical Service', in W. Franklin-Mellor (ed.), *History of the Second World War: Casualties and Medical Statistics* (London, 1972), 793.

6 Frederick Cartwright, *A Social History of Medicine* (London, 1977), 169.

7 Hardy, *Health and Medicine in Britain Since 1860*, 104.

8 For accounts of Fleming's work see Ronald Hare, *The Birth of Penicillin and the Disarming of Microbes* (London, 1970).

9 John Ellis, *The Sharp End: The Fighting Man in World War II* (London, 1990), 170.

10 Cartwright, *A Social History of Medicine*, 148.

11 Hardy, *Health and Medicine in Britain Since 1860*, 136.

12 In his article on the trials of penicillin in the Second World War, Peter Neushul argues that military intervention with medicine ensured that the development of penicillin from its experimental stages to a mass produced drug was shortened in an unprecedented way. Peter Neushul, 'Fighting Research: Army

Participation in the Clinical Testing and Mass Production of Penicillin During the Second World War', in Roger Cooter, Mark Hamson and Steve Sturdy (eds), *War, Medicine and Modernity* (Stroud, 1998).

13 Ellis, *The Sharp End*, 170.

14 Those who survived with a disability during the Second World War was 14%, whereas in the First World War it was 8%. Franklin-Mellor, *History of the Second World War*, 445.

15 Douglas Guthrie, *A History of Medicine* (London, 1945), 350.

16 Lionel Whitby, 'The Transfusion of Blood and Other Fluids', in Sir Zachary Cope (ed.), *History of the Second World War: Surgery* (London, 1953), 47.

17 Ibid., 50.

18 It was noted that 80% of those badly injured went back to flying duty and only 5% had been invalided out of the Service. Memo to Sir Charles Portal from Archibald McIndoe (1944), AIR 8/796, National Archives, London. See also *The Lancet* (6 May 1944), 609.

19 McIndoe's patients wrote about their experiences, and were also the subjects of books about the Guinea Pig Club, a group formed during the war comprised solely of burned airmen. For personal testimonies see Richard Hillary, *The Last Enemy* (London, 1961); William Simpson, *The Way of Recovery* (London, 1944); and Peter Williams and Ted Harrison, *McIndoe's Army* (London, 1981).

20 See Brenda McBryde, *A Nurse's War* (London, 1980), for details of her personal experience of field hospitals during the Second World War.

21 The Corps was mainly staffed with volunteers; in 1938 there were 1,500. Jane Wicksteed, *The Growth of a Profession* (London, 1948), 132.

22 *British Medical Journal* (19 August 1939), 419.

23 Jean Barclay, *In Good Hands: The History of the Chartered Society of Physiotherapy 1894–1994* (Oxford, 1994), 125.

24 Gordon Phillips, *Best Foot Forward: Chas A. Blatchford and Sons Ltd. 1890–1990* (Cambridge, 1990), 84.

25 This operation was performed far more extensively in the United States than in Britain. Henry H. Kessler, *Cineplasty* (Springfield, K, 1947), ix, 51.

26 'Unfit Recruits', *British Medical Journal* (11 December 1937), 1204.

27 Ibid., 1204.

28 Research Board for the Correlation of Medical Science and Physical Education, *The Sub-standard Recruit* (1943), CMA SA/RBC C.7/4, Wellcome Trust, London.

29 *Report of the Inter-departmental Committee on the Rehabilitation and Resettlement of Disabled Persons* (1943), CAB 117/145, National Archives, London.

30 Services Sub-Committee, 'The Sub-standard Recruit' (undated, but the Services Sub-Committee first met in December 1943), CMA SA/RBC C7.4, Wellcome Trust, London.

31 'Rehabilitation in the Army', *British Medical Journal* (13 March 1943), 338.
32 Ibid., 338.
33 Ibid., 338.
34 D. Silbey, 'Bodies and Cultures Collide: Enlistment, the Medical Exam and the British Working Class, 1914–1916', *Social History of Medicine*, Vol. 17, No. 1 (2004), 61–76.
35 Stanley D. Large, 'Rehabilitation', *Journal of the Royal Army Medical Corps*, Vol. LXXX, No. 3 (March 1943) and No. 4 (April 1943), 123, 175.
36 Richard M. Titmuss, *Problems of Social Policy* (London, 1950), 480.
37 Ibid., 478.
38 For a discussion of terms, see *British Medical Journal* (24 March 1941), 793.
39 *Tomlinson Report of the Inter-departmental Committee on the Rehabilitation and Resettlement of Disabled Persons* (1941–43), CAB 117/145, National Archives, London.
40 R.G. Henderson, 'Rehabilitation at an EMS Hospital', *The Lancet* (3 June 1944), 734.
41 'Resettling Disabled Persons', *British Medical Journal* (5 April 1958), 818.
42 *The Lancet* (29 July 1944), 131. For work on early rehabilitation methods, particularly those of Robert Jones, see Alan and Malkin, 'The Conquest of Disability'; Watson, *Civilisation and the Cripple*; and Anderson, *A Record of Fifty Years' Service to the Disabled.*
43 *British Medical Journal* (17 October 1942), 466.
44 'Provided the error is recognised early': quote from an unnamed commanding officer of a rehabilitation centre, *The Hospital*, Vol. 41, No. 7 (July 1945), 211.
45 War Cabinet Home Policy Committee Social Services Section (26 February 1941), CAB 117/145, National Archives, London.
46 Emergency Medical Services, Memorandum No. 6, *The Organisation of a Hospital Rehabilitation Department* (1943), FD 1/6811, National Archives, London, 2.
47 Ibid., 8.
48 The apparatus and its name underwent a number of changes. The apparatus was originally called 'Slings and Pulleys', then 'Treatment by Suspension' and finally the 'Guthrie-Smith Apparatus'; *St Mary's Hospital School of Physiotherapy (Swedish Institute) Magazine* (1954), 8.
49 Olive F. Guthrie-Smith, 'Rehabilitation Exercises', *Journal of Massage and Medical Gymnastics* (October 1940), 3.
50 Nellie Lanckenau, 'Rehabilitation by Modern Methods of Exercise', in W.B. Doherty and D.D. Runes (eds), *Rehabilitation of the War Injured: A Symposium* (London, 1945), 618.
51 Service Sub-Committee of the Research Board for Correlation of Medical Science and Physical Education, *Report on Wounded and Disabled, Part III* (15 March 1944), CMA SA/RBC C7.4, Wellcome Trust, London.

52 Elvira Hobson, *Physiotherapy in Paraplegia* (London, 1956), 77.
53 For more detailed examination of Stoke Mandeville, see Sir Ludwig Guttmann, *Spinal Cord Injuries: Comprehensive Management Research* (Oxford, 1973); Joan Scruton, *Stoke Mandeville: Road to the Paralympics* (Aylesbury, 1998); and John Surtees, *Chaseley: A Home from Home* (Eastbourne, 1997).
54 Reginald Watson-Jones, 'Rehabilitation in the Royal Air-Force', in Doherty and Runes (eds), *Rehabilitation of the War Injured*, 439.
55 R.N. Houlding, 'Rehabilitation of Injured Air Crews in Great Britain', in ibid., 443.
56 George H. Dobney, 'Work on the Land: Its Potentialities for Resettlement of the Disabled', *Rehabilitation*, No. 4 (May 1952), 6.
57 Text *Return to Action*, INF 6/1260 (1947) National Archives, London, 2.
58 Ministry of Labour and National Service, 'Egham Rehabilitation Centre' (no date but likely 1946), LAB 18/367, National Archives, London.
59 Franklin-Mellor, *History of the Second World War*, 100.
60 Letter to Miss Lloyd-Williams, Secretary of the Research Board, Ling Association from K. Digby-Bell, Surgeon Captain of the Medical Department of the Royal Navy (14 January 1944), CMA SA/RBC C7.5, Wellcome Trust, London.
61 *Report on the Wounded and Disabled*, Part III, Services Sub-Committee of the Research Board for the Correlation of Medical Science and Physical Education (15 March 1944), CMA SA/RBC C.7.4, Wellcome Trust, London.
62 Franklin-Mellor, *History of the Second World War*, 444.
63 Ibid., 439.
64 *Report on the Wounded and Disabled*, Part III.
65 'Concessions to Injured Servicemen', *Manchester Guardian* (19 December 1945).
66 The Egham Centre in Surrey was one of the largest government-run rehabilitation centres. *The Lancet* (29 April 1944), 596.
67 Ministry of Labour and National Service Pamphlet 'Roffey Park, Horsham', undated, presumably 1943, FD 1/6809, National Archives, London.
68 Pamphlet from Egham Centre in Surrey, Ministry of Labour and National Service PL 137/1943, October 1943, FD 1/6809, National Archives, London.
69 Cooter, *Surgery and Society in Peace and War*, 199.
70 Memorandum, Rehabilitation, Training and Employment of Disabled Persons (November 1941), CAB 117/145, National Archives, London.
71 *Tomlinson Report of the Inter-departmental Committee on the Rehabilitation and Resettlement of Disabled Persons.*
72 'Health of Industrial Workers', *The Times* (1 March 1943).
73 Harold Balme, *The Unfit Made Fit: Britain Advances* (London, 1943), 9.
74 'In England Now', *The Lancet* (19 February 1944), 260.

75 *The Lancet* (10 February 1945), 196.
76 Memo from Howie Mitchell, Ministry of Labour and National Service, Industrial Rehabiliation Centres Change of Name (9 November 1946), LAB 16/462, National Archives, London.
77 Mark Harrison, *Disease and the Modern World* (Cambridge, 2004), 149.
78 *Report of the Inter-departmental Committee on the Rehabilitation and Resettlement of Disabled Persons* (January 1943), CAB 117/145, National Archives, London.
79 Ibid., 2.
80 W.L. Buxton, 'Industrial Rehabilitation Units: A British Experiment', *International Labour Review*, Vol. 67 (1953), 535.
81 London County Council Minutes Rehabilitation and Resettlement of Disabled Persons – Report of Inter-departmental Committee (27 July 1943), CAB 117/145, National Archives, London, 5.
82 Fraser, 'Employment of the Disabled', 280.
83 London County Council Minutes *Rehabilitation and Resettlement of Disabled Persons* – Report of Inter-departmental Committee.
84 The report made a possible exception for miners.
85 The Committees Bevin referred to were investigations into the rehabilitation of disabled persons headed by Sir Edward Forber for the Ministry of Health and another under J.M. Glen for the Ministry of Labour and National Service. Memo from Ernest Bevin, War Cabinet Home Policy Committee on Rehabilitation of Disabled Persons (13 February 1942), CAB 117/145, National Archives, London.
86 For a discussion of labour and the Services see David Englander, 'Soldiers and Social Reform in the First and Second World Wars', *Historical Research*, Vol. 67, No. 164 (1994).
87 By 1940, there was a significant rise in accidents from the previous year; 33% in engineering works, 47% in the making of machines and 21% in chemicals. There was an increase in the number of explosions, not only in munitions factories, but also in flour mills and cattle feed factories. *Annual Report of the Chief Inspector of Factories*, Cmd 6316 (1940), CMA SA/RBC C8.9, Wellcome Trust, London.
88 Memo from R.P. Williamson, Ministry of War Transport, to S.G. Holloway, Ministry of Labour and National Service (13 June 1945), LAB 20/1, National Archives, London.
89 Report by H. Balme for the Ministry of Health, *Rehabilitation in the New Health Services* (1945), FD 1/6810, National Archives, London.
90 E.A. Nicoll, 'Rehabilitation of the Injured', *British Medical Journal* (5 April 1941), 506.
91 Balme, *Rehabilitation in the New Health Services.*
92 Angus Calder, *The People's War: Britain 1939–1945* (London, 1997).
93 Titmuss, *Problems of Social Policy*, 478.

94 According to its official history, the Infantile Paralysis Fellowship assisted in helping the government form policy, when a member of the association wrote to Ernest Bevin with details on how those with polio could help in the war effort. Barry North, *Something to Lean On: The First Sixty Years of the British Polio Fellowship* (South Ruiship, 1999), 6.

95 Humphries and Gordon, *Out of Sight*, 129.

96 There is some disagreement on this point. *The Western Daily Press*, 22 February 1943, as cited in Calder, *The People's War*, 387, quoted 300,000, whereas Humphries and Gordon, *Out of Sight*, 133 put the figure at 500,000.

97 One of these women performed her civil duty with a good deal of seriousness and managed to 'track down' and report two men who had been using petrol illegally. *British Deaf News*, Vol. 1, No. 5 (September–October 1955), 147.

98 Penny Summerfield, *Reconstructing Women's Wartime Lives* (Manchester, 1998), 217–18.

99 *Report of the Inter-departmental Committee on the Rehabilitation and Resettlement of Disabled Persons.*

100 Letter from B.C. Tilghman, Chairman of Directors, George Richards and Co., Ltd, to Lord Woolton, Minister of Reconstruction (16 December 1943), CAB 117/145, National Archives, London.

101 'Restoring the Disabled', *The Times* (24 October 1941).

102 'War Work By Deaf and Dumb', *The Guardian* (6 September 1941).

103 *The New Beacon* (15 August 1940), 158.

104 By 1945, 2,000 blind people were engaged in industry. Michael W. Royden, *Pioneers and Perseverance: A History of the Royal School for the Blind, Liverpool (1791–1991)* (Liverpool, 1991), 210.

105 *The New Beacon* (15 August 1940), 157.

106 Many deaf volunteered for some form of National Service. *Deaf Quarterly News* (January–March 1940), 9.

107 This system operated around Bristol. Gloria Pullen and Rachel Sutton-Spence, 'The British Deaf Community During the 1939–1945 War', in Renate Fischer and Harlan Lane (eds), *Looking Back: A Reader on the History of Deaf Communities and their Sign Language* (Hamburg, 1993), 173.

108 Ibid., 173.

109 Calder, *The People's War*, 32.

110 Brooke, 'Emergency Medical Service', 643.

111 *British Medical Journal* (22 March 1941), 445.

112 Sheila Smith, *Still Unique After All These Years: A History of Blanche Nevile School* (London, 1995), 23.

113 Royden, *Pioneers and Perseverance*, 184.

114 'The Schools in War-Time', *Teacher of the Deaf*, Vol. XXXVII (December 1939), 220.

115 Royden, *Pioneers and Perseverance*, 184.
116 Chailey also took in children, either with raid shock or injured as the war progressed. Kimmins, *Chailey Heritage*, 8.
117 Vera Dean, *Three Steps Forward* (London, 1957), 17–83.
118 Pritchard, *Education and the Handicapped*, 207.

4

Fit: the process of rehabilitation

The Royal Air Force captured the public's imagination. In the summer skies of 1940, during the Battle of Britain, spectators witnessed skirmishes that cemented the RAF's position as the nation's protectors. Acclaimed as Churchill's 'Few', their position as national heroes was augmented by accounts of their insouciant bravery.[1] The *Illustrated War News* described in detail aircrew's bravery, exploits and value to the war effort. Indeed, the pilots, clad in silk scarves and sheepskin jackets posing for photographs on the wings of their fighter planes, were the epitome of glamour.[2] The RAF combined new technology and old-fashioned British dogged persistence at fighting. From its inception the RAF had formed 'traditions of informality, heavy drinking, collective and individual modesty and habitual understatement'.[3] In *Postscripts*, J.B. Priestley noted the 'informality' of airmen.[4] Their old-fashioned notions of chivalric masculinity ensured RAF aircrew fit perfectly the public's need for heroes. Michael Paris argues that this was already well established by the 1930s as airmen represented a new kind of chivalry associated with new technology and hope that the tide of future warfare would be altered by air supremacy.[5] Memories of mud and the depressing stalemate of the Western Front in the First World War were obliterated by high technology aircraft piloted by brave, dashing young men.

In addition to its role as defender of the nation, the RAF was important for a number of reasons. Transport was an important function as the nature of battle required mobility, and the wounded had to be moved to hospitals for treatment as quickly as possible. Mark Harrison details the RAF's role as transporters of wounded in his book on the Second

World War.[6] Between D-Day on 6 June 1944 and VE Day on 8 May 1945, the RAF carried 77,348 sick and wounded men back to Britain for treatment.[7] The RAF had a number of roles to play in the war, so their fitness was highly important.

The fittest men went into the Royal Air Force. The 'Boys in Blue' held positions that were highly risky; training them was expensive and initially time consuming, although that shortened as the war progressed. It was imperative that aircrew remained fit, and the chapter will discuss the way that their fitness, both physical and mental, was judged, and, after injury, the nature of their return to fitness after a programme of rehabilitation.

This chapter explores the nature of rehabilitation in the RAF. Particular emphasis is made of rehabilitative work in the RAF, as the restoration of their fitness was vital for winning the war, which was associated with the RAF's role in maintaining public morale. This chapter also demonstrates the enduring power of the RAF, and the importance of its medical officers. The influence associated with its medical officers was a reflection of the RAF's value to the war effort. Rehabilitation re-established levels of fitness and much experimental work on it was conducted in the RAF centres. Due to the nature of injuries, much rehabilitative work focused on orthopaedics. In addition to the danger that flying presented to bones, the skin was at risk; burns were a new type of injury associated with flying. The flexibility of rehabilitative practice was evident in the way that these burned airmen were treated. The chapter juxtaposes the tough, physical methods employed in orthopaedic centres with the social rehabilitation practised in burns units.

Fitness for the Royal Air Force

Fitness was vital for selection for the RAF. Not only was the imperative to be fit, but also to embody the ethos of the RAF; therefore 'fitness' was about character in addition to ability. Only the fittest were selected to undergo pilot training. They underwent tests for their ability and physicality, including vision and reflex testing. Pilot training took months and was to a high standard, especially in the early stages of the war, as during the Battle of Britain in 1940 training was accelerated.[8] Mechanics and air crew, such as navigators, also needed expensive and lengthy training using high technology equipment to maintain and fly aircraft. Fitness had to be maintained. Mechanics, radar operators and crew, in addition to pilots, were highly technically trained and expensive to retrain or replace.

In particular, care had to be taken with these highly strung air crew who were just as likely to take risks when they were off duty. Pilots' off-duty exploits caused numbers of accidents and fatalities. In 1941 there were 4,379 athletic injuries in the RAF, and 38 resulted in death. The number of fatalities rose in 1943 to 49, owing to the high number of deaths by drowning.[9] In whatever way they were injured, RAF personnel had to be returned to fitness quickly, and that fitness level had to be high. Those who remained disabled after injury were returned to service in different positions if their disability made their previous job unfeasible. In some high profile cases, residual disability was no barrier to performance, and double amputee pilot Douglas Bader was considered doubly heroic; fighting Germans and overcoming disability. Additionally, the RAF's location on mainland Britain meant that disability was not necessarily a barrier to war service. Another double leg amputee, Colin Hodgkinson, transferred to the RAF from the Fleet Air Arm as he was unable to walk easily on aircraft carriers' decks.[10] Others with disabilities associated with the RAF, the 'back-room boys' as they were known, were employed at the highest levels. Air Commodore Huskinson was living in London, researching the types and effects of German bombs. He was blinded during a bombing raid in 1941, and after a short recovery, continued to run the RAF armament department for the duration of the war.[11]

Rehabilitation in the RAF

The RAF embodied notions of rehabilitation, for medical, economic and social reasons. This chapter now turns to rehabilitative treatment of those injured while in the RAF. Rehabilitation was particularly important in this Service. The nature of injuries associated with aircraft presented specific difficulties for surgeons and doctors. Bodies were at a premium in this Service; as Liddell-Hart reminds us, 'Men, not planes, were Dowding's main worry.'[12]

The first hospital for the RAF was established in 1918 at Hendon and specialised in the exclusive treatment of RAF personnel.[13] By 1940, treatment was divided into three parts: necessary surgical treatment and restoration of function, followed by removal to a rehabilitative unit for recovery for further treatment.[14] The RAF embraced the centralised system of care that became a hallmark of British military medical treatment during the war. Army casualties were generally placed in EMS hospitals – but those in the RAF were moved to special hospitals as soon as they could be transferred, usually within ten days.[15]

Figure 4.1 Rehabilitation in the Air Force, some in uniform (reproduced with permission of the Wellcome Library, London)

The RAF was a thoroughly modern Force requiring the most innovative medical treatment. A number of accidents specific to air warfare were identified and steps taken to minimise the damage to expensively trained pilots. Due to flying at high altitude, many aircrew lost fingers and toes to frostbite and suffered ear problems due to the lack of pressurised cabins. Crash injuries could result in multiple fractures, burns and other specific types of injuries. Many pilots who survived a serious crash were badly hurt. The safety harness, devised to save pilots from serious injury if they crashed, increased numbers of compression fractures, yet saved lives.[16] Specific injuries required new methods of treatment and each nation used technology and medical expertise to ensure pilots kept flying. German pilots returned to flying duty much faster than their Allied counterparts as Kuntscher nails were used to repair fractures to the long leg bones.[17] Americans reduced the number of fractures from parachute landing by adopting the British method of landing with feet together, instead of apart.[18] It is important not to ignore ground crews, radar operators and other ancillary staff who were exposed to risk from bombing in above ground operations buildings close to airfields. They were also provided with high levels of care and rehabilitation if they were injured.

Activity at RAF rehabilitation centres was relentless. One of the reasons for the success of the RAF rehabilitation campaign was the belief that, 'Rehabilitation does not begin with recreation and games; it begins with work and very hard work.'[19] Orderlies were trained to provide five minute exercise sessions every hour while patients were still in bed in the wards. Active therapy was prescribed over passive treatment. Physiotherapy was used sparingly 'because some patients are only too happy to lie at their ease on a couch and receive treatment, which, for remedial purposes, is a poor substitute for their own activities'.[20] Physiotherapy was considered insufficiently harsh for injured aircrew, which is interesting in the light of research on the First World War by Ana Carden-Coyne and Beth Linker, who challenge the perception that physiotherapists merely applied gentle massage, and show that they could, indeed, be quite brutal.[21] Remedial exercises and games were key in treatment. Much active treatment for rehabilitation consisted of physical training (PT) and sport, and men were divided according to their fitness levels. The 'nearly fit' class participated in remedial exercises and swimming; and the 'fit' class patients participated in organised activities. Early rehabilitation in the RAF consisted of individualised programmes, but upon a member gaining an improved level of fitness, patients were organised into playing sports. Playing as a group instilled a sense of camaraderie that reinforced teamwork, essential to being part of a military unit. Teamwork was an important component of military service, and was reinforced in rehabilitative practices. The essence of fitness for military service was the ability to participate in team sports and be part of an organisation, with everyone 'doing their bit' to help their side achieve victory.

Despite its reputation for informality, the RAF maintained stringent distinctions between ranks in its medical and rehabilitative practices. Even on the sporting field, divisions were evident, as it reinforced class distinctions that existed in the RAF. Generally, PT classes were segregated for officers and non-commissioned ranks. When the Officers' Hospital at Torquay was destroyed by enemy action, officers were taken to Loughborough to continue their rehabilitation but were kept separate from the ranks.[22] Instructors were chosen carefully, as aircrew were known to be temperamental; and as they were highly important to the war effort, their wishes were often indulged. Drill sergeants were not notable for their success in motivating aircrew to perform their exercise regimes. It was highlighted in a 1941 report that 'it seemed that the discipline and somewhat unimaginative routine of drill and physical instruction failed to secure the co-operation of the sick and injured'.[23] Aircrew responded more positively to other fitness instructors, including athletes, footballers and other sportsmen who were more successful at motivating them. These physical fitness officers 'provided the necessary psychological incentive by virtue of their personalities, being frequently chosen from among the well-known figures of the world of sport, who were often adept at maintaining the difficult balance between authority and informality'.[24] One of the Physical Fitness Officers at Loughborough, the largest of the RAF's rehabilitation centres, was a former tennis professional at Wimbledon, and one of the Medical Officers was a former first class rugby player.[25] Aircrew maintained a level of respect for the non-professional sports stars such as athletes and rugby players, associated with their own class, and were less likely to relate to a drill sergeant who would enforce notions of military obedience, which were anathema to aircrew.

Class divisions were also evident in the types of sport played and PT practised in rehabilitation units. There was a presumption that ranks would want to play different sports from officers, which was narrated through specialists who instructed them in sport and games. Those in the ranks were instructed in football by well-known players.[26] This demonstrated the influence of the RAF, further highlighting its uniqueness and importance, yet it also reinforced class divisions and segregation. A similar situation existed for PT instructors; officers were led in their exercises by athletes while the ranks' PT instructors were often school masters.[27] Injured men also responded well to being led by disabled ex-servicemen, who often had poorly united fractures and were used in RAF rehabilitation centres as physical training instructors. Civilian consultant surgeon to the RAF, Reginald Watson-Jones, wanted disabled ex-servicemen in orthopaedic rehabilitation centres because their disabilities gave them a special understanding of the difficulties associated

Figure 4.2 Football match, 'Knees vs. Ankles' Royal Air Force (reproduced with permission of the Wellcome Library, London)

with rehabilitative training, and were also what Watson-Jones called the 'right type'.[28]

Rehabilitation took place within the mind as well as the body, as the association of wellness between them was well established in medical thinking. After their experiences of patients with shell shock in the First World War, the Services were very concerned about the impact of war neurosis, and the RAF had engaged a psychiatrist and a neurologist from Guy's Hospital in the 1930s.[29] For men in the RAF, a healthy and confident mind was also a competitive one. Established to increase patients' competitive feelings, winning games was likened to conquering one's body. Activities were undertaken by the rehabilitating patients at RAF centres, including rambling, cycling, swimming, dancing, fencing, skipping, climbing and dribbling a football, as they instilled 'a high measure of confidence and satisfaction in the patient'.[30] In addition to using sport as a series of rehabilitative exercises geared toward personal recovery and the resumption of a positive attitude, the RAF used sporting competition between men to hasten their mental, as well as their physical recovery. Patients were categorised by a combination of their physical fitness and mental progress. Nevertheless, it was noted that rehabilitation was not just an internal exercise by the patient to conquer negative thoughts. Rehabilitation of the mind could be affected by a doctor's approach to his patient. An article in *The Lancet* detailed the impact that surgeons with poor attitudes had on a patient's recovery:

> One most skilful surgeon, known as 'The Fuehrer' because of his unbending attitude, sent to our rehabilitation centres patients with straight limbs but sadly warped minds. Another was an indifferent surgeon but a man of great personality, and he sent me with not so straight limbs but with a spirit which nothing could quell.[31]

Rehabilitation centres

The RAF carefully planned its system of medical care when war broke out. In 1940, the first rehabilitation centre for RAF patients was opened and, as is evident from Air Ministry files, the RAF regarded itself as wholly distinct from other Services. The Officers' Hospital was originally the requisitioned Palace Hotel in Torquay, Devon, well known as a holiday resort during peacetime. For those in the ranks, an Airmen's Convalescent Depot was opened in Blackpool.[32] Blackpool was a holiday resort in the north of England, but it did not have the cachet of Torquay where

Table 4.1 Injuries and Diseases Treated in RAF Orthopaedic Centres, 1941–44 (D-Day)

Major fractures and dislocations	19,122
Fractures and burns	159
Penetrating joint wounds	124
Soft tissue wounds	1,058
Internal derangements of knee	4,808
Other joint injuries	1,339
Tendon and muscle injuries	1,312
Nerve injuries	499
Amputation stump disabilities	233
Gangrene	35
Arterial injuries	32
General orthopaedic cases	6,368
TOTAL	35,089

the officers were sent to recover. As casualties increased, so did the number of centres operated by the RAF. In 1941, bed numbers increased and new centres were opened: Hoylake was opened in August of that year with 100 beds; Cosford in September with 200 beds and Blackpool was enlarged to accommodate 500 aircrew and ground personnel.[33] The Officers' Hospital expanded to house 250 officers at Torquay. By the end of the war the RAF had nine rehabilitation centres dotted around the country: Cosford, Halton, Ely, Rauceby, Church Village, Weeton, Wroughton, Loughborough and Hoylake, which treated over 35,000 injuries (see Table 4.1).

The rehabilitation unit at Cosford was closed in November 1942 when the spacious Loughborough Engineering College was taken over by the RAF. All patients were transferred from the less salubrious amenities at Cosford to improved conditions at Loughborough.[34] Loughborough was a perfect location for a rehabilitation unit – it had good playing fields, a large gymnasium and a swimming pool.[35] Owing to requirements for specialist care and their long period of treatment, burns patients were treated mainly at East Grinstead in Kent by Archibald McIndoe and his specialist medical team, but a few were treated at other centres. After the Officers' Hospital at Torquay was destroyed by enemy action, a number of officers were sent to Loughborough and, in addition, Mongewell Park in Berkshire was opened and some officers were moved to the large house where they underwent rehabilitation exercises, played golf and punted on the river.[36] Loughborough was large, with accommodation for over 500 men, approximately 309 officers and 202 airmen when at full capacity.[37] To outside views, the rehabilitation centre looked more like a holiday camp than a hospital, but this was the atmosphere that medical staff and administrators worked hard to create.

Patients mixed freely with locals and recovering men participated in social events held in the local area. Within ten days of opening, patients at the centre were contacted by local football clubs at Leicester, Nottingham and Derby. It was noted in the RAF Operations Record that 'visits were made to each club in turn as guest of the Club'.[38] These visits to sporting events were frequent and large scale; the operations record states on 6 March 1943 that a 'bus load' of patients went to Derby football club as guests of the team.[39] In addition to visits to local sporting events, Loughborough's rehabilitation centre provided a social locus for patients and local people. Much of the social activity was centred on sport. In July 1943, some of the more fit patients played a game of cricket with the local Brushworks factory as part of activities for the Wings for Victory week.[40] As a showpiece of the importance of rehabilitation regimes, Loughborough also received a number of visitors, sporting, medical and industrial. Visitors from Armed Services from other Allied nations came to play sport, including the Norwegian Army Team in September 1943.[41] Games and sports demonstrations were held for the amusement of local people and patients; in 1944 American paratroops participated in a sports day and patients were reported to be 'very interested' in the demonstration game of baseball.[42] While patients and public were entertained, four American generals and six colonels of the US Air Force visited, and were reportedly 'very impressed' with the officers' enjoyment of group activities, reporting they did not have a unit of this kind.[43] Industrial medical officers visited the centre to ascertain how RAF rehabilitative practices could be transferred to industry to ensure that workers, who were vital to the war effort, could be rehabilitated in the quickest possible time.[44] Loughborough cemented the effectiveness of rehabilitation methods, and provided an example for other interested groups to educate themselves on the importance of rehabilitation regimes to maintain numbers for total war.

Notwithstanding the holiday atmosphere at RAF rehabilitation centres, air and ground crew were there for a specific purpose and doctors at the units ensured that patients recovered in the quickest possible time. Even for the RAF, with its reportedly lax attitudes to rules and regulations governing military life, expediency was important in rehabilitation, geared toward resumption of military service in as short a period of time as possible. Occupational therapy was precisely that, retraining for previous occupations – there were very few baskets woven by members of the RAF. Reginald Watson-Jones, as consultant surgeon to the RAF, would not endorse occupational therapy unless it was specifically geared toward resumption of military duties. He wrote in the *British Medical Journal*: 'There can be no possible doubt that the danger of patients' being buried alive in a workshop is even more grave than the former danger of patients' being buried in a massage department.'[45] In order to strengthen and relax stiffened fingers, games of tiddley winks were played and clay models were made as they were fun activities that helped restore function.[46] Nevertheless, battle readiness was the most important result of rehabilitation for the RAF and it started early in the programme. One report in *The Lancet* noted: 'While still in plaster they attend wireless refresher courses and are given tuition in navigation, Link trainer flying, air-craft recognition and gunnery.'[47] For air gunners, part of rehabilitative practices consisted of target range and clay pigeon shooting.[48] While enjoyable, it served to reinforce training and ensured that crews did not have to re-learn skills. At a rehabilitation centre, a training workshop was established for technicians, and wireless operators were provided access to apparatus to maintain their level of expertise in addition to rounds of gymnastic and sporting therapy.[49] At another unit for aircrew, a fuselage was installed to test the fitness level of pilots.[50] Known as 'Synthetic Training', these experimental practices were expanded in July 1944 to ensure that all aircrew were battle ready as well as rehabilitated.[51] Maintaining familiarity with Air Force technology and skills learned while in the Service ensured that the newly rehabilitated were able to participate fully in their functional capacity as soon as they were returned to their units.

Discipline at rehabilitation centres

The RAF requisitioned the Palace Hotel in Torquay, Devon, a popular holiday resort for a rehabilitation centre for its officers in 1939. It had a putting course, swimming pool, squash courts, gymnasium and an indoor tennis court.[52] In addition to the 'Programme of Work', which consisted of hours of remedial exercises and rambles, games of cricket and golf tournaments were held.[53]

Torquay was full of affluent evacuees who treated RAF officers royally and there were complaints levelled to authorities about a lack of discipline at the centre. Often administrators turned a blind eye to the antics of aircrew, owing to their bravery in the face of danger. There may have been other reasons for the gentle treatment of aircrews. An article in *The Lancet* noted that aircrews 'are trained to be aggressive in the highest degree, and unless wisely handled they are liable to project this aggression to doctors, hospitals and rehabilitation centres'.[54] One RAF report stated, 'The fighting spirit of these pilots had been stimulated to the highest degree and they regarded any control as a fit opportunity for violent reaction.'[55] One of the only ways to control these recalcitrant pilots and stop them going off in groups to Torquay in the evening and making nuisances of themselves was to install a bar that sold wine and beer in the hospital.[56] One of the biggest problems for the administrators of the unit was ensuring that officers participated in their rehabilitation. In order to keep them in the hospital, administrators organised dances, a cinema and concerts to keep officers occupied.[57] Other activities included swimming competitions, squash games, golf, tennis and even a hospital magazine was started.[58] It was difficult to get aircrew to stay in the gym to do their exercises so a coffee and milk bar was installed.

However, there were other distractions. One report from the RAF Officers' Hospital stated:

> Patients were referred to [the instructor] by the officer in charge of the surgical division, but there was no effective check on attendance and, because the Massage Department was situated at the opposite end of the hospital to the gymnasium, it is probable that patients were to be found more often in the Massage Department than in the gymnasium.[59]

The Massage Department treated over 1,000 cases per month in 1940, and the attraction for this type of treatment, apart from being able to lie down, was probably because many of the therapists were female.[60] The administrators kept trying to instil military discipline. Even the hospital's décor was changed in an attempt to remind officers of the nature of their attendance. The gym was decorated with a frieze of an airman going into hospital on crutches, performing exercises and returning fit.[61] While most pilots and aircrew entered the spirit of rehabilitation with a certain degree of enthusiasm, levels of interest in their rehabilitation were often associated with being monitored and provided with privileges that were not provided to others in the Services.

Discipline continued to be problematic among officers, reflecting their special status within their Service and the minds of the public.

As we have seen, administrators endeavoured to entertain the men, and provide them with many activities. One of the issues highlighted was that there were insufficient ways for the officers to entertain themselves, including no emphasis on occupational therapy. As we have seen, Watson-Jones did not endorse occupational therapy unless it was directly linked to function in the Service. In a letter between medical officers at different centres, one is criticised by the other for his lack of emphasis on occupational therapy in an article written on rehabilitation in the *British Medical Journal*:

> Occupational Therapy is also relegated to the background. This is a pity as the brain is a very important part of the human body, and so much is done for the brute muscle in man but so little for his brain. At Torquay he is entertained in every way, except made to think about his work in future, whether it is to be in the Services or otherwise. I know all work and no play makes Jack a dull boy, but all play is equally bad, and is liable to bring out the worst in one's instincts.[62]

Rehabilitation and burns

Rehabilitation for burns cases employed a different regime from the active orthopaedic centres. For the RAF, the multiple injuries and burns that resulted from flying accidents exhibited a new war horror. In particular, plastic surgeon Archibald McIndoe's work on the treatment of pilots' burns has received much attention from historians – the bravery of the pilots in spite of horrific injuries has been a popular topic for books about medical treatment in the Second World War.[63] McIndoe himself has been the subject of a number of biographies.[64] Burns were not limited to the RAF, but the scale of burns and the techniques developed to treat them in addition to the concentration of aircrew at East Grinstead, tell an interesting story about the psychology of rehabilitation in the RAF, and the way that different injuries were treated within regimes designed to get aircrew back to work as soon as possible. The burns units in RAF hospitals employed a type of social rehabilitation, particularly at East Grinstead. While the numbers of burned aircrew were small, as we can see from the table, the impact of the work at East Grinstead and the ability of these men to capture the public's imagination cannot be underestimated.

Many of the books written by pilots who had survived their burns detailed the regime at East Grinstead; saline baths and numerous skin graft operations with periods of recovery in between was often the

Table 4.2 Number of aircrew plastic surgery cases treated at Queen Victoria Hospital, East Grinstead, 1939–44

1939	6
1940	120
1941	120
1942	150
1943	187
1944 to September	137
Total	720

Source: CAS Memo, 30 October 1944, AIR 8/796, National Archives, London.

schedule for a number of months. Isolation from general wards was important in the first stages as those with burns were highly prone to infection. Early in the war, many of the men were housed in maternity wards, as these wards were isolated on account of puerperal sepsis.[65] This close proximity established a close camaraderie between patients and staff. Rehabilitation at East Grinstead was certainly less organised than in the orthopaedic units and the atmosphere was much more casual. Burns to the hands were often so severe that others had to light and fill fellow-patients' pipes.[66] As soon as the men were able to use their hands they were encouraged to use them. However, the delicate nature of their skin, grafts and risk of infection made a great deal of active movement impossible. It took burned pilot Tom Gleave months before he was able to walk as his legs had been badly burned and he required a number of skin grafts.[67] Aircrew attended East Grinstead for surgery, and after they had recovered from it, went to RAF Convalescent Homes to recover. Many of them could not use their hands, like well-known pilot Richard Hillary, so were not enthusiastic about going to Homes with squash and tennis courts and golf courses.[68] However, some burns patients went to the Officers' Hospital at Torquay in the latter stages of their rehabilitation and were able to go walking across the moors and swimming in the sea. Some burns patients were eventually able to take part in a limited way in the physical training exercises at Torquay and then Loughborough.[69] The rehabilitation required for these men in particular was social rather than physical.

Social rehabilitation required the participation of others and, as we have seen, rehabilitation was an exercise in large-scale cooperation. We will turn now to the regime at East Grinstead to explore the way that social rehabilitation worked in this particular context. Social rehabilitation was specific to acceptance associated with injuries that caused disfigurement. This was not a new idea – disfigurement had been a feature of the First World War. Certain benches were painted blue during and after the First World War for the use of those with facial disfigurement so that members of the public would not sit there and be shocked by what they saw. However, unlike those men who had removed themselves from society, sitting on blue benches to isolate themselves from a horrified public, or wearing masks to hide their faces from fearful eyes, the burned airmen at East Grinstead were paraded before a local community who were asked to accept them. While in the hospital, men were allowed to look at themselves in mirrors. As with rehabilitation, a number of groups had to cooperate to ensure that social rehabilitation was an effective treatment. As we will see, the Air Ministry had to rethink its attitude to early discharge, military discipline in hospital was suspended, those in the hospital had to work in highly unusual circumstances, and the local community had to suspend their horror at the effect of burns sustained by aircrew. McIndoe received assistance from the Services but also from local people around East Grinstead who offered a supportive environment to the burned airmen.[70] Locals visited the hospital, took the men out to parties and dances, drank with them in the local pub, and endured their drunken antics. At the hospital, nurses also had to endure aircrew's pranks and sexual advances, despite McIndoe's assertion that he felt the same level of protection for his nurses that he did his daughters and that his patients were to leave them alone to do their work.[71] In order to ensure that social rehabilitation was successful, the men were allowed to indulge a type of hyper-masculinity, where sexual harassment of nurses was not punished. However, some nurses' certainly maintained discipline in the wards – Richard Hillary was separated from his friend by the matron as their behaviour was deemed to be unacceptable.[72] Nevertheless, due to their position as officers and the sacrifice of the skin on their bodies to the war effort, in conjunction with the indulgence of doctors at the hospital, the War Office, administrators and, in particular, Winston Churchill, whose attitude to the RAF was willingly supported by the public, the burned pilots' behaviour at East Grinstead was tolerated and indulged. Archibald McIndoe was instrumental in the operation of East Grinstead, and the attitude of nurses and the public to 'his boys'. He was very protective of 'his boys', and military discipline in the hospital was virtually non-existent. McIndoe ignored rank and there was no segregation at East Grinstead, unlike in other rehabilitation centres and hospitals in the RAF.[73] One patient noted: 'It wasn't a hospital, it was just a big comfortable hotel . . . There was a big barrel of beer at the end of the ward and you could help yourself.'[74] McIndoe's close association with them resulted in the establishment of the Guinea Pig Club, a group of airmen on whom McIndoe experimented with new reconstructive surgery techniques. McIndoe was highly influential, and the chapter will now focus on the role of these consultant surgeons in the RAF.

The role of consultant surgeons in rehabilitation

Medical specialists were brought in to advise the Services in the early part of the war. Many of these senior specialists did not enlist in the Services, but retained their civilian status. Consultants who advised the RAF were very involved in patient care at the highest level. Medical specialists in charge of caring for RAF personnel often rejected military rules surrounding patient care, putting the needs of patients ahead of established regulations. In particular, two consultant surgeons, orthopaedic surgeon Reginald Watson-Jones, who was attached to the RAF as a civilian consultant, and burns specialist Archibald McIndoe, influenced senior members of the RAF to relax strict military protocol.

Part of the reason that these surgeons were able to maintain their independence was that they did not join the Forces. Unlike many surgeons and doctors during the First World War, their civilian status allowed them a degree of independence. Some surgeons enlisted – neurosurgeons Hugh Cairns and Geoffrey Jefferson made an agreement that one would enlist in order to be the 'inside man', whereas the other would remain outside the Services in order to influence medical practice in the Forces. Watson-Jones and McIndoe continued to enjoy an association with the RAF but, free from the threat of military discipline, they were able to criticise the standard of care provided to those undergoing treatment and rehabilitation, and challenge the rules governing medical care in the RAF. One of the reasons why these surgeons were taken seriously is the level of dedication and their results. Medical expertise in rehabilitation was highly valued, as the system returned men to the fighting more rapidly. Unlike the First World War, senior consultants more readily questioned decisions taken by military authorities surrounding medical care. In 1941 Reginald Watson-Jones and B.H.C. Matthews, a doctor of applied physiology, were attached to the RAF.[75] Upon Watson-Jones' appointment letters were sent at the highest levels of the Air Ministry, which expressed mild concern at his plans for a special orthopaedic service in RAF hospitals.[76] Yet the Air Ministry usually took Watson-Jones' directions. It is testament to the faith in rehabilitative therapy that when building work at Hoylake was delayed in 1941 and Reginald Watson-Jones complained, his letter to Air Commodore Lydford noted, 'it is required for rehabilitation of air crew – I would be much obliged if you could get this matter hastened'.[77] Watson-Jones complained in 1942 that facilities at Cosgrove were insufficient to rehabilitate aircrew and he had drawn attention to 'the appalling conditions under which skilled airman are living at Cosford – conditions that limit their total recreation space to 6 feet by 4 feet'.[78] Cosford was closed and all of those patients were moved to the newly opened unit at Loughborough. Between 1942 and 1943 the average incapacity period for orthopaedics was 15 weeks, as multiple fractures took a long time to heal.[79] As we have seen, aircrew were engaged in a number of activities in those 15 weeks. When concern was expressed about the period of time it took to rehabilitate a pilot who had broken bones in a crash, Watson-Jones wrote a letter to Sir Charles Portal:

> Quite unlike the average run of Army casualties the pilot fractures two, three or all four limbs; he fractures each limb in many places; he often fractures many limbs and also the spine; he may even fracture his spine at seven different levels.[80]

Under a combination of highly effective RAF organisation and advice from Watson-Jones, orthopaedic rehabilitation centres achieved very good results. In 1942 and 1943, Loughborough returned 62% of orthopaedic cases of aircrew to full flying duties.[81] Figures show that by the end of the war RAF orthopaedic units had returned 85% of injured pilots to full flying duty.[82]

Although Watson-Jones was not enlisted in the Services, his loyalty to his war activities and the RAF in particular was paramount. When Watson-Jones was asked by the Ministry of Fuel and Power to establish a rehabilitation service for injured workers, he was immediately approached by the Air Ministry and reminded of his commitment to them. Watson-Jones wrote back to the Air Ministry, assuring them that his service to the RAF was his 'first duty'.[83]

One of the most problematic rules was time limits set out in Service regulations. Military rules dictated that injured personnel had a specific time in which to recover before they were discharged. Generally, that did not allow sufficient time to ensure that the patient was fully rehabilitated, nor to know for certain whether he was able to remain in the Service.[84]

If an airman was discharged before what was termed 'surgical finality' was reached, it could cause him extreme financial and social difficulty. Another well-known surgeon attached to the RAF, plastic surgeon Archibald McIndoe, was extremely perturbed about this situation. As we have seen, McIndoe was a highly regarded burns specialist, who spent much of the war at East Grinstead reconstructing airmen's faces and performing hundreds of skin grafts. McIndoe wrote to Air Chief Marshal Sir Charles Portal in 1944 about the problems faced by the air crew:

> He feels primarily that the service in which he has taken an active part and for which he has sacrificed so much, has discarded him as useless and that this uselessness will pursue him into civilian life. The RAF uniform is the accepted reason for disfigurement and to continue wearing it for as long as possible saves the injured man from considerable embarrassment and awkward explanations. The mere fact that he is retained in the service until the period is overcome (and it varies very much with the individual) is the best guarantee of his satisfactory rehabilitation and resettlement. I might point out that his rehabilitation is not a matter of regaining physical strength and power, as is the case with orthopaedic injuries, but is closely connected with his social readjustment.[85]

At East Grinstead, results were better than expected. By 1944 approximately 23.7% returned to flying duties, 53.3% returned to duties other than flying, 5% were invalided out of the Forces and 18% were still undergoing treatment.[86] McIndoe pointed out that 'not a few of these apparently "hopeless" cases have actually returned to flying duties after more than two years' hospital treatment'.[87] McIndoe noted one reason that rehabilitation in the RAF achieved such good results was because men remained in their RAF uniform. Refusing to wear the blue hospital uniform was yet another way that the RAF demonstrated its difference from other Services. This was partly because while wearing hospital blues a member of the Services was not allowed to enter licensed premises.[88] Going to the pub was an important part of social rehabilitation, as we saw earlier in the chapter. In addition, once a man was invalided out of the Services, his pay was cut in half and he was charged for his medical care: 19s a week for NCOs and 4s per day for officers.[89] Had he been able to remain in the Services, his medical care would have been provided free. As McIndoe stated: 'That is to say if the airman has given to the Service almost all he has to give except his life, then under the present regulations the Service must wash his hands of him'.[90] The pride of serving in the RAF and their continued camaraderie were vital to successful rehabilitation. As guardians of the public faith, aircrew also believed that their Service was as loyal to them as they were to it, and would look after them if they were badly injured. One of the reasons for the delay in departure from the RAF was to prevent a sense of abandonment experienced by the men.

Watson-Jones agreed with McIndoe's sentiments, and in a letter pointed out the danger of early discharge to the mental health of RAF personnel:

> It is clear from the many letters and observations that supreme confidence in their own medical service is at least one important factor in maintaining morale and fighting spirit. As Lord Moran put it; 'The greatest contribution the medical service has made to the Royal Air Force is in the elimination of fear'. Exactly the opposite influence is to be expected when a pilot realises that if he injures himself a little more severely he will be denied the facilities he knows and be discharged as soon as it is clear that he is of no further use.[91]

As Martin Francis reminds us, the RAF hierarchy approached the issue of fear 'as a collective problem'.[92] The hierarchy expended much time and effort on ameliorating fear, and Watson-Jones' letter reminded the authorities that the practice of early discharge was adding to fear and affecting aircrews' combat ability.

Chief of Air Staff, Sir Charles Portal was influenced by these two charismatic surgeons. He wrote in a memo that 'high morale in the worst cases naturally encourages high morale in all the others', which was almost a direct quote of McIndoe from a letter sent to Portal only a month before.[93] By the end of the war, a member of the Forces could stay in for treatment for 8 months; however, in some cases it took 14 months to complete rehabilitation. This occurred mainly in burns cases where the number of operations a patient averaged was 12.[94] Partly as a result of the intervention of notable surgeons, and also the high standing of aircrew in the government and public consciousness, standard invaliding procedures in the RAF were not followed – generally a 'blind eye' was turned to the length of time that rehabilitation took, especially in burns cases.[95] If an officer was disabled but continuing in the Services, he was retained as long as his illness lasted less than 18 months.[96] There were debates surrounding the special treatment meted out to aircrew even after the war and the Admiralty argued that it would also have to follow the RAF because it also had badly injured men who required long courses of treatment.[97] This loyalty coupled with an individual's identity with the RAF continued long after the war was over. In 1946, a meeting of the National Advisory Council on the Employment of the Disabled made reference to a scheme that allowed members of the RAF to continue to wear their uniforms while undertaking factory work 'as an aid to their recovery'.[98]

The influence of these two surgeons was pervasive; they communicated with men in the highest echelons in the RAF, highlighting the value placed on medical consultants in the Services during the Second World War, particularly in regard to rehabilitation. Between them, Watson-Jones and McIndoe influenced the way that men injured while in service with the RAF were treated. Both of these surgeons believed that the medical care in the RAF ought to reflect the high status of aircrew in particular, and the RAF's treatment of them.

Despite the efforts of doctors to rehabilitate them, the impact of residual disability for some patients was too much for them to continue working in the RAF. A combination of good medical care and a concentration on rehabilitation ensured that those whose disability prevented them from remaining in the Forces could continue working in a civilian capacity. Indeed, their association with the RAF continued, as many discharged men were employed through the Ministry of Aircraft Production, in factories or farms, or with the RAF sea-rescue squads.[99] As we have seen, many men returned to full military duties in the RAF after rehabilitation. There were a number of reasons why people with disabilities were able to stay within the RAF. To train technicians, support staff and aircrew was expensive, so their retention in the Service made sound economic sense. Alternative jobs were made available for those who could not return to their previous job. Aircrew and technicians were based in Britain, which allowed pilots such as Douglas Bader and Colin Hodgkinson to fly despite being double amputees, as their environment was stable and they had access to technology which aided their function. Mobility was less of an issue when in mainland Britain, as aids could be procured and maintained. When Bader was shot down and ended up in a prisoner of war camp, in order to halt his many escape attempts, his captors confiscated his artificial limbs.[100] There was also a strong sense of loyalty from inside and outside the RAF, and the public and the chiefs of staff of the RAF wanted to ensure that these men, to whom such a commitment was made and who carried the nation's hopes on their shoulders, would be cared for by a grateful nation.

Long-term impact of rehabilitation after the war

After the war was over, the RAF continued to hold an important place at the forefront of rehabilitative medicine. Fighters and bombers were required and new and innovative types of aircraft were flown and tested; thus there were still incidences of injury, as well as accidents sustained by young men working in a highly competitive and dangerous environment. Rehabilitation was still needed. By 1950 there were three rehabilitation units operated by the RAF. Mongewell Park was still a functioning unit for officers; Collaton Cross near Plymouth and Chessington in Surrey continued to provide services for RAF personnel.[101] The largest centre, at Loughborough was no longer required and it was closed on 1 July 1946.[102] The Army and Navy, whose rehabilitation services were less established, did not maintain rehabilitation units after the war. Instead, the RAF's rehabilitation units were used by other Services. The Navy sent its patients to Mongewell Park and when that was closed to Headley Park. The Army continued to use its Convalescent Home at Osborne House on the Isle of Wight, originally Queen Victoria's holiday home on the island which was not technically a rehabilitation unit. Instead, Army personnel went there to rest after injury.

The special nature of RAF rehabilitation units was maintained after the war. In some cases, the mixing of the Services at rehabilitation centres became problematic. In a letter to the Director General of Medical Services for the Navy from Air Marshal P.C. Livingston, it was carefully explained that Headley Court had been a gift from the Chartered Auctioneers' and Estate Agents' Institute. Under the terms of the gift, the only members of the Forces to be treated there were the RAF aircrew. What was also problematic is that at all RAF rehabilitation centres, officers and other ranks were mixed in the gymnasium, swimming pool and while undergoing treatment, yet maintained separate accommodation and eating areas. This presented a problem for the Navy, as officers and men were not allowed to mix. While an exception might be made for naval personnel who had been in the fleet air arm, at Headley Court Army personnel were still excluded.[103] The complex nature of this gift of Headley Court, which was bestowed on the RAF for its efforts during the Battle of Britain, was problematic for one Army officer, Major Aitken, who had contracted polio and had rehabilitative treatment at Mongewell Park until it closed in 1949. Such were the specific instructions of the gift that despite letters to the King's Assistant Private Secretary, Michael Adeane, from Major Aitken's father, there was nothing that could be done and Major Aitken was supposed to be moved to Collaton Cross. That the RAF occupied a special position was further evidenced by a note by Livingston which read that Major Aitken would not have been discharged from the RAF 'while he was still likely to improve in his physical condition because we would have felt that the importance of improving him far outweighed the letter of the law'.[104]

The impact of rehabilitation services in the RAF was long lasting and the principles that had been established at the centres were practised long after the war was over. In 1948, a film was made about medical rehabilitation in the RAF by Mr N.M. Richards, to which Air Marshal Livingston added a soundtrack in 1949.[105] Reginald Watson-Jones showed the film to groups of surgeons at medical conferences and it was received with a great deal of enthusiasm. So much so, that Watson-Jones wrote to Air Marshal Livingston, asking if he might take a copy of the film to Australia as it would be 'wonderful to spread the RAF gospel there as well'.[106] The film was shown to physical training instructors and medical officers who had enlisted in the RAF. There was also a suggestion that it be used in recruiting drives and be presented to medical and civilian audiences as a documentary.[107] As late as 1956, the Royal Society of Medicine hosted a symposium on rehabilitation, which celebrated the fifteenth anniversary of organised rehabilitation in the RAF.[108]

Rehabilitation methods were transferred to civilian life. The efficient and successful rehabilitation methods of the RAF were held up as an example to the rest of the Forces and indeed the whole country. As Reginald Watson-Jones wrote in the *British Legion Journal*,

> That which has been achieved in one military service, and is now being attempted in the civilian service of coal mining, and in the industries of Birmingham, can be achieved in the country as a whole. Every disabled person can be treated, rehabilitated and resettled with no interruption and no break in continuity.[109]

This could only be achieved, according to Watson-Jones, if the medical and social practitioners on whom rehabilitation depended, co-operated.[110]

Although injuries from trauma and life in the Services were treated with rehabilitative methods, other conditions presented particular problems for the RAF. It was difficult, in some cases, to be certain of the duration required for recovery and then a period of rehabilitative therapy for some diseases. Polio presented a particular problem for the RAF during and after the war. Between October 1949 and October 1950, 23,044 cases of polio were treated at the RAF Physical Medicine Centres.[111] The long-term effects of polio were difficult to judge and varied widely from patient to patient. Therefore it was generally accepted that those affected by polio would stay in the Services until they achieved a level of function and their 'future could be foreseen'.[112] It was reported by Squadron Leader

Mason, specialist in physical medicine, that the average beneficial time of treatment was 18 months, but in some cases there was still improvement after two years. Therefore, it was agreed that all long-term cases be reviewed after 18 months and again two and a half years later if it was required.[113] Essentially polio cases could stay in the Forces for up to two years on full pay. Many of these cases went to RAF rehabilitation units to benefit from treatment regimes provided there.

Conclusions

The RAF ran its rehabilitation centres in its own way during and after the war. Early in the war, rehabilitation centres were established to deal with specific injuries associated with aircrew. Pilots in particular underwent extensive training which was lengthy and costly. Owing to the risky nature of flying, many trained men only went on one mission, so it was important to maintain pilot numbers.

As a special service, with a place in the hearts of the British public and the State, the RAF, supported by eminent consultant surgeons such as Archibald McIndoe and Reginald Watson-Jones, was able to run its medical services independently, more so than the Army and the Navy. Owing to its position in the military hierarchy, and its importance in the mind of the public, the RAF was able to retain its special status in the realm of rehabilitation. It had its own rehabilitation centres, and rapidly moved its men from an EMS hospital to one of its own rehabilitation units. It did not follow the usual rules relating to discharge, generally ignoring the rules adopted by the other Services, 'turning a blind eye' to those that stayed in the Service longer than they should have under the rules. The specialists who provided medical expertise to the RAF colluded in its unique position and certainly gained concessions that doctors in the Army and Navy seemed unable to procure. Both Watson-Jones and McIndoe used the special nature of the RAF to break standard military rules, such as the wearing of uniforms while recovering in hospital. The notion that they would receive excellent medical care should they be injured alleviated the problem of fear in aircrew. These support systems within a Service that regarded loyalty to it above all other things assisted in reducing the number of breakdowns in health. Different aspects of rehabilitation were employed to achieve the best results. Social rehabilitation was generally more psychological than physical. For aircrew who had suffered burns, the typical round of rehabilitative therapy was not suitable, as the delicate medical condition of burns patients did not allow them to participate in the rough and tumble of the rehabilitation centres established for those with orthopaedic injury. Instead, parties and outings replaced PT and sports. The methods of rehabilitative therapy were not prescriptive when it came to restoring the vital services of the RAF.

After the war, the RAF continued to enjoy its special status. It was seen as an example of high quality rehabilitative therapy and the successes of the RAF in this field were celebrated long after the war was over. The RAF's medical treatment was held up to others as an example of excellent quality care. Consultant surgeons such as Watson-Jones held up the RAF as an example for rehabilitative practices in civilian life.

Notes

1 B.H. Liddell-Hart, *History of the Second World War* (London, 1970), 93.

2 The scarves were actually adopted to protect their necks from the stiff collar and tie worn when flying which would chafe against their skin with g-forces; the sheepskins were worn to protect against the cold of high altitude.

3 Calder, *The People's War*, 142.

4 J.B. Priestley, *Postscripts* (London, 1940), pp. 39–43.

5 See Michael Paris, 'The Rise of the Airmen: The Origins of Air Force Elitism', *Journal of Contemporary History*, Vol. 28, No. 1 (January 1993), 123–41.

6 See Mark Harrison, *Medicine and Victory* (Oxford, 2008).

7 Theodore James, 'A History of the Medical Branch of the Royal Air Force', *Adler Museum Bulletin*, Vol. 10, No. 2 (1984), 6.

8 M.A. Liskutin, *Challenge in the Air: A Spitfire Pilot Remembers* (London, 1988), 75.

9 In 1943 45 men drowned, one was paralysed in a diving accident and three died from football injuries. S.C. Rexford-Welch, *The Royal Air Force Medical Services: Vol. 1: Administration* (London, 1954), 568.

10 See Colin Hodgkinson, *Best Foot Forward: The Autobiography of Colin Hodgkinson* (London, 1957).

11 See P. Huskinson, *Vision Ahead* (London, 1949).

12 Air Chief Marshall Sir Hugh Dowding was the Commander-in-Chief of Fighter Command. Liddell-Hart, *History of the Second World War*, 93.

13 Joan Lane, *A Social History of Medicine: Health, Healing and Disease in England, 1750–1950* (London, 2001), 183.

14 Rexford-Welch, *The Royal Air Force Medical Services: Vol. 1*, 314.

15 Draft Minutes of Meeting with Director-General of Medical Services of consultants in Surgery, Orthopaedic Surgery and Plastic Surgery (15 December 1941), AIR20/9919, National Archives, London.

16 R.N. Houlding, 'Rehabilitation of Injured Air Crews', *British Medical Journal* (27 September 1941), 429.
17 James M. Banovetz, 'The Development of Orthopaedics in 20th Century Warfare', *Iowa Orthopaedic Journal*, Vol. 17 (1997), 38.
18 See David LeVay, *The History of Orthopaedics* (Park Ridge, New Jersey, 1990).
19 Watson-Jones, 'Rehabilitation in the Royal Air-Force', in Doherty and Runes (eds), *Rehabilitation of the War Injured*, 428.
20 Houlding, 'Rehabilitation of Injured Air Crews in Great Britain', in ibid., 445.
21 See Ana Carden-Coyne and Beth Linker, 'Strength and Science: Gender, Physiotherapy and Medicine in Early Twentieth Century America', *Journal of Women's History*, Vol. 17, No. 3 (2005), 105–32; Ana Carden-Coyne, 'Painful Bodies and Brutal Women: Remedial Massage, Gender Relations and Cultural Agency in Military Hospitals, 1914–18', *Journal of War and Culture Studies*, Vol. 1, No. 2 (2008), 139–58.
22 Minute 20 from file DGMS/55 – Orthopaedics, Visit to RAF Rehabilitation Unit, Loughborough (2 December 1943), AIR 49/359, National Archives, London.
23 Report: *Physical Fitness Officers and Physical Training Instructors* (undated, presumably 1941), AIR 49/359, National Archives, London.
24 Rexford-Welch, *The Royal Air Force Medical Services: Vol. 1*, 321.
25 *The Hospital*, Vol. 41, No. 7 (July 1945), 212.
26 R. Watson-Jones, 'Rehabilitation in the Royal Air-Force', *British Medical Journal* (March 28, 1942), 405.
27 RAF Operations Record, RAF Medical Rehabilitation Centre, Loughborough, AIR 29/767 (1942–44), National Archives, London.
28 Letter to Air Marshal Sir Harold Whittingham from R. Watson-Jones (4 September 1942), AIR 20/9919, National Archives, London.
29 Ben Shephard, *A War of Nerves: Soldiers and Psychiatrists 1914–1994* (London, 2002), 168.
30 *Organisation of Classes* (no date but probably 1945), AIR 49/359, National Archives, London, 2.
31 H. Osmond Clarke, 'Orthopaedic and Rehabilitation Service of the Royal Air Force', *The Lancet* (18 May 1946), 721.
32 The Palace Hotel was requisitioned in October 1939. Minute 20 from file DGMS/55 – Orthopaedics, Visit to RAF Rehabilitation Unit, Loughborough (2 December 1943), AIR 49/359, National Archives, London.
33 Ibid.
34 The aircrew from Cosford exhibited surprise when they were told that they did not have to carry their own utensils and that they would be waited on by waiting staff. RAF Operations Record, RAF Medical Rehabilitation, AIR 29/767 (1942–44), National Archives, London.

35 Minute 20 from file DGMS/55 – Orthopaedics, Visit to RAF Rehabilitation Unit Loughborough, 2 December, 1943, AIR 49/359, National Archives, London.
36 Repatriated POWs were also sent there for 'mental rehabilitation'. RAF Operations Record, RAF Medical Rehabilitation AIR 29/767, National Archives, London.
37 Minute 20 from file DGMS/55 – Orthopaedics, Visit to RAF Rehabilitation Unit Loughborough, 2 December, 1943, AIR 49/359, National Archives, London.
38 RAF Operations Record, RAF Medical Rehabilitation, AIR 29/767 (1942–44), National Archives, London.
39 Ibid.
40 Ibid.
41 Ibid.
42 Ibid.
43 Ibid.
44 Ibid.
45 Watson-Jones, 'Rehabilitation in the Royal Air Force', 406.
46 *The Hospital*, Vol. 41, No. 7 (July 1945), 214.
47 'Rehabilitation in the RAF', *The Lancet* (6 May 1944), 608.
48 Rexford-Welch, *The Royal Air Force Medical Services: Vol. 1*, 323.
49 Minute 20 from file DGMS/55 – Orthopaedics, Visit to RAF Rehabilitation Unit Loughborough (2 December 1943), AIR 49/359, National Archives, London.
50 Watson-Jones, 'Rehabilitation in the Royal Air-Force', 406.
51 RAF Operations Record, RAF Medical Rehabilitation AIR 29/767 (1942–44), National Archives, London.
52 Rexford-Welch, *The Royal Air Force Medical Services: Vol. 1*, 315.
53 *Royal Air Force Officers' Hospital, Torquay – Programme of Work* (1941), AIR 20/9919, National Archives, London.
54 Osmond Clarke, 'Orthopaedic and Rehabilitation Service of the Royal Air Force', 722.
55 Report: *RAF Hospital for Officers, Torquay* (undated, presumably 1941), AIR 49/359, National Archives, London, 3.
56 Ibid.
57 Rexford-Welch, *The Royal Air Force Medical Services: Vol. 1*, 316.
58 Report: RAF Hospital for Officers, Torquay (undated presume 1941), AIR 49/359, National Archives, London.
59 Report: *The Development and Organisation of the Physiotherapeutic and Rehabilitation Departments at the Royal Air Force Officers' Hospital* (20 August 1941), AIR 49/359, National Archives, London.
60 Ibid.
61 Rexford-Welch, *The Royal Air Force Medical Services: Vol. 1* (1954), 318.

62 Letter to R.N. Houlding from H.E. Whittingham (28 September 1941), AIR 20/9919, National Archives, London.

63 See E.R. Mayhew, *The Reconstruction of Warriors: Archibald McIndoe, the Royal Air Force and the Guinea Pig Club* (London, 2004); Edward Bishop, *McIndoe's Army: The Story of the Guinea Pig Club and its Indomitable Members* (London, 2001).

64 See Hugh McLeave, *McIndoe: Plastic Surgeon* (London, 1961); Leonard Moseley, *Faces From the Fire: The Biography of Sir Archibald McIndoe* (London, 1962).

65 G.H. Morley, 'The Saline Bath Treatment of Burns', in Cope (ed.), *History of the Second World War*, 314.

66 Tom Gleave, *I Had A Row With A German* (London, 1941), 94.

67 Ibid., 93.

68 Hillary, *The Last Enemy*, 194.

69 William Simpson, *I Burned My Fingers* (London, 1956), 114.

70 Richard Battle, 'Plastic Surgery in the Two World Wars', *Journal of the Royal Society of Medicine*, Vol. 71 (1978), 846.

71 Williams and Hamson, *McIndoe's Army*.

72 Hillary, *The Last Enemy*, 205.

73 Simpson, *I Burned My Fingers*, 65.

74 Flight Sergeant Alan Morgan quoted in Williams and Harrison, *McIndoe's Army*, 17.

75 The job of these civilian consultants was to ensure medical officers were appropriately qualified, advise on arrangements, be available for consultant work, act as technical advisor to the director general of medical services, and provide a report for the Annual Health Report and the History of the War. Air Ministry Order A.187/41, *Medical Branch Consultants* (undated, presumably 1941), AIR 20/9919, National Archives, London.

76 Correspondence between Air Marshal Sir Christopher Courtney, Air Marshal Sir Harold Whittingham and Air Vice-Marshal W. Tyrrell (21 July–25 October 1941), AIR 20/9919, National Archives, London.

77 Letter to Air Commodore H.T. Lydford from Air Marshal Sir Harold Whittingham (18 September 1941), AIR 20/9919, National Archives, London.

78 Letter to Air Marshal Sir Harold Whittingham from R. Watson-Jones (10 September 1942), AIR 20/9919, National Archives, London.

79 *Analysis of Disposal of Orthopaedic Cases from RAF Medical Officers' Rehabilitation Unit, Loughborough, Year beginning 1 December 1942 ending 30 November 1943* (no date, presumably 1943), AIR 20/9919, National Archives, London.

80 Memo to Sir Charles F.A. Portal from Reginald Watson-Jones (4 November 1944), AIR 8/796, National Archives, London.

81 Thirty-one per cent went back to full flying duty and 7% were found fit for ground duty. *Analysis of Disposal of Orthopaedic Cases from RAF*

Medical Officers' Rehabilitation Unit, Loughborough, Year beginning 1 December 1942 ending 30 November 1943.

82 *The Hospital*, Vol. 41, No. 7 (July 1945), 216.

83 Letter to Air Marshal Sir Harold Whittingham from R. Watson-Jones (26 November 1942), AIR 20/9919, National Archives, London.

84 Letter to Air Chief Marshal Sir Charles F.A. Portal from Archibald McIndoe (14 October 1944), AIR 8/796, National Archives, London.

85 Ibid.

86 CAS Memo (30 October 1944), AIR 8/796, National Archives, London.

87 Letter to Sir Charles Portal from Archibald McIndoe (4 November 1944), AIR 8/796, National Archives, London.

88 Simpson, *I Burned My Fingers*, 91.

89 Letter to Sir Charles Portal from Archibald McIndoe (14 October 1944), AIR 8/796, National Archives, London.

90 Letter to Air Chief Marshal Sir Charles F.A. Portal from Archibald McIndoe (19 October 1944), AIR 8/796, National Archives, London.

91 Memo to Sir Charles F.A. Portal from Reginald Watson-Jones (4 November 1944), AIR 8/796, National Archives, London.

92 Martin Francis, *The Flyer: British Culture and the Royal Air Force 1939–1945* (Oxford, 2009), 106.

93 CAS 3942 from Sir Charles Portal (3 December 1944) AIR 8/796, National Archives, London.

94 E.R. Mayhew, *The Reconstruction of Warriors* (London, 2004).

95 Letter to Air Chief Marshal Sir Charles F.A. Portal from Archibald McIndoe (14 October 1944), AIR 8/796, National Archives, London.

96 Note by the Parliamentary Secretary of the Admiralty, War Cabinet Memo, Committee on Service Pay and Allowances (10 April 1945), AIR 7/796, National Archives, London.

97 Ibid.

98 Minutes from National Advisory Council on the Employment of the Disabled (10 March 1946), LAB 18/148, National Archives, London.

99 'Rehabilitation in the RAF', *The Lancet* (6 May 1944), 609.

100 Paul Brickhill, *Reach for the Sky* (London, 1955), 281.

101 Letter to Gordon C. Touche, MP, from Major Hugh Aitken (11 May 1949), AIR 20/9923, National Archives, London.

102 RAF Operations Record, RAF Medical Rehabilitation Centre, Loughborough, AIR 29/767, National Archives, London.

103 Letter to Surgeon Vice-Admiral C.E. Greeson, from Air Marshal P.C. Livingston (22 June 1950), AIR 20/9923, National Archives, London.

104 AUS Note from P.C. Livingston (2 February 1950), AIR 20/9923, National Archives, London.

105 Memo from P.C. Livingston, ADST (Films) Medical Rehabilitation in the Royal Air Force (30 April 1949), AIR 20/9923, National Archives, London.

106 Letter from Sir Reginald Watson-Jones to P.C. Livingston (21 March 1951), AIR 20/9923, National Archives, London.
107 Memo, *Rehabilitation Film*, AIR 20/9923, National Archives, London.
108 Programme of *Symposium of Medical Rehabilitation in the Royal Air Force* (12 December 1956), AIR 20/9923, National Archives, London.
109 Reginald Watson-Jones, 'All Must Co-operate', *British Legion Journal*, Vol. 25, No. 5 (May 1945), 85.
110 These included the doctor, surgeon, nurse, physiotherapist, gymnast, almoner, resettlement officer and industrialist. Ibid., 85.
111 *Return of Treatments at Physical Medicine Centres During the Twelve Months Ending October 1950*, AIR 20/9923 (1954), National Archives, London.
112 Minutes from a conference held at Central Medical Establishment (13 March 1950), AIR 20/9923, National Archives, London.
113 Ibid.

5

Men: masculinity and rehabilitation

One of the most important objectives in rehabilitation was to restore a sense of identity. But nowhere was the success of rehabilitation as a method of restoring a sense of manhood more strongly tested than at the Spinal Unit of the Stoke Mandeville Hospital in Aylesbury.[1] This chapter will trace the events that led up to its establishment and will examine the treatment provided to men who were paralysed and whose masculine identity was called into question. Stoke Mandeville set out to restore this sense of manhood, stressing courage in the face of adversity, with an emphasis on games sport and military camaraderie. This chapter details the development of Stoke Mandeville's rehabilitative methods, including competitive recovery: the use of sport and techniques of daily living geared toward the restoration of masculine identity.

Rebuilding a strong sense of masculinity was particularly difficult in men with spinal paralysis. The chapter examines the combination of physical and social rehabilitation at Stoke Mandeville, and its redefinition of a useful masculine body. Graham Dawson reminds us that 'masculinities are lived out in the flesh, but fashioned in the imagination'.[2] The subject of masculinity and war has fascinated historians; raising issues about gendered selves and the ways in which identity is shaped.[3] However, war causes ambiguity in gender roles, as noted by Penny Summerfield and Corinna Peniston-Bird: 'the meaning of masculinity as well as femininity was plunged into uncertainty by total war'.[4] Structured norms of male and female roles were easier to maintain and control in times of peace. But men's bodies were altered physically and emotionally by war. One of the constant pressures was the fear of the individual being feminised by injury. As men who embodied strength and virility, those in the Services related to their bodies as fit and healthy.[5] Sonya O. Rose points out that the association between masculinity and fit men had grown throughout the twentieth century and was celebrated in conflict.[6] Rose has argued that in the Second World War, men focused less on heroics and more on restrained courage. As we have seen, the heroes from St Dunstan's in the First World War represented sacrifice as heroic stoicism. In the Second World War, another type of hero was associated with the quietly courageous workers who joined the Forces to defeat Hitler.

This industry-based form of heroism is juxtaposed with what Martin Francis in his essay calls the 'old-style, public school, visions of chivalric masculinity'.[7] Behaviours that were tolerated in the expression of masculinity differed among the Services. As we have seen, the RAF embodied the more traditional notions of heroic masculinity. Courage was appreciated but chivalry was celebrated. It was perhaps necessary, for a country involved in a global war and one hugely dislocated by its effects, to view disabled men waging a war not merely against the Germans and their allies, but the adversary represented by their disability.

Disablement was another challenge to the nature of gender and a threat to embodied identity. As we have seen, much of the literature on war, masculine identity and disability focuses on the First World War.[8] Joanna Bourke, and more recently Ana Carden-Coyne and Wendy Jane Gagen, have highlighted the conflict between masculinity and disability, and put forward arguments for the ways in which masculine status was renegotiated.[9] Many of these arguments centre on the seminal work of R.W. Connell.[10] Gagen uses a theory of 'hegemonic masculinity' and argues that it was possible to renegotiate an individualised masculine identity. Carden-Coyne goes beyond this to suggest that several competing forms of masculinity ensured that identity was maintained in a number of ways.[11]

Much has been written about Stoke Mandeville, mainly by people who worked there. This chapter does not wish to replicate those useful stories; instead it will offer an insight into the role of rehabilitation as it relates to restoring masculinity. Those at Stoke Mandeville had a particular and difficult challenge, as the men with spinal paralysis experienced initial stages of severe depression and hopelessness. The chapter will detail Stoke Mandeville's work and its own particular brand of rehabilitation, which combined specific medical treatment with a regime to restore feelings of independence, employability and physical prowess.

Spinal paralysis before 1944

At the beginning of the Second World War, the outlook for servicemen with spinal injury was as poor as it had been in 1918. Mortality, within the first few months of the onset of paralysis, was between 47 and 65%.[12] Within three years the death rate for spinal injury had increased to 80%.[13] Death followed complications such as bed sores and urinary tract infections. Most patients were confined to hospital, and the medical routine was generally limited to massage and occupational therapy.[14] Wasting from inactivity meant patients were unable to sit up, and this resulted in a helpless, prone state. Wheelchairs were difficult to procure, although some had access to a spinal carriage, in which the patient would lie on pillows. These carriages resembled adult-sized perambulators, which a nurse would push around. For more mobile patients with lesions lower down the spine, sticks were placed either side of the carriage, enabling them to push themselves, with a motion reminiscent of a skier. It was felt that those with spinal paralysis were hopeless cases. Those who surmounted the odds and survived beyond three years were 'doomed to spend the rest of their lives as pensioners at home or in institutions for incurables dependent on other people's assistance, and, as a rule, given no incentive or encouragement to return to a useful life'.[15]

There were exceptions to this prognosis. Before the Second World War, some with spinal injury were better placed than others, having resources to pay for treatment and assistance at home. For some, good medical care and a healthy diet reduced the weakening effects of spinal injury. One woman wrote, 'I began to live a normal life again, going out in a wheeled-chair and being carried from a car to visit friends and cinemas and theatres. I even started going to a few dances again and watching others doing what I had loved best of all before.'[16]

While some paraplegics reconstructed their lives, British doctors could do little to improve paraplegics' experience. A physiotherapist recalled, 'I well remember an orthopaedic surgeon telling me how much it distressed him that all he seemed able to do for these patients was to discuss the string bags which they were making.'[17] The making of string bags was part of a long tradition of occupational therapy. Rehabilitative methods, such as prone remedial exercises and physiotherapy, were not used for the bedridden. New methods of rehabilitation bypassed those with spinal injuries until the war was almost over. As we will see, rehabilitative regimes for the spinal injured were evolving, but an organised, systematic treatment routine for servicemen and women was not realised until 1944.

In the early part of the war, there were few established centres for spinal treatment in Britain.[18] In total, 12 spinal units were set up attached to neurological, neurosurgical, orthopaedic, psychiatric and urological units.[19] The apparent neglect of rehabilitative practice had a deleterious effect on patients at these centres who suffered from the common complications of bed sores and bladder infections. In some cases, surgeons even amputated paralysed patients' legs, assuming they were useless and that amputation would prevent further complications.[20]

One rehabilitation unit succeeded where others had failed. The regime at the Stoke Mandeville Hospital near Aylesbury proved highly effective. While many factors ensured Stoke Mandeville's success, the application of rehabilitative practices by a German Jewish neurosurgeon certainly increased survival rates. In March 1939, Ludwig Guttmann and his family escaped Germany, owing to the efforts of the British Society for the Protection of Science and Learning.[21] Arriving in Oxford, Guttmann worked under Sir Hugh Cairns.[22] Like Geoffrey Jefferson in Manchester and Norman Dodd in Edinburgh, Cairns was a pioneering specialist in neurosurgery.[23] He and Jefferson were responsible for the organisation of neurosurgery in Britain from 1939 until Cairns joined the Royal Army Medical Corps, when control of civilian responsibilities passed wholly to Jefferson.[24] Guttmann worked on comparative nerve regeneration in rabbits at the Department of Zoology and Comparative Anatomy with J.Z. Young and Peter Medawar.[25] When war broke out in September 1939, Guttmann offered to join the Services, but was told by Cairns that he should wait as there was a plan to open a wing of the Wingfield-Morris Hospital at Oxford for peripheral nerve injuries.[26] Later, he was asked by Dr George Riddoch, Chairman of the Nerve Injury Committee of the Medical Research Council, (MRC), to review the state of spinal surgery, the nervous system's recovery and rehabilitation.[27]

Why did the MRC call for a report? Although Guttmann assumed that new treatments owed much to his efforts, other factors also influenced the MRC. According to Guttmann's unpublished autobiography, Riddoch was not happy with the work being carried out in the spinal units, as survival rates were not improving above what they had been in the First World War.[28] At the end of 1941, the first symposium on rehabilitation after injuries to the central nervous system was held by the Section of Neurology at the Royal Society of Medicine in London.

Papers on head injuries were delivered by Britain's notable neurosurgeons, Hugh Cairns and Geoffrey Jefferson, but there were no papers on spinal injuries.[29]

Even though Britain boasted high calibre neurosurgeons, the care of peripheral nerve injuries was delegated to orthopaedic surgeons. Thus, Herbert Seddon, an orthopaedic surgeon, was put in charge of the spinal injury centre at the Wingfield-Morris Hospital in 1940.[30] The spine was treated as a broken bone, and where there was no damage to the spinal cord, treatment was based on the premise that it restored mobility. However, orthopaedic surgeons were not equipped to treat patients whose nerve injuries resulted in paralysis. The idea that neurosurgeons could do a better job came from the United States and Germany. It was argued that the number of casualties that American orthopaedic surgeons treated meant they were unable to effectively look after such specialised cases as the spinal injured, and as a result neurosurgeons had been drafted in to treat them.[31] The MRC report may have been inspired by the perceived success of American neurosurgeons.[32] The British worked closely with the Americans after they entered the war in 1941.[33] Additionally, innovations in medical technology such as the Stryker bed were part of a growing interest in spinal injury.[34]

Guttmann's report detailing his methods of treatment was submitted to the Peripheral Nerve Committee of the MRC in 1941.[35] Guttmann's radical ideas came from experience at a hospital in Germany. The particular case concerned a young miner who had had his spinal cord crushed in an accident, and who died, not from his injuries, but from complications that were essentially preventable. Guttmann wrote,

> During the following weeks I saw this fine, strong man rapidly deteriorate and become increasingly emaciated as a result from sepsis from urinary infection and sloughing, multiple bedsores until he died just five weeks after his injury.[36]

The MRC was impressed with Guttmann's proposal to cure patients by using rehabilitative practice and surgery. Guttmann gained their confidence, and they recommended he put his theories into practice at Stoke Mandeville.[37] The Stoke Mandeville Unit for the Spinal Injured opened in February 1944 with little fanfare, one ward and 28 beds.[38] This small number was likely to grow as the Unit was opened specifically to treat the high number of casualties expected from the D-Day landings in June.[39] Initially Stoke Mandeville was ill-equipped to deal with the special requirements of the spinal injured; 18 of the 28 standard mattresses needed replacing with sorbo-rubber mattresses and the metal bedpans supplied were exchanged for rubber ones which prevented bed sores.[40] Plaster beds, the traditional method for transporting soldiers with spinal injury, could be devastating for a patient with paralysis. The resulting loss of sensation would mean that he would not feel pain from pressure, and bed sores would form. Generally, patients were transported back to Britain reasonably quickly, but even a week on a plaster bed was detrimental to even the most robust.[41] Returning from a distant theatre, such as Asia, a soldier could be lying catheterised on a plaster bed for several weeks without being moved. Guttmann suggested that the Services use pillow packs as the plaster beds were contributing to the pressure sores which threatened the patient's chances of survival, so the practice was changed. As soon as the patient arrived at Stoke Mandeville, he was placed on pillow packs and moved regularly. In order to receive a good standard of care, the Medical Services sent those with peripheral nerve injuries back to the UK, but in some cases this could take months, which was detrimental to the patient's health.

Life at Stoke Mandeville

The war left a permanent, physical mark on men with spinal injuries. The prospect of permanent disability was devastating. Many were severely depressed and a number attempted suicide. It became the function of doctors, nurses and physiotherapists to aid in the process of rehabilitation.[42] The restoration process extended to the mind as well as to the body. Steps were taken to minimise stress, and provide an encouraging and constructive environment. Competition was seen as a positive aspect of the rehabilitative process and was encouraged. The Service Sub-committee of the Research Board for the Correlation of Medical Science and Physical Education noted: 'The importance of the morale factor cannot be overstressed. It is essential to remove the inertia and despondency of hospitalisation and to restore this will to get well.'[43]

At Stoke Mandeville, the Director heartily endorsed this sentiment: 'The creation of a cheerful atmosphere and good morale in the ward cannot be stressed too much. The whole unit must be deliberately impregnated with enthusiasm.'[44] Guttmann also suggested 'empathy on the one hand and firm handling on the other'.[45] He found that patients' accounts were useful in helping the newly disabled men. One of Guttmann's patients wrote in 1943 that 'one of the most difficult tasks of a paraplegic is to cheer up his visitors'.[46] Guttmann and his staff tried to educate the family and friends of paralysed servicemen to 'understand' as opposed to 'pity' the men.

Guttmann's treatment regime combined new and established therapies.[47] Many medical problems were solved by simple common-sense. To prevent bed sores patients were turned in their beds regularly, which took four orderlies and a supervisor.[48] Infection of the urinary tract was alleviated by regular disinfecting of the urinary system or by installing supra-pubic catheters, which were fitted into the bladder above the pubis.[49] New drugs including penicillin were particularly useful in the treatment regime of the spinal paralysed.[50] With his Oxford connections, Guttmann obtained penicillin, as Lady Florey, wife of Hugh Florey, would bring small supplies to Stoke Mandeville.[51]

From its establishment in 1944, the daily routine of the Spinal Unit was a combination of contemporary practice and new treatments devised by Guttmann. Military discipline served to reinforce masculine norms of behaviour. Despite an initial lack of enthusiasm from staff who believed that there was little that could be done for these patients, physiotherapy and remedial exercises were instigated.[52] There was a definite concentration on bodily movements that matched the role of the military male. Patients were encouraged to exercise in bed as soon as they were able. In order to make patients maintain correct posture, they were given mirrors – a form of visual–sensory–motor interaction which reflected the straight spine of the military body.[53] George Mosse argues that the male body is central to the conception of manliness and to regain control of an aspect of their corporeality, such as an upright position in bed, would have contributed to the refashioning of male identity.[54]

In addition, Guttmann instructed his staff to throw medicine balls at patients while they were confined to bed.[55] Other exercises were also prescribed, and specialised equipment was designed to build up supportive muscle in the mobile part of the body. The Stoke Mandeville Bed Cycle was developed specifically for these bed exercises.[56] While the patient was still in the ward, curing through competition began. This proved very successful, as most patients were young men, eager to outdo one another, and Guttmann exploited their competitive instincts. Most rehabilitative units encouraged competition between patients; it redirected their focus from emasculated invalid toward the natural male state of rivalry.[57] The RAF used such methods to great effect. At Stoke Mandeville, contests were held including timed 'dressing exercises' in which patients got out of bed, dressed themselves, and got into their wheelchairs.[58]

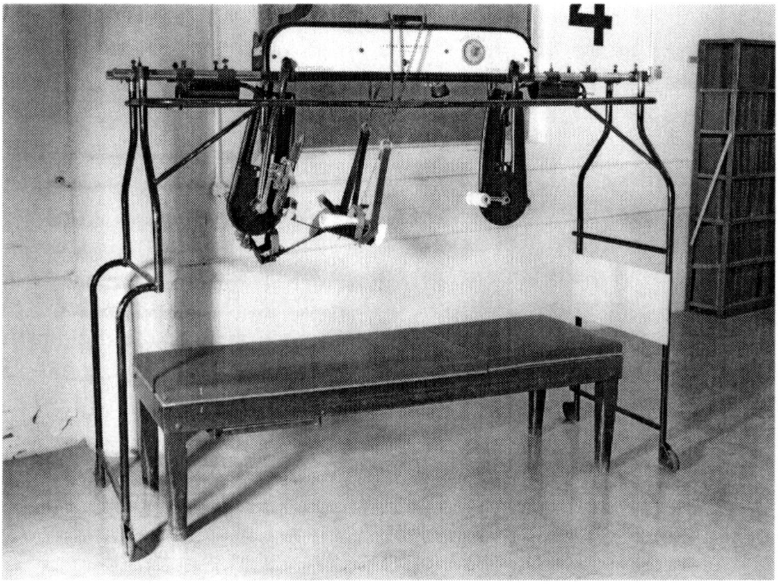

Figure 5.1 Stoke Mandeville bed cycle, 1949, which was one of the specialised types of equipment designed at Stoke Mandeville by Ludwig Guttmann (reproduced with permission of the Science Museum, London)

Even while bed-bound or on the wards, such activities became part of a routinised, disciplined system.

Following the initial phase of the rehabilitation process, patients graduated from the ward to the physiotherapy room, where they performed exercises, firstly on the Guthrie-Smith apparatus.[59] The exercises gradually became more advanced. Much of the equipment was standard gymnasium apparatus and served to re-establish patterns of masculine behaviour. Patients would practise hitting a punchball from their wheelchairs, and performed tasks requiring strength, such as pulling themselves upright and using their arms to support themselves between parallel bars. The idea was that the patient would be able to develop compensatory muscles in the upper torso, in order to sit up in their wheelchair. Most patients at Stoke Mandeville had wheelchairs provided by the Ministry of Pensions from 1944. The spinal carriage, for so long the hallmark of the helpless invalid, was not considered suitable. Even so, the wheelchairs provided were large and cumbersome, weighed about 50 pounds and looked like leather armchairs on wheels. They had to be pushed by a helper, so it was virtually impossible for a patient to venture out of the hospital grounds on his own. In order to gain any independence of movement, a patient had to build up his muscles sufficiently to be able to push the wheels of his chair.

Cheerfulness and positive thinking were not enough to overcome boredom. Repetitive exercises and physiotherapy were insufficiently stimulating and could not be practised all day long. Patients devised their own activities in order to pass the time and amused themselves with a dramatic society, and a choir that treated the entire hospital to carols at Christmas.[60] Volunteers and staff at Stoke Mandeville also gave the men some sort of social life, for example by pushing them to the pub in the evenings. Such visits attempted to get men out of hospital, but also to restore a sense of the familiar. Fortunately, there was no shortage of helpers, as 'the war-time spirit was very much in evidence and these severely disabled ex-servicemen were welcomed everywhere'.[61] Trips to the local cinema in Aylesbury were regular events, and as there was no space for wheelchairs, men had to be taken out of their chairs and carried to the seats. One of the patients recalled, 'the patience of the attendants at the local cinema would be required to lift as many as six of us at a time into seats'.[62] Additionally, films were delivered to the hospital and shown weekly. Many famous entertainers came to Stoke Mandeville, such as Dame Margot Fonteyn and others from the Royal Ballet who danced for the patients.[63]

Activities were organised in such a way as to put meaning and purpose into life. The British Legion established a special paraplegic branch at the hospital in 1945. Two years later, this branch established a magazine, called *The Cord*, whose purpose was to inform patients and others about paraplegia. *The Cord* was full of medical advice, such as how to avoid complications such as bed sores and recurring urinary tract infections. Guttmann was a regular contributor. Other articles included information about pensions, taxation and employment opportunities, engagement and wedding announcements, teasing references to patients who had left the hospital and descriptions of sexual exploits (especially with nurses in the cupboards at Christmas parties), which helped establish masculine camaraderie. Military regimes were observed. In 1949 42 paralysed ex-servicemen were sent to the seaside for a holiday. The enlisted men went to Prestatyn and the officers went to Rustington in Sussex. Bathers were wheeled down to the water's edge or were taken down by donkeys and lifted into the water to swim. One woman said that they 'quickly get a new outlook on life when they find they can still take part in sports and pastimes. That's half the battle.'[64]

Thanks to these efforts, permanent hospital life was no longer the destiny of men with spinal paralysis; still, some stayed up to four years before they were deemed ready to leave the hospital. After their rehabilitative treatment was finished, a few returned to their homes and others moved to affiliated institutions. At these places, patients could live and work with a degree of independence. Some lived permanently in large private houses such as Chaseley Home in Eastbourne, which accommodated single men who had left Stoke Mandeville. Chaseley was to have been a convalescent home for blind soldiers, but Guttmann persuaded the owner, Lady Michaelis, to give her house and 50,000 pounds to maintain paraplegics.[65] This opened in 1946, as did a spinal section at the Star and Garter Home in Richmond, run by the Ministry of Pensions.[66] In the same year, the British Red Cross and the Order of St John established Lyme Green Settlement in Macclesfield.[67] Both Lyme Green and Kytes Estate,[68] near Watford, were settlements where specially adapted homes were built in the late 1940s for both single ex-servicemen and those with families.[69] These were located close to potential employment opportunities at nearby industrial parks.[70] The Duchess of Gloucester House, previously the Osterley Hotel, opened in 1949, and gave a home to single men, operating in a similar way to Chaseley.[71] The Thistle Foundation was officially launched by the Queen Mother in Edinburgh in 1950.[72] The Foundation supplied specially adapted houses for paralysed ex-servicemen. A Clinic was attached to the grounds where the houses were located and the men took part in sport and also were under the watchful eye of an orthopaedic surgeon, a consultant physician and a number of physiotherapists.[73]

But Stoke Mandeville remained a constant part of the men's lives. Guttmann was consultant to the affiliated homes, and when any man relapsed he could return to Stoke Mandeville for treatment. Patients continued to practise rehabilitative activities in their new accommodation, and *The Cord* kept them abreast of each others' activities.

The establishment of homes for the paralysed helped normalise life. But returning to work was the ultimate test of rehabilitation. Stoke Mandeville's Occupational Therapy Department taught carpentry and other skills, and patients were sent out on work placements.[74] Many settlements set up for paraplegics were located reasonably close to industrial areas where the men could, in principle, find employment.[75] Those hospitalised at Stoke Mandeville were ex-Service personnel and entitled to preferential employment under the Disabled Persons (Employment) Act 1944, yet suitable work was difficult to procure. Transport was problematic, and wheelchairs' dimensions hampered access. Continuity in employment was sometimes difficult to maintain as health breakdowns were common: patients had problems with their supra-pubic catheters and a bed sore could re-hospitalise a man for months.

Sport and games

While working toward full rehabilitation, a job and independence, men had to find something to do. In the early days, work was sporadic, fitness a slow process, and the choir, the cinema and films were not enough to prevent boredom. Recreational games became a popular way of passing the time. Patients at Stoke Mandeville played darts, skittles and snooker at the hospital and at the local pub.[76] These activities were easy to play from a wheelchair.

The first moves toward sport and games came not from the medical establishment, but from the patients themselves. In 1944, Guttmann watched from a window while staff had a break outside, throwing a ball to each other. As the patients in their wheelchairs watched, staff started including some patients in the game.[77] Guttmann noticed the body movement of the patients and how the effort of catching the ball made them bend and stretch. After this incident, throwing balls became part of the exercise regime. On another separate occasion, again in 1944, Guttmann discovered a number of patients pushing themselves around in their wheelchairs, attempting to hit a wooden puck with upended walking sticks.[78] Guttmann saw this game as yet another way to alleviate boredom and depression, and got into a wheelchair in the gymnasium and began to practise what he dubbed 'wheelchair polo':

> I tried to move about and, using the curved handle of a walking stick to hit the ball and chased after it. Simultaneously, I tried to prevent my opponent in another wheelchair . . . from counteracting my movements.[79]

There seems to be no reason why the game was called 'polo' and not hockey. The notion of the wheelchair as a type of 'horse' may have given rise to its name. Whatever the case, this game was the first developed in Britain specifically for wheelchair players, and was played regularly at Stoke Mandeville, pitting teams of patients against orderlies and physiotherapists. For able-bodied players, unfamiliarity with the wheelchair and its sudden movement led to many more bruises than their disabled opponents suffered.[80] Photographs depict men in shirtsleeves with knitted waistcoats and blankets covering their legs, hitting the ball around the gymnasium. The patients responded to questions by the British Legion for an article on their activities saying that they were 'warm':

> That word was what the doctor wanted to hear. The game was invented by the specialist in charge of the Spinal Injuries Unit to invigorate the body and promote the blood circulation, to keep the man's intelligence lively and his healthy limbs supple.[81]

There were no particular rules to wheelchair polo, no team names or fixtures. The ungainly wheelchairs hampered competition and caused frustration; nonetheless the games were played with great enthusiasm. Even the Occupational Therapy Department became involved; in July 1945, the Woodwork Department made goalposts with nets and 12 mallets.[82] Despite enthusiasm, the game was eventually abandoned because of 'possible head injuries being caused by the excitement created by the game, the swinging mallet frequently being in contact with the heads of the players'.[83] Participants did not share this concern. One recalled that, 'if you didn't come out of your chair at least once during the course of this game, you were considered by the other lads to be a cissy'.[84] Men stressed their determination to remain manly, even if it meant hurting themselves in the process.

Although wheelchair polo lasted only a few months, its impact was considerable, as it was the first wheelchair team sport played in Britain. By early 1945, it had been replaced by wheelchair netball, which was considered a safer option.[85] Such games whetted patients' appetite. Most sports were selected by Guttmann, who subsequently chose archery because it built up compensatory muscles in the torso, strengthening the patients' upper body, and was more interesting than repetitive movements. It was also a skilled, non-contact sport, which did not require a great deal of equipment, and patients could devote as much or as little time to it as they wished. It was also an activity which the able-bodied and disabled, men and women could play together. Guttmann invited the champion English archer Frank Bilson to Stoke Mandeville to teach patients and physical instructors how to shoot.[86] Archery proved a popular pastime and, as with wheelchair polo, the Occupational Therapy Department was put to good use in constructing suitable equipment.[87]

In archery, as with most activities at Stoke Mandeville, there was a large element of rivalry and an ad hoc competition was established between the different wards. This competition expanded quickly and became formalised. On 28 July 1948 an archery competition was held on the lawns outside Stoke Mandeville.[88] The Star and Garter Home's Spinal Unit was challenged to a match, as remedial exercise and sport continued to be practised at all of the Homes in which Guttmann was a consultant.[89] Sixteen competitors participated, including two female patients from Stoke Mandeville.[90] The Star and Garter emerged victorious, and were awarded the Challenge Shield, which was specially made for the first contest. While archery eventually became an important sport for disabled people, shooting was only part of the festivities at Stoke Mandeville that day. The main focus of the celebration was a visit from the Minister of Pensions, Hilary Marquand, who presented the patients with a 'Paraplegic Bus' to help them go on outings and to work.[91] Both the *Bucks Herald* and *The Cord* reported on the Minister's visit and the gift of the bus.[92] The competitive spirit between the Homes made this a popular event, and when the decision was made to hold another competition in 1949, the numbers taking part increased to 60.[93]

As there was no visit from the Minister of Pensions in 1949, the archery and netball competitions received little coverage outside the individual hospitals and Homes. But the new, and safer, sport of wheelchair netball joined archery in the calendar of events in 1949. The faster paced netball proved more popular than sedentary archery with gate-paying spectators; 'netball, in particular, seems very well patronised. It seems to be as good a crowd-drawing game as soccer.'[94] Although each team included ex-servicemen, a women's only team and a group of Polish ex-servicemen also competed at the sports day in the archery rounds. The women were drawn from paralysed servicewomen at Stoke Mandeville and the Polish soldiers came from a home in Penley in Wales.[95] Neither team excelled on the day, but *The Cord* commended the 'sporting' attitude of the Poles.[96]

After 1949, paraplegic games became an established event, yet they remained part of the treatment regime. In 1950, the competition was renamed the Stoke Mandeville Festival of Sport, after the British Festival of Sport. During the Festival at the Empress Hall in London, two teams of paraplegics played a game of wheelchair netball in front of a crowd of 10,000 and disabled archers shot against some of the top archers in England.[97] This event gave the spectacle of competitive paraplegic sport its first real public exposure outside Aylesbury.

This new awareness had a wider impact as patients who had been paralysed in industrial accidents took part in the Festival at Stoke Mandeville for the first time. They were mainly coal miners from the north of

England.[98] For the first time the Olympic sport of javelin throwing joined archery and netball as a main event.[99] Javelins were also used in therapy for building muscles in the upper torso and arms, as throwing was more exciting than remedial exercises. The spirit of competition, so important at Stoke Mandeville, added to the fun. As its popularity grew, competition intensified.[100] While it would be misleading to suggest that those taking part practised religiously, training did take place. Individuals focused on specific events, encouraged by Guttmann as part of the ongoing fitness programme.

While games and sports were important, their function was mainly medical. While no 'cure' could be effected, minimising disability was the principal aim. Moreover, patients were examined by Guttmann for research purposes. Like the burned airmen at East Grinstead, Guttmann's patients were guinea pigs. He often put them into what they dubbed his 'sweat box', where he tested the effects of temperature regulation, continuing work he had begun prior to taking up a position in the Spinal Unit.[101] After 1946 he conducted research on the effects of postural change on the cardiovascular system and sexuality of paraplegics and quadriplegics, which was a subject doctors did not discuss with patients.[102] However, research tackled the subject with sensitivity, new methods for conception were developed, and later research revealed that paralysed men were able to father children.[103]

While the remedial aspect was still paramount, the Stoke Mandeville Games became a regular feature of the English summer. In addition to the obvious physical benefits of having a fitter, stronger body, participation in sport minimised the consequences of disability in the eyes of society, helping the men to gain employment and independence.

Although Stoke Mandeville grew in reputation, it was not necessarily an exemplary centre as far as its attitude toward the government plan of employment was concerned. The main purpose of rehabilitation centres was to assist their patients back into the workforce. On this subject, the views of Guttmann and the Ministries diverged. In 1948, a representative of the Ministry of Labour and National Service went to Stoke Mandeville to examine levels of training in the workshops. As usual, the visit was an excuse for Guttmann to get his patients to show off their proficiency in sport. The visitor reflected:

> There were some excellent demonstrations including basketball and badminton by the women. Dr Guttmann has also introduced archery as he finds it excellent for developing shoulder muscles.[104]

However, the provision of employment was less of a priority. There seemed to be no training provision for women, nor was there any administrative help in finding new homes.[105] Generally, Stoke Mandeville focused on the interests of men with contemporary expectations of masculine roles. Early experiments were conducted with a group of male patients, given training at a factory in Aylesbury. Men had to be lifted into the back of a truck to be taken to and from work and, while they were keen, the experience was not repeated until better transport became available in 1948.[106] Other jobs were also investigated. Chick sexing, which was apparently a closely guarded secret of the Japanese, was thought to be a very good occupation for ex-servicemen in wheelchairs. Training took two years, but eventually the successful chick sexer could be employed, earning £500–800 per year.[107]

In October 1948, the Ministry of Pensions announced that it would be providing cars and £45 a year for their maintenance to those ex-servicemen and women with 100% disability.[108] At a time when new cars for the general population were in short supply, this gain for paraplegics was heralded as a significant step in recognising the needs of those with severe disability.[109]

In hindsight, Stoke Mandeville and its affiliates were anomalous in the experience of rehabilitation and resettlement. Whereas many centres such as Egham and Garston Manor used remedial exercises and games for the injured as a way to return them to fitness, Stoke Mandeville focused more on the medical aspects of recovery through sport and games, and less on employment. Possibly, the explanation may lie in the fact that the Ministry of Pensions oversaw Stoke Mandeville, and the Ministry of Labour and National Service was in charge of centres such as Egham. Although Guttmann said that he wanted 'to transform a severely disabled person into a tax payer', this meant more to its patients in terms of equality than in terms of employment.[110] Stoke Mandeville's focus on sport reflects the fact that treatment for the spinal injured was still in its infancy, and doctors were still experimenting with different therapies. Essentially, Stoke Mandeville was doing its job as a hospital, and its doctors were working with patients to regain their independence.

Interest in rehabilitation of the spinal injured expanded throughout the late 1940s. In 1949, the British Council for Rehabilitation established a specialist department that dealt specifically with the spinal paralysed. The purpose of the National Association for the Paralysed was to ensure cooperation between those interested in their welfare, to represent them and to provide information about their needs to wider interests.[111]

Conclusions

Stoke Mandeville's Spinal Unit produced good results.[112] Patients gradually found jobs through a combination of their own efforts and the assistance provided by the Disabled Persons (Employment) Act of 1944. On the whole, men from the Forces responded well to its tough competitive regime. No doubt this was in part a way of regaining or refashioning a sense of masculine identity. However, military discipline may have had some bearing on the patient's willingness to undergo a rehabilitation regime based on competitive games. As noted by Joan Scruton, Guttmann's personal assistant for many years:

> There was no question of whether the patient *wanted* to undertake sport – like work, Sir Ludwig introduced it into the dynamic treatment programme of spinal cord injuries with the same importance as that of bladder or skin care.[113]

Rehabilitation at Stoke Mandeville was a structured method reaching disabled people who had previously been considered beyond help, as the war unlocked knowledge into alternative treatments for spinal paralysis.[114] Rehabilitation knew no boundaries; it was systematically applied to all bodies, and could be restructured to gain specific results. As Christina Jarvis notes, 'The war wounded male body and efforts to rehabilitate it highlight the centrality of servicemen's bodies in constructing national self-definitions as well as the performative nature of masculinity.'[115] What made Stoke Mandeville special? It was partly due to the physical inactivity and damaged morale that resulted from paraplegia and the time that recovery took for the patients; but also partly due to Guttmann's single-minded pursuit of results, and the cheerful and competitive atmosphere worked particularly well with its majority of young ex-servicemen. However, Stoke Mandeville had less success in other areas, such as employment, but there may have been a number of reasons for this. Systems were established to return men to the fighting during the war, and these were not applicable to the men of Stoke Mandeville. In addition, it was not until after the war that an organised system to employ disabled ex-servicemen in civilian life was set up, and that may have impacted on employment opportunities for those at Stoke Mandeville. The hospital's legacy, however, was associated with the development of international disability sport, as it actively pursued recognition for its sporting achievements within wider society. The meanings associated with sport, with fitness and the male body gave Stoke Mandeville a spectacular opportunity to reinvent a recognisable notion of the self and a vision of the whole man vital to physical and mental health.

Notes

1 There were only 650 spinal paralysed who survived the Second World War but their position in the rehabilitative processes and its effects were central. Ludwig Guttmann, *Spinal Cord Injuries: Comprehensive Management and Research* (Oxford, 1973), 7.

2 Graham Dawson, *Soldier Heroes: British Adventure, Empire and the Imagining of Masculinities* (London, 1994), 1.

3 Books on the development of masculine identity include Michael Roper and John Tosh (eds), *Manful Assertions: Masculinities in Britain Since 1800* (London, 1991); and George L. Mosse, *The Image of Man: The Creation of Modern Masculinity* (New York/Oxford, 1996).

4 Penny Summerfield and Corinna Peniston-Bird, *Contesting Home Defence: Men, Women and the Home Guard in the Second World War* (Manchester, 2007), 15.

5 See Christina S. Jarvis, *The Male Body At War: American Masculinity During World War II* (Dekalb, 2004).

6 Sonya O. Rose, 'Temperate Heroes: Concepts of Masculinity in Second World War Britain', in Stefan Dundink et al. (eds), *Masculinities in Politics and War: Gendering Modern History* (Manchester, 2004), 185–6.

7 Martin Francis, 'The Domestication of the Male? Recent Research on Nineteenth and Twentieth Century British Masculinity', *Historical Journal*, Vol. 45, No. 3 (2002), 637–52.

8 Other works have examined a number of wars in relation to cultural production such as literature in wars other than the First. See K.J. Phillips, *Manipulating Masculinity: War and Gender in Modern British and American Literature* (New York, 2006) and Paul R. Higate (ed.), *Military Masculinities: Identity and the State* (New York, 2003).

9 See Bourke, *Dismembering the Male*; Carden-Coyne, *Reconstructing the Body*; and Gagen, 'Remastering the Body, Renegotiating Gender', 525–41.

10 See R.W. Connell, *Masculinities* (Cambridge, 1995).

11 See Gagen, 'Remastering the Body, Renegotiating Gender', 525–41; Carden-Coyne, *Reconstructing the Body*.

12 Guttmann, *Spinal Cord Injuries*, 5.

13 R.O. Ward, 'The Management of the Bladder in Spinal Injuries', in Henry Hamilton Bailey (ed.), *Surgery of Modern Warfare* (Edinburgh, 1944), 661.

14 Being forced to lie down when disabled was not confined to the spinal paralysed. Vera Dean, who had cerebral palsy, was forced to spend a significant amount of time in bed in hospital. See Dean, *Three Steps Forward*.

15 Susan Goodman, *Spirit of Stoke Mandeville* (London, 1986), 98.

16 *The Cord*, Vol. 3, No. 1 (Autumn 1949), 26.
17 *The Cord*, Vol. 17, No. 1 (Winter 1964/65), 40.
18 Throughout the war, twelve spinal units were established at Warrington, Basingstoke, Sheffield, Leeds, Worcester, Newcastle, Cardiff, Llandrindod Wells, Edinburgh, Stanmore and Leatherhead outside London as well as Stoke Mandeville. That is not to assert, however, that the treatment at these other institutions was the same as at Stoke Mandeville. Guttmann, *Spinal Cord Injuries*, 7.
19 Unpublished autobiography, Ludwig Guttmann, Guttmann Papers, PP/GUT/A.7 Box 4, Wellcome Trust, London, n.d., 162.
20 Ibid., 164.
21 For more details on émigré surgeons see Paul Weindling, 'The Impact of German Medical Scientists on British Medicine: A Case Study of Oxford', in Mitchell G. Ash and Alfons Söllner (eds), *Forced Migration and Scientific Change: Émigré German-Speaking Scientists and Scholars After 1933* (Cambrige, 1996), 86–114. An account of Guttmann's life can be found in Goodman, *Spirit of Stoke Mandeville.*
22 Unpublished autobiography, Ludwig Guttmann, Guttmann Papers, PP/GUT/A.7 Box 4, Wellcome Trust, London, n.d., 162.
23 For details on Geoffrey Jefferson's early career see Stella V.F. Butler, 'Academic Medicine in Manchester: The Careers of Geoffrey Jefferson, Harry Platt and John Stopford, 1914–39', *Bulletin of the John Rylands University Library of Manchester*, Vol. 87, No. 1 (2005), 133–54.
24. Peter H. Schurr, *So That Was Life: A Biography of Sir Geoffrey Jefferson* (London, 1997), 199.
25 Peter Medawar won the Nobel Prize for tissue transplantation.
26 Unpublished Autobiography, Ludwig Guttmann, Guttmann Papers, PP/GUT/A.7 Box 4, Wellcome Trust, London, n.d., 140.
27 There are arguments surrounding the year in which the reports were requested: Guttmann cites 1939 while other sources state it was 1941. IWM Sound Archive 4596/03, Interview with Ludwig Guttmann, 18 February 1980.
28 Unpublished Autobiography, Ludwig Guttmann, Guttmann Papers, PP/GUT/A.7 Box 4, Wellcome Trust, London, n.d., 157.
29 Jefferson had written on spinal injuries in the 1920s and 1930s. See Geoffrey Jefferson, 'Discussion on Spinal Injuries: Section of Orthopaedics', *Proceedings of the Royal Society of Medicine* (1927), 625–48; 'The Treatment of Spinal Injuries', *The Practitioner*, Vol. 130 (1933), 332–41; 'Concerning Injuries of the Spinal Cord', *British Medical Journal*, Vol. 2 (December 1936), 1125–30.
30 Unpublished Autobiography, Ludwig Guttmann, Guttmann Papers, PP/GUT/A.7 Box 4, Wellcome Trust, London, n.d., 145.
31 Medical Department, United States Army, *Surgery in World War II: Vol. II, Neurosurgery* (Washington DC, 1959), xii.

32 There is no actual evidence of this, but the timing of the call for Guttmann's report (of which no copy exists) and the Americans' entry appears to be causal.
33 Medical Department, United States Army, *Surgery in World War II*, xii.
34 The Stryker bed was developed in 1937 and used extensively to turn patients to prevent bed sores. See James C. Breneman, *The Stryker Story: Homer's Iliad* (Kalamazoo, 1993).
35 Guttmann assisted in the establishment of this Committee in 1939. Ludwig Guttmann, 'Services for the Treatment and Rehabilitation of Spinal Paraplegics and Tetraplegics in Great Britain', *Trends in Social Welfare* (Oxford, 1965), 319.
36 Goodman, *Spirit of Stoke Mandeville*, 29.
37 The EMS acquired the hospital in 1939. Originally the Stoke Mandeville Hospital had been a centre for contagious diseases and later for war wounds and plastic surgery. See J.P. Reidy, 'The Formation and Early History of the Stoke Mandeville Plastic Surgery Unit', *British Journal of Plastic Surgery*, Vol. 39 (1986).
38 Hobson, *Physiotherapy in Paraplegia*, 2.
39 By August 1944, there were 50 patients at Stoke Mandeville. Surtees, *Chaseley*, 13.
40 Unpublished Autobiography, Ludwig Guttmann, Guttmann Papers, PP/GUT/A.7 Box 4, Wellcome Trust, London, n.d., 166.
41 During the D-Day landings, in 90% of cases the time from wounding to arrival in a British hospital was one week. F.A.E. Crew, *Army Medical Services: Campaigns Vol. IV* (London, 1962), 615.
42 For an interesting discussion on the ways that cultural tradition affects modes of behaviour in disabled men see David Gerber, 'The Rise and Representation of Repertory of Self-Presentation Skills in a World War II Disabled Veteran', *Journal of Social History*, Vol. 27, No. 1 (Autumn 1993), 5–27.
43 Service Sub-Committee of the Research Board for the Correlation of Medical Science and Physical Education, *Report on the Wounded and Disabled*, Part III (15 March 1944), CMA SA/RBC C 7.4, Wellcome Trust, London.
44 Guttmann, 'The Treatment and Rehabilitation of Patients with Injuries of the Spinal Cord', in Cope (ed.), *History of the Second World War*, 499.
45 Unpublished Autobiography, Ludwig Guttmann, Guttmann Papers, PP/GUT/A.7 Box 4, Wellcome Trust, London, n.d., 186.
46 Ibid., 186.
47 Medical Research Council Report, *Injuries of the Spinal Cord and Cauda Equina* (1924), FD 4/88, National Archives, London. This book identified both urinary tract infections and bed sores as a problem for those with spinal injury during the First World War and suggested ways in which they might be avoided, such as using 'water mattresses'.
48 Hobson, *Physiotherapy in Paraplegia*, 12.

49 In some cases, supra-pubic catheters were removed after bladder control had been regained. *The Cord*, Vol. 2, No. 1 (Autumn 1948), 23–8.

50 For details on penicillin see Robert Bud, *Penicillin: Triumph and Tragedy* (Oxford, 2007).

51 Scruton, *Stoke Mandeville*, 41.

52 Ludwig Guttmann, 'Victory Over Paraplegia', in Fraser (ed.), *Conquest of Disability*, 65.

53 Unpublished Autobiography, Ludwig Guttmann, Guttmann Papers, PP/GUT/A.7 Box 4, Wellcome Trust, London, n.d., 181.

54 Mosse, *The Image of Man*, 24–50.

55 Goodman, *Spirit of Stoke Mandeville*, 143.

56 This equipment looked somewhat like a regular bicycle and was attached above the patient's bed. The patient gripped handles with his hands, and his feet and legs were attached to a type of pedal, which the patient rotated. Hobson, *Physiotherapy in Paraplegia*, 30.

57 *The Cord*, Vol. 17, No. 1 (Winter 1964/65), 71.

58 The record for the dressing competition stood at four minutes. Ludwig Guttmann, 'Rehabilitation After Injuries', in Olive Guthrie-Smith (ed.), *Rehabilitation, Re-education and Remedial Exercises* (London, 1949), 445.

59 The Guthrie-Smith apparatus is described in chapter Two.

60 Scruton, *Stoke Mandeville*, 19.

61 Surtees, *Chaseley*, 31.

62 *The Cord*, Vol. 17 (Winter 1964/65), 61.

63 Scruton, *Stoke Mandeville*, 23. Dame Margot Fonteyn returned with her husband Roberto Arias in 1964 when he was shot in the spine and made quadriplegic. He was treated for many months at Stoke Mandeville.

64 'Paralysed Men Go for a Swim', *British Legion Journal*, Vol. 29, No. 11 (November 1949), 217.

65 Surtees, *Chaseley*, 15.

66 As mentioned in chapter One, the Star and Garter first opened in 1916. *The Star and Garter Home Annual Report*, 1950.

67 *The Guardian*, 14 July 1945. A notice announcing the opening also appeared in *The Lancet* (21 July 1945), 95.

68 Although Kytes Estate was associated with Stoke Mandeville, it did not participate in many of Stoke Mandeville's sporting activities.

69 *The Cord*, Vol. 1, No. 1 (Autumn 1947), 10–13.

70 Kytes opened in 1947. *The Cord*, Vol. 17, No. 1 (Winter 1964/65), 27.

71 *The Cord*, Vol. 3, No. 3 (Spring 1950), 8.

72 Scruton, *Stoke Mandeville* 49.

73 Pamphlet from The Thistle Foundation (1953), MH55/2159, National Archives, London.

74 The first of these was in 1944. Guttmann, *Spinal Cord Injuries*, 10. Hobson, *Physiotherapy in Paraplegia*, 84.

75 Both Kytes Estate and Lyme Green were located in proximity to industries. Guttmann, 'Services for the Treatment and Rehabilitation of Spinal Paraplegics', *Trends in Social Welfare*, 329–30.
76 Hobson, *Physiotherapy in Paraplegia*, 83.
77 Surtees, *Chaseley*, 60.
78 Goodman, *Spirit of Stoke Mandeville*, 142.
79 Ibid., 142.
80 Unpublished Autobiography, Ludwig Guttmann, Guttmann Papers, PP/GUT/A.7 Box 4, Wellcome Trust, London, n.d., 192.
81 'Paralysed Men at Work', *British Legion Journal*, Vol. 25, No. 3 (March 1945), 50.
82 *The Cord*, Vol. 17, No. 1 (Winter 1964/65), 56.
83 Ibid., 57.
84 Ibid., 60–1.
85 Although it was named netball, from photographs and descriptions of the game, it appears that the game was wheelchair basketball, which was played in the USA. Guttmann, *Textbook of Sport for the Disabled*, 23.
86 *The Cord*, Vol. 17, No. 1 (Winter 1964/65), 43.
87 Parker, *The Cord*, Vol. 17 (Winter 1964/65), 57.
88 The archery competition was held on the same day as the opening ceremony of the 1948 London Olympics.
89 Guttmann was also a consulting surgeon at the Star and Garter Home in Richmond. He also persuaded Frank Bilson to instruct there and procured equipment in order for those at the Star and Garter to practise.
90 Joan Scruton, 'Sir Ludwig Guttmann: Creator of a World Sports Movement for the Paralysed and Other Disabled', *Paraplegia*, Vol. 17, No. 1 (May 1979), 52.
91 *The Cord*, Vol. 1, No. 4 (Summer 1948), 23.
92 The *Bucks Herald* got Guttmann's initial wrong, citing it as 'H'. *Bucks Herald* (6 August 1948).
93 Goodman, *Spirit of Stoke Mandeville*, 149.
94 Ibid., 23.
95 Penley was also administered by the Ministry of Pensions and formed a hospital and rehabilitation centre for Polish soldiers who had fought under British Command since 1942. See MH 120/8, History of Penley (undated but probably 1961), National Archives, London.
96 *The Cord*, Vol. 3, No. 1 (Autumn 1949), 22.
97 The event was organised by the Central Council for Physical Recreation. *The Cord*, Vol. 3, No. 4 (Summer 1950), 9–10.
98 Ibid., 19.
99 Archery was not an Olympic sport at that time, although it had been in the 1900, 1904 and 1908 Games. At Antwerp in 1920 it was included but then it disappeared again until the Munich Olympics of 1972. *Chronicle of the*

Olympics (New York, 1998), 223–84 (results pages). Whereas javelin was an individual event in the Olympics, javelin throwing at Stoke Mandeville was a variation on the able-bodied event, as it was the combined score of a team of two.

100 Whereas in 1949, *The Cord* had referred to the Polish soldiers as 'sporting', the following year they took the Archery Shield and continued to be champions for several years afterwards.

101 Scruton, *Stoke Mandeville*, 41.

102 Put very simply these experiments were largely trying to find out why paraplegics would faint when moved from horizontal to vertical. Guttmann, *Textbook of Sport for the Disabled*, 41.

103 Guttmann, *Spinal Cord Injuries*, 641.

104 Report by Norah Hill on her visit to Stoke Mandeville (25 October 1948), LAB 18/469, National Archives, London.

105 The report noted that 90% of hospital leavers found employment through their own efforts. Ibid.

106 Scruton, *Stoke Mandeville*, 20.

107 'Chick-Sexers', *British Legion Journal*, Vol. 27, No. 4 (April 1947), 90.

108 *The Cord*, Vol. 2, No. 2 (Winter 1949), 7.

109 Morgan, *The People's Peace*, 33.

110 Scruton, *Stoke Mandeville*, 19.

111 Pamphlet from the National Association for the Paralysed (1949), MH 55/2159, National Archives, London.

112 There was no mention of Guttmann's early rehabilitative work in *The Lancet* or the *British Medical Journal.*

113 Scruton, 'Sir Ludwig Guttmann', 52.

114 See Cooter, 'Medicine and the Goodness of War', 147–59.

115 Jarvis, *The Male Body at War*, 88.

6

Revealed: women and rehabilitation

On 30 September 1943 and 1 January 1944, an advertisement headed 'Blitz Aftermath' appeared in *The Times*, recounting the story of an ambulance driver blinded in a bomb blast. What was striking about this advert for St Dunstan's was that the ambulance driver featured was a woman.[1] The advert reflected the dangerous tasks that women, even as official non-combatants, performed during the war. In the Second World War, women moved from the role of supporters, distant from battle, to what cultural commentator J.B. Priestley referred to as 'soldier-civilians'.[2] Women's wartime role required fortitude. Strength, although generally seen as a masculine construct of physicality, was much in evidence as women supported men fighting in distant places, aided in protecting the nation and supported their families while enduring privation.

Large numbers of women participated in the war in a variety of roles in industry and the Services. Membership of the ATS peaked in 1943 at 214,420.[3] As they became exposed to greater personal risks in the Second World War, women naturally were more prone to injury and disablement. This chapter examines women's experience of rehabilitation and disablement during a war that, 'for the duration', eased rigid gendered identity. As we have seen, in creating a number of physically disabled people, the war touched a wide spectrum of the population. It also altered perceptions of ability; disabled people were provided with opportunities for war work due to labour shortages. Disabled women were also able to take advantage of the relaxation of limitations for employment opportunities due to the doubly disadvantageous problem of their perceived lack of ability and their gender, and participate in a range of wartime activities alongside able-bodied people. As non-combatants exposed to aerial bombardment on mainland Britain, women civilians and those in the Services who were disabled came under wartime legislation. The chapter examines the way that exposure to the threat of permanent disablement was expressed in gendered arguments about equal compensation for women performing wartime duties. Additionally, the practice of rehabilitation and the methods employed to ensure that women were engaged will be discussed. A system that was designed with men in mind had to be readjusted to fit large numbers of female participants. New regimes of rehabilitative therapy emerged, and the chapter will concentrate on the effect of rehabilitation on women. Finally, the chapter concentrates on provisions made for disabled women once they were rehabilitated or discharged, and their newly negotiated relationships with the Ministry of Pensions and the Ministry of Labour and National Service immediately following the war.

Cultural histories of the body and of war have concentrated on the experience of men, although there have been a number of more recent studies on the nature of gender in war and whether or not war alters conceptions of gender for its duration.[4] Indeed, historians have tended to remain focused on the impact of war on women's identity and the restoration of gender roles following conflict. Men's bodies have historically been more affected by war as combatants, and historically women's supporting role has not exposed them to physical dangers in the same way as men. Wars fought far away from home and communicated by letter from the field of battle meant that women were removed from the experience as well as the physical danger. In addition, the association between war and masculinity has tended to push women further to the margins. Men's bodies were validated by war; women's were not. Generally, the historical voices of women in wartime are less audible when masculine traits are valued, celebrated and remembered. As Lucy Noakes has observed, 'Women's memories of wartime are less likely to appear in official discourse; memories of bombardment, grief or simply coping with the wartime exigencies of family, work and shortages of food and fuel are far less likely to be memorialised than the experiences of male combatants.'[5] Susan Grayzel argues that during the First World War, women in the home remained symbolically central to the nation, despite men's place as fighters.[6] In the Second World War, the woman at home was additionally struggling with mortal danger. As J.B. Priestley noted in his *Postscripts* broadcast on the BBC on 22 September 1940:

> For this is total war; and total war is war right inside the home itself, emptying the clothes cupboards and the larder, screaming its threats through the radio at the hearth, burning and bombing its way from roof to cellar. It's ten times harder being a decent housewife and mother during such a war than it is being a soldier. You have to make a far greater effort to keep going, for you've no training and discipline to armour you.[7]

Disabled women were not featured in popular heroic narratives of war, and as such, their experience was largely private. This can be problematic for historians, searching for experiences to construct a representative history of disabled women in the Second World War. There were obvious differences between disabled women and men, despite efforts by the State to provide for women. Women who were already disabled or became disabled as a result of war were perceived in a different way from men, by society and the State. One of the ways that this difference was obvious was the way disabled men and women were represented in contemporary media. Men who were disabled or disfigured were retained in the Forces if possible and viewed as romantic heroes fighting for their country. Women were not, yet they required a particular type of strength to endure war privations. No matter what J.B. Priestley said in his BBC broadcasts, it was not heroic to do housework and feed children without the benefit of aids or home adaptations. Generally, disabled women were not closely associated with a domestic role, except in the position of an enfeebled dependant, relying on institutional and familial support. Problematically, independent life was not easy for disabled women. Only those with wealthier families could afford to live independently as there had to be sufficient money to hire an assistant and find a place to live that suited their needs. Domestic concerns were not associated with heroism. The public's imagination was captured by men who overcame adversity such as Douglas Bader. A pilot who overcame the fact that he was a double leg amputee and flew airplanes defending his country from the Luftwaffe was exactly the type of hero to appeal to the public. If women were seen as heroes, it was able-bodied women working for the Special Operations Executive (SOE) or romanticised figures of the French Resistance. Disabled women working in factories or offices or helping with support services were not considered heroic.

The *British Medical Journal* reflected on issues regarding women's participation in the war, noting, 'For the first time in history a vast number of our young women are receiving a regimental training in discipline and arduous communal living.'[8] Conversely, this readjustment which impacted heavily on able-bodied women may have had less of an impact on disabled women as they often lived in communal settings, institutions or at home with their families. Their societal role was rarely associated with that of wife and mother. In addition to traditional gendered associations, disabled women's bodies were even less suitable than able-bodied women's for supporting conflict.

Women and war

Due to difficulties inherent in the study of women's role in war, historians have produced innovative ways to explore wartime experiences of them. Women's role as war workers has been the focus of a number of studies relating to the First and Second World Wars.[9] Methodological shifts have provided a wealth of rich material. For example, oral history has provided details of women's wartime experiences.[10] Dorothy Sheridan has used the rich source of the Mass Observation Archive to collate accounts of women's wartime activities.[11] Additionally, works have approached women and war from a cultural perspective, and considered women's lives through activities such as cinema and popular culture.[12] The value of cultural readings of combatants, either wounded or disabled, is significant, and similar methodologies have been applied to women's experiences during war. This is especially important for the Second World War when the 'front' was mobile and large numbers of women became directly engaged in the war. Participation was inadvertent and official. Employment in the Women's Auxiliary Air Force (WAAF) peaked in 1943 at 178,689.[13] Sonya O. Rose has explored women's experience and the multiplicity of identities they constructed in their relationship with the State, and how that was embodied in their sense of national identity.[14] Penny Summerfield and Corinna Peniston-Bird's cultural history relocates women in the Home Guard, which replaces previous historiographical accounts and popular understanding.[15] Histories have also uncovered women's role as combatants in the Forces, particularly the ATS and Home Guard.[16] Tessa Stone's research into women's integration in the WAAF demonstrates that the members identified with their membership of a military service, and less with their gender.[17] In addition, I would contend that the close association with the high public profile that was associated with the RAF that was examined in chapter four also reflected women's identity. Consequently, women in the Second World War permeated further into 'men's territory' than previously realised.

Women's efforts were not limited to the Home Front. Nursing was one of the ways that women featured in war, in a role that essentially nurtured and inspired wounded bodies to rehabilitate and resume their task as combatants. Women's role of healer complemented the male role of combatant. Since Florence Nightingale, 'the lady with the lamp', whose nursing career has been mythologised in books and film, the role of women as nurses has been a traditional way of historicising women's wartime experiences.[18] The role of nurses was embodied in medicine and concomitantly the military, which provides historians with sources to trace their histories.[19] Recent works include Janet Lee's history of the First Aid Nursing Yeomanry in the First World War, where mainly upper-class women challenged hegemonic gender roles and created new wartime identities.[20] Classic texts such as Anne Summers' *Angels and Citizens* delineate conflicting roles of nursing and participation in the mass carnage of the First World War. Professionalisation, argues Summers, was offered to women in their position as nurses, and many women embraced their newly discovered status.[21] Moreover, in her book on nurses in the Second World War, Penny Starns highlights the nature of militarisation in nursing and ways in which this association benefited in protecting nurses' hard-won professional standing.[22] Biographies of nurses and their war work have been published, and writer Monica Dickens published an amusing account of her nursing experiences in the popular book, *One Pair of Feet*.[23] Other work has explored the role of women in medical professions other than nursing. Ana Carden-Coyne and Beth Linker have focused on physiotherapists, their relationship with male bodies and their role as professional practitioners.[24]

Women's work

With the coming of World War in 1939, British women experienced discrimination as their bodies were not valued in the same way as men's. War duties increased the possibility of being permanently disabled, yet compensation was gender related. The government awarded differing levels of compensation to men and women for home guard duties such as fire watching and operating searchlights for anti-aircraft units. Officially, women were not authorised to fire guns and participate in dangerous war work.[25] In the case of total disablement for men, under the Personal Injuries (Emergency Provisions) Act of 1939, a maximum of 49 shillings a week was provided to a married man with dependent children. For women the rates were two-thirds of this, which mirrored their rates of pay in the Civil Defence Services.[26] There were complaints about this disparity for those involved in 'warlike operations', which amounted to between 25 and 50%.[27] This difference in remuneration for war-related injury raised the question of equal pay for equal work, which had been much debated since the nineteenth century. A letter to *The Times* in October 1939 enquired:

> Under what system of calculation is it deduced that single disabled women can manage on 10s less a week than single disabled men. Women have to pay exactly the same rent, taxes, for medical care, food and every other living expense as men do; and it should be remembered that there are many women to-day wholly dependent on their own earnings.[28]

Although the question of equal pay for equal work was centrally important to women, the government granted few concessions.[29] In 1942, the Minister of Pensions, Sir Walter Womersley maintained unequal rates of compensation for disablement, apparently at the urging of Ernest Bevin, Minister of Labour and National Service, who feared any change would raise the spectre of equal pay, causing industrial disruption, which would have dire consequences for wartime production.[30]

> The claim ignores the general inequality of earnings as between men and women, which is relevant, whatever may be the circumstances of the injury, to the measure of compensation to be accorded to those prevented from, or handicapped in, following their normal occupation. What on the face of things appeared equal compensation would, in effect, be a greater relative degree of compensation to women than to men.[31]

However, opposition to equal compensation was dismantled in late 1942. In January 1943 a royal warrant gave the same rates of compensation for death and permanent disablement to men's and women's dependants.[32] Despite continuing resistance from Womersley, the pressure applied by groups such as the Equal Compensation Campaign Committee ensured that by April 1943 differing levels awarded for disablement to civilian men and women had been abandoned.[33]

As we have seen, total war required bodies. The shortage of manpower opened employment opportunities for women and disabled people as many came forward to assist in the war effort. As the response was not as great as anticipated, conscription was introduced for women between 20 and 30 years of age in December 1941.[34] Certain jobs were deemed suitable for women, which freed up men to fight. Plans were made to increase the number of women working in certain industries, including the production of artificial manure and fertiliser and boot and shoe making.[35]

While able-bodied women were conscripted, disabled people were not. However, disabled men and women volunteered for jobs including fire watching and stretcher bearing.[36] For many, this was the chance to perform some sort of paid work, an opportunity which until then had not been available to them. The government recognised the enthusiasm for disabled women to work, and made efforts to place them in industries that needed workers. Special programmes were established to provide skills training for disabled women and men, and by 1941 the Interim Scheme for the Training and Resettlement of Disabled Persons in Industry was providing opportunities for employment in war industries and freing up able-bodied men to participate as combatants.[37] The requirement for bodies lifted restrictions on disabled people's employment, and both men and women were able to benefit from paid work.

Although all disabled people, regardless of gender, benefited from this training, it was financially more advantageous for men than for women. Indeed, there was a discrepancy in the amount paid by the Ministry of Labour and National Service during the training. Men received higher wages although there is no evidence that men and women were trained differently. A man over 21 years of age received 42 shillings a week whereas a woman got 33 shillings.[38] There was also a disparity in the extra allowances paid to disabled men and women while they were taking up training. Although all trainees received equal recompense for travel and meals, men received a dependants' allowance of 7 shillings 6 pence, but a woman with a dependent adult was eligible only 'in certain circumstances'.[39] Despite this inequity, the Interim Scheme was judged to be a success, and between 300,000 and 500,000 people with varying disabilities found work. Although disabled women were generally paid less, the shortage of labour enabled them to enter the workforce. As the majority of women were civilians, the opportunity to work and earn their own living was a welcome way to contribute to the war effort and gain some personal independence. Some disabled women were unable to do industrial work. Instead they continued producing piecework, which was often shown alongside disabled ex-servicemen's work at exhibitions around the country. At one exhibition in London in 1940, disabled women displayed woollen coats and skirts that they had made.[40]

In the desperate struggle to find workers, especially for the munitions industry, levels of fitness grading were relaxed and many disabled women went to work in factories. Although disabled people were technically not Grade A fit, as long as the disability did not affect a woman's working capacity, she would be passed as able to work. Indeed, the notion of 'fitness' was very elastic. The job was judged to fit the person, as opposed to a person's fitness for a job. Thus, Ms B, a profoundly deaf woman, was passed fit and sent to work in a munitions factory after she finished her education at a deaf girls' school.[41] She was surprised at being passed and when interviewed said, 'I didn't think they'd pass me fit . . . they passed anyone in the war.'[42] Probably unknown to Ms B, some disabilities were particularly sought after for certain jobs, and deafness was considered an advantage in shell assembly given the lack of safety equipment to protect hearing. Many deaf people worked in isolation areas making shells where the noise level was damaging to those who had higher levels of hearing.[43] The dangers of munitions work were such that Ms B was disabled further when a faulty detonator blew up in her hands, leaving her with only part of her left hand and her little finger on her right.[44] After rehabilitation, which took about a year, she resumed her factory work as a messenger girl. Despite being disabled even further, disabled bodies like Ms B's acquired a value, distinct from able-bodied women, at times specific to wartime exigencies.

As disabled people were employed in factories, local papers lauded their assistance. Both the *Deaf Quarterly News* and the *Birmingham Post* reported the story of a deaf woman who had contracted polio, but who had been trained for work in a local factory. According to the newspapers, the disabled woman had been instrumental in increasing the output of the factory. This increase in productivity was explained thus: 'they put the deaf girl between two of the most talkative employees, and output has considerably increased'.[45] Such stories depicted disabled workers as valuable, and furthermore demonstrated that disabled women could be productive war workers. Other newspapers detailed the redeployment of disabled women into war work. In 1942, the *Daily Mirror* reported that 12 blind women had been moved from their jobs making baskets, as supplies of raw materials had ceased, into a factory to examine finished machine parts, which they did by feeling them.[46] In addition to factory work, disabled women were employed in the Auxiliary Territorial Services and the Women's Land Army. Ms H., who worked for the Women's Land Army, was pronounced Grade A fit although she had tuberculosis of the knee and was unable to bend her leg more than halfway.[47] She was put to work on a dairy farm, and managed to keep her disability a secret by maintaining the strength in her knee by walking long distances and cycling regularly.[48] In the Land Army, women were often discriminated against as being unsuitable for heavy farm labour, so it was no wonder that Ms H. wanted to keep her disability a secret – not only did she have a disability, she was also a woman. Ms S. was called up in 1943 and because she had worked with the Red Cross she was able to join as a VAD. However, her foot prevented her from nursing so she was judged A2, and became a secretary to one of the psychiatrists.[49] Indeed, the necessity of maintaining a large workforce to maintain a war economy ensured that those without full mobility were not exempt.

Initially, women's disabilities may have had a catastrophic effect, but did not express themselves within a gender argument. Rather, the disability had to be overcome. Disease was a more common occurrence than injury in the ATS. The incidence of tuberculosis was higher among women than men.[50] A young woman in the ATS who became deaf after contracting cerebro-spinal meningitis wrote in a journal for deaf people that initially she was depressed about her deafness but wrote triumphantly about regaining her pre-war employment as a shorthand typist. The social side of life was not neglected. She also wrote about going to dances and that she was never short of partners.[51]

Paid work was not the only way in which disabled women assisted the war effort. Disabled women supported the servicemen and women by providing home comforts through the Women's Voluntary Service for Civil Defence (WVS) and the Women's Institute. Clemency Greatorex, who had severe asthma, was told to go and join the WVS as 'they'll take any old crock'.[52] She ran a housewives service which settled evacuees, billeted factory workers and took meals in great secrecy to workers building the Mulberry harbour for the D-Day landings. Other women with disabilities collectively worked on more traditional war work for women. One blind women's group knitted articles such as socks and hats for men at the Front.[53] Another group of blind women donated the pension increase they received in 1941.[54] Disabled women were anxious to be seen to 'do their bit' for the war effort and be good citizens.[55] One disabled woman left a note for her daughter, telling her that she had finally managed to find a way to help, washing the feet of French servicemen who had been evacuated from Dunkirk.[56]

During the war, some disabled women's employment position was precarious; particularly those with more severe cognitive disabilities. John Groom's Crippleage, which had been operating since 1863 in London, ran advertisements in *The Times* requesting donations to provide for approximately 300 disabled women who were employed making artificial flowers.[57] The money earned from this activity paid the women's keep. Making artificial flowers and basket weaving provided employment for a number of disabled women; however, demand for these items was limited in wartime, and if women were permanently institutionalised and could not switch to employment associated with wartime production, the war adversely affected their lives.

Rehabilitation

While women who were disabled before the war looked for ways to fulfil their patriotic duty, others who were injured as a result of bombing or war service sought or were prescribed rehabilitative treatment. Servicemen and injured workers often had rehabilitation thrust on them. Essentially, it was designed for men to regain strength and independence, which was judged their preserve. Prior to the war, women were exempt from rehabilitative processes in industry as the association between dependence and femininity was established.[58] During the Second World War this was not the case, as war expediency reduced emphasis on the limits of gender. Like men, women's bodies needed to be repaired and rehabilitated quickly. Women disabled as a result of the war had specific entitlements as war wounded, one of which was inclusion in the rehabilitation system. Their injured and ill-prepared bodies were not to be abandoned by an ungrateful State.

Indeed, for women whose disabilities would not result in discharge from the Services, institutions were established to administer their rehabilitation. Similarly to the fitness depots established between the wars for men discussed in chapter three, women's bodies needed to be trained for war. Like men, their bodies were often found wanting. In early 1942, a Committee was established to report on amenities and welfare services for women recruits into the ATS and WAAF. In the same year the *British Medical Journal* reported that there was a 'marked improvement . . . in physique, poise and self-confidence of the recruits'.[59] Rehabilitative regimes were put into practice for the State to prepare its women, as well as its men, for the physical and emotional strain of war.

Initially, rehabilitation units for women were similar to those established for men. Women's participation in rehabilitation was another aspect of military service that was novel for women and also for those responsible for its establishment and administration. A report from the ATS noted: 'Rehabilitation in the ATS is still in an experimental stage . . . because experience in the rehabilitation of women in other walks of life is almost non-existent and policy, method and training have to be worked out from scratch.'[60] The need for different rehabilitation programmes for men and for women was demonstrated in the same report. While women benefited from the training and industrial rehabilitation regimes, the benefits of physical rehabilitation were not as obvious. Women attended one of the rehabilitation centres set up along lines similar to those for injured men. These were established for the ATS in the Red Cross and Order of St John Auxiliary hospitals. Upon arrival women were divided into four medical grades. The Grade 1 group combined bed rest with sitting PT exercises, and were exempt from scrubbing, digging and exercising outdoors, whereas Grades 3 and 4 exercised outdoors and had an hour of PT in the morning.[61] Since the rehabilitation system had been devised and established for men, the success rate was high for male patients. The competitive atmosphere, military discipline and the strong emphasis on sport were extremely successful.[62] But whereas men enjoyed rehabilitation regimes, reports noted that women had to be coaxed to perform any kind of physical activity. The report detailed, 'in its [exercise's] absence, tend to sit about over the fire or on the lawns and on their return to their units are found to be unfit for a full day's work'.[63] The system of competitive recovery, established during the First World War and implemented in the Second World War, was unsuccessful in establishing systematic physical rehabilitative practices for women. Women participated in exercises, drill and physical movements, and there was less emphasis on competition and games as rehabilitation regimes for women became established. Nevertheless, women were forced to participate in activities to fulfil their rehabilitation, although the definition of 'physical activities' was wide ranging and could be domestic in nature, such as scrubbing and cleaning in addition to drill and exercise. At Roffey Park in Sussex, women patients spent some time in the kitchens, where they were instructed in the principles of healthy cooking, particularly in the preparation of vegetables and salads.[64]

At Stoke Mandeville, women participated in the same programmes as men, as detailed in chapter Five. Although few in number, they performed rehabilitative exercises and participated in the archery competition and, in some cases, in wheelchair netball with their male counterparts. There are no reports of women's participation in the short-lived wheelchair polo competition. While they did participate, the emphasis on competition was not as manifest as it was for men. Disablement was seen as a process in which the body was weakened, made more dependent and passive. Rehabilitation therapy at Stoke Mandeville was about making the body strong and independent, despite severe disability. For women, whose identity was not bound up in the essentially male characteristics that rehabilitation sought to rediscover, the philosophy of competitive sporting endeavour at Stoke Mandeville was a less successful aid to recovery. Women's fitness took on a different identity. Industrial fitness and training for work were very important for women; they participated in activities in the hospital workshops, making products alongside male patients. An enterprising woman fashioned a smoking apparatus by which a fellow patient would be able to smoke, as he was unable to use his hands.[65] Other women retrained in new jobs such as teaching and administration, although, as previously noted in chapter Five, the system was ad hoc and not particularly geared toward women's specific needs. As we will see, full rehabilitation by living and working in the community was more difficult for women in wheelchairs than it was for their male counterparts.

Disabled civilians and Service women were treated differently, despite government assurances that all war wounded would be treated equally. Disabled servicewomen were provided with training in different locations, but this was for reasons associated with military service. The Royal National Institute for the Blind opened centres where blinded women civilians were retrained for work. They also played non-competitive games to instil confidence. Blind women played golf at the RNIB's training centre where the unfamiliar terrain provided useful training in moving around on uneven surfaces.[66] Servicewomen who were blinded went to St Dunstan's, which only accepted those enlisted in the Forces for training at its centres. Rehabilitation regimes did not differ greatly if the disability was permanent, although similarly to men, efforts were made to limit the impact of disability in ensuring that a certain level of function was attained before discharge. There is little evidence to suggest that disabled women were retained in the Services after disablement to the same extent that disabled men were.

As we have seen, rehabilitation associated the physical and mental, although bodily rehabilitation was the main aim of the Services. The connection between body and mind would usually be served by a busy, activity-centred atmosphere where the body and mind would be busily engaged in rehabilitation. Where the body went, the mind would naturally follow. Essentially, if the body was busy the mind would be too. The expectation of women being able to withstand the stress of membership in the Forces was lower than that of men. Maintaining morale in the home was one matter, the stress of a masculine environment was another. Women who had a breakdown in their mental health did not usually undergo rehabilitation in the Forces; instead they were discharged relatively quickly. Conversely, men tended to be retained, treated and then rejoined their Service, as research had been conducted between the wars to ensure that the numbers of men affected by neurosis were reduced. Figures from the ATS show women had high rates of discharge; 50% of all discharges were on account of 'mental disorders'.[67] The high rates may have been associated with the Army Act of 1941, which gave the ATS full military status and, in doing so, ensured that its members could not leave at will.[68] Provision was made for women with nervous disorders, but generally that led to discharge if the problem was not easily solved.[69]

The Ministries

As we have seen, rehabilitation was a highly bureaucratic process. During the war, two Ministries oversaw disablement: the Ministry of Pensions and the Ministry of Labour and National Service. Each had a different function and agenda. It was the role of the Ministry of Pensions to restore disabled Forces personnel to health and provide them with pensions and other means of support. The Ministry of Labour and National Service intended that rehabilitated disabled people returned as 'useful' members of society. The Ministry of Pensions, while not affording the same standards of assistance, attempted to meet the needs of both men and women. The Ministry of Labour and National Service, led by Ernest Bevin, organised industrial rehabilitation centres where disabled women could take retraining courses.

For some women, injuries caused by war service dramatically altered their bodies. During the First World War women were not entitled to compensation for injuries. Even disabled nurses were given merely a promise that any claims would be 'considered'. Nurses could apply for a pension or a gratuity in lieu as well as asking for payments for retraining.[70] But a woman who had served in the war did not merit the award provided to a man who had been injured while fighting. Women who applied after the First World War to the Ministry of Pensions were war widows, not injured civilians; the State's job was to support the absent father, who had given his life for his country. Women's relationship with the Ministry of Pensions changed between the First and Second World Wars. For the first time, women were entitled to compensation directly in the form of pensions for war injuries resulting in permanent disablement.

While this form of assistance was ostensibly on offer, gender bias was still very much in evidence. It was not always easy for women to claim a pension or even a one-off payment. The Ministry of Pensions recognised shortcomings in the system rather late, announcing in 1948 that, 'From its inception in 1917 the Ministry's concern has naturally been centred in the main on males.'[71]

By the end of the war the number of women injured or permanently disabled with dependants to support had added another 17,500 people to the Ministry's already significant responsibility. To its credit, the Ministry recognised that the requirements of these new pensioners would be different, and despite the discrepancy in numbers attempted to respond to requests. The medical and cosmetic requirements of female pensioners were different from those of their male counterparts; they had roles as wives and mothers, as well as wage earners. Indeed, the Ministry itself posed the question, 'Do we, in determining the degree of disablement, give proper weight to the effect of the war disablement on the function of child bearing and on "cosmetic value"'?[72] As Sonya O. Rose has demonstrated, the necessity of looking good despite the exigencies of war was seen to be an important facet of women's identity.[73]

The Ministry of Pensions did allot a certain bearing on cosmetic value, which was evident in the issue of artificial limbs. Both women and men were given free artificial limbs if amputation had been caused by war service or as a result of an air raid. But more attention was paid to the aspects of aesthetic appeal of artificial limbs for women than for men. 'The wooden limb is preferred by many women as giving a better cosmetic result and causing less damage to stockings.'[74] Although aluminium legs were lighter and had superior moveable joints, women preferred wooden legs. It was easier for wood to mimic the curved shape of a woman's calf. The shortage of feminine necessities meant that women would go to great lengths to ensure their stockings were protected. As shown in chapter two, heavy wooden legs were readily discarded by men during the First World War in favour of lighter weight aluminium, which was disguised by trousers. Although women did wear trousers in industry and farming, most service uniforms were a jacket and skirt. The exposure of women's legs meant that aesthetic matching was preferred over function. Moreover, in the inter-war period, the demand for prostheses had declined, and the Ministry of Pensions had discarded wooden limbs available for those for whom ease of movement was less of a consideration.

The other issues relating specifically to women were those of childbirth and the family. Despite their wartime service, women were expected to maintain their domestic responsibilities. Without many labour-saving devices and displaced family and friends, bringing up a child could be a heavy burden, especially on a disabled woman. Women with paralysis or other pelvic injuries had trouble carrying a child to term and had to have Caesarean sections, which were dangerous and costly.[75] Before the advent of reliable birth control methods, sterilisation was one way in which women were able to exercise control. Many wanted to limit the size of their families. Letters arrived at the Ministry from women pensioners requesting funds for sterilisation.[76] Mrs L. became a paraplegic when her pelvis was crushed when an air raid shelter collapsed. She subsequently had one child who was born blind. After a second child was born she wrote to the Ministry of Pensions requesting assistance with sterilisation.[77] Another woman wrote to the Ministry of Pensions to say that she wanted to be sterilised and wanted the Ministry to pay because both she and her husband had tuberculosis.[78] The Ministry's willingness to consider such requests demonstrated an acceptance of the real needs of women pensioners. The fact that women wrote such letters at all revealed the lack of assistance available to disabled women; yet these women felt a sense of entitlement, that they had recourse to assistance from the Ministry that had been the preserve of wounded male soldiers. It also demonstrates the perception that disabled women were limited in their ability to manage their families. The increasing role of the State with plans for a National Health Service put forward by the Beveridge Report in 1942, and the belief that the war would result in an altered society, ensured that the State would take a more accountable role, particularly when a disability was incurred in war service.[79] However, the State's responsibility would only go so far. If a disabled woman wished to have a larger family, she could not expect the State to assist her outside the boundaries of the strict regulations that were established. Nevertheless, if a disabled woman wanted to limit the size of her family by being sterilised, then the State willingly financed the procedure.

Disabled women were often seen as perpetual spinsters, their disability making them ill-equipped to withstand the physically demanding role of motherhood and running a home. The institution or shared all-female home was the domestic space allocated to women with disabilities. When the traditional role of wife and mother was re-established, disabled women, whether injured before or during the war, returned to their homes like many of their able-bodied counterparts. For some, this domestic role was more physically challenging than for able-bodied women, a fact acknowledged by the Ministry of Pensions. In 1948 it noted:

> For example, the housewife whose domestic duties involve . . . all the primary functions (I submit) of the female sex, suffers, I suggest a more severe physical impairment by an above the knee amputation than does the average male clerical worker, similarly handicapped.[80]

But there was little provision to retrain disabled women for domestic duties, and there was little available immediately following the war. The overarching perception of disabled women having a limited presence in the domestic sphere may have been one of the reasons why there was little training for disabled women to manage their homes. One household training unit was established at the Devonshire Royal Hospital in 1953.[81] The Ministry was aware of the difficulty, but devoted more assistance to limiting families than for re-equipping disabled women for domestic life.

Accusations of unfairness and insufficient payments had been levelled at the Ministry since 1917. During the Second World War, new rules were established in an effort to improve the lives of male and female pensioners. Disabled women were entitled to some supplements, and rules governing the burden of proof were relaxed to ensure they received the maximum available. A disabled pension was awarded on the basis of degree of disability, with each part of the body being given a particular value.[82] Pension systems were more even-handed for women and men, and both had recourse to appeal if they felt their disability had been judged unfairly. Certain supplements were available; money was available for the excess wear and tear that their disability placed on clothes, and was often awarded to paraplegics and amputees.

The other benefit previously unavailable to women was the Constant Attendance Allowance. This concession for disabled ex-servicemen, established after the First World War, enabled them to live independently. The Allowance was restricted to those with 100% war disability, which included spinal paralysis and multiple amputations. It was awarded to women from 1941.[83] During the Second World War, only 230 women were given the Constant Attendance Allowance, which provided them a sum to pay for a carer to assist them with necessities of daily living. Initially, the payment was £75 a year for female officers and 15s a week for those in the ranks.[84] However, the increased amount of £100 was still insufficient as a full salary for a carer, so the disabled person's pension or other income was needed to make up an attendant's wage. The Allowance was geared more to the needs of men than of women. If a man was married, he could use the money to augment his family income, and his wife performed the role of carer. An article in *The Times* stated: 'A wife is probably the best attendant a disabled man could have, and it does not appear unreasonable that she should be provided for as a wife.'[85] However, for single disabled women, with no recourse to a wife, the Allowance did not provide enough support. One woman summed up the frustration in *The Cord*, the journal for the Paraplegic Branch of the British Legion at Stoke Mandeville. She wrote, 'if I were a man, I should immediately marry a capable woman, preferably a nurse, and all my troubles would be solved!'[86]

The pensions system also treated disabled women and men differently. Women disabled while serving who could not be redeployed in the Forces were pensioned out at two-thirds the rate of men. There were also supplements for which women were ineligible, including the Special Hardship Allowance and the Unemployability Supplement, which were made to men who found it difficult to find work. During the early stages of the war, women's dependants were not compensated for at the same rate as men's, but this inequality was resolved and by 1943 women officers' dependants were also compensated at the same rate as men's.[87] Despite some gains, gendered differentiation was still evident in the system of financial support afforded to men and women who were disabled. This discrimination also affected women married to disabled men. Financial assistance only benefited a married couple if they had been married before the man became disabled, and any children born after permanent disablement were not included in benefits.[88]

Independence came at a price, and was often out of the reach of disabled women. Accommodation was difficult to procure, particularly for the more severely disabled paraplegics. Better management of complications associated with paraplegia had improved survival rates, but health breakdowns could occur at any time so some paraplegics preferred to live within the confines of a medical institution, where expertise was readily available. Others preferred a more independent life, choosing one of the several Homes. Most of the places were occupied by men, and there were none for women. When places for women paraplegics became available, the gesture was small scale, with only 6 beds out of 78 made available at the Duchess of Gloucester House in Isleworth in 1949.[89] Owing to their needs and the severe housing shortage, by the early 1950s many disabled women continued to be forced into institutionalised settings. As one wrote to a paraplegic journal in 1951, 'The women pensioners in this hospital are certainly not catered for on an equal footing with the men. Those of us who have no home to go to are kept in hospital indefinitely because no accommodation is available.'[90] Others had to return to their families, and remain there. Some were able to secure home loans from the various Auxiliary Services but these were limited. Daily living continued to be a struggle for many disabled women, whether married or single.

Although finding accommodation was difficult, disabled women received benefits designed to lift the pressure of daily living. The most seriously disabled people, those considered 100% disabled including double leg amputees and those with spinal paralysis, were given a motorised wheelchair by the Ministry of Pensions. The motorised chair was incapable of carrying more than one person, so it was impossible for disabled people to go out with their families. Additionally, the motorised chairs were mechanically unreliable with no roof so the driver was exposed to the vagaries of the British climate. By 1948 adapted four-door cars were produced and funded by the Ministry. Generally, men received cars more quickly, and disabled women had to make do with the motorised wheelchairs for a longer time. When the first disabled woman received her car the achievement was reported in the *Manchester Guardian* of 19 November 1948. The delay in the supply of cars reflected problems in post-war production, but some attributed it to the lower status of women, and single women without children in particular.

When a war-disabled woman's basic support needs had been met through the Ministry of Pensions, her case was transferred to the Ministry of Labour and National Service. If she returned to domestic activities, her involvement with the State was limited to the Ministry of Pensions. However, if she went to work then the Ministry of Labour and National Service was vital. The Ministry worked to find the many places for men and women returning from the war. The most important piece of legislation for disabled people was the 1944 Disabled Persons (Employment) Act, which recognised disabled men's and women's capacity to work, and will be discussed at length in the next chapter. Moreover, it reflected a change in attitude, however temporary, toward physically disabled people in the mainstream workforce. The Act was discriminatory as it gave special consideration to war disabled, but it did not discriminate on grounds of gender.[91] However, available jobs were limited. Occupations for trainees listed 'for women only' included parachute-making machinists and sewing for 'women only'.[92] Similar to disabled men, women's preferential employment was in low-skilled jobs.

New establishments were set up for women who wanted to work while others expanded their premises. Nonetheless, women and men were often segregated during training. In 1948, land was purchased on the outskirts of Farnham for Woodlarks, a residential workshop for women only, where toys were made.[93] Queen Elizabeth's Training College in Leatherhead had trained disabled men since 1934. In 1949, an advertisement appeared in *The Times* asking for donations to the College to train disabled women.[94] Advertisements from private charities asking for donations suggested that some women were having difficulty finding work through official channels, and more required training, or sheltered employment. Presumably the Disablement Resettlement Officers (DROs) assumed the mantle of women's resettlement as well. However, there is little on their work with women, although a note in one file details the efforts of a DRO on behalf of a 21 year old woman invalided out of the ATS, who could not continue her pre-war position as a sales assistant due to a leg injury. The DRO found her work as a clerk in the Ministry of National Insurance.[95] The taking up of positions and training was sporadic. In 1946, only 12 disabled women had taken advantage of opportunities for ex-Service personnel to work in agriculture by training on farms.[96] As we will see in the next chapter, Remploy was established after the war to provide employment for severely disabled people, but women may not have been able to avail themselves of this service. Generally, training for new types of jobs was gendered and segregated.

Conclusions

Pragmatism gave rise to women's roles in the Forces during the Second World War. As noted by D'Ann Campbell, 'necessity, once it was dire enough, could overcome culture'.[97] Not only women, but disabled women, considered the most helpless owing to a combination of their gender and disability, performed war work. This wartime expediency impacted on able-bodied and disabled women, providing employment to women already disabled, and those women disabled through war service were rewarded, in part, for their sacrifice. Disabled women were retrained and relocated in industry. As war pensioners, disabled women were allowed to share some of the preferential treatment that disablement in war afforded to men. Disabled women were not held back legislatively, and for the first time experienced, in a small way, preferential treatment. They were not as well recompensed by the pension system as men were, but the State assisted women with a range of medical issues, including fertility, sterilisation and aesthetics. While not represented as heroic, disabled women were given some means to manage their disability in relation to the demands of family, work and social life. However, as many historians have noted, independence was limited to wartime, and when the war was over women returned to lives centred around home and family. This was problematic for disabled women. The argument put forward by historians that women maintained their status as guardians of the State, what Higonnet calls the 'universally protonatalist climate' of Britain after the war, and their participation in the war was only for the duration of hostilities, did not always apply to disabled women.[98] Unlike their able-bodied counterparts, disabled women were not seen as material for motherhood, although many were mothers. Disabled women were seen as passive; cared for rather than being carers. While male war wounded were, through rehabilitation, rescued from emasculation, women were not. A sense of independence was tolerated in disabled women as their disability prevented them from having a full life, that of wife and mother. The Ministry of Pensions did not devise ways to assist disabled women with their families. Rather it assisted them to limit the size of their families, thereby reducing their dependence on the State. They were exempt from participating in the thrust to re-populate after the war; their status as mothers was diminished. Some, who did not marry, whether through choice or unavailability of partners, had to return to the family home or remain institutionalised, as their disability and lack of fiscal support through limited work opportunities or low pension rates, forced them to remain dependent on the State. Disabled women participated in the war in a number of capacities, and enjoyed freedom from gendered roles as much as their able-bodied counterparts.[99] For those that were disabled as a result of the conflict, State support became more available and women enjoyed many of the benefits afforded to disabled men.

Notes

1 Between 1942 and 1945, St Dunstan's ran a total of 26 advertisements in *The Times*, but only two featured the story of the woman blinded in the bomb blast. The others were general and did not feature either a man or a woman although all of the advertisements mentioned 'men and women blinded in war service'.

2 Priestley, *Postscripts*, 68.

3 Lucy Noakes, *Women in the British Army: War and the Gentle Sex, 1907–1948* (Abingdon, 2006), 125.

4 For a discussion of this see Ruth Roach Pierson, 'Beautiful Soul or Just Warrior: Gender and War', *Gender and History*, Vol. 1, No. 1 (Spring 1989), 77–86.

5 Lucy Noakes, 'Review Article: Gender, War and Memory: Discourse and Experience in History', *Journal of Contemporary History*, Vol. 36, No. 4 (2001), 664.

6 Susan R. Grayzel, *Women's Identities at War: Gender, Motherhood and Politics in Britain and France during the First World War* (Chapel Hill, 1999).
7 Priestley, *Postscripts*, 78.
8 'Welfare in the Women's Services', *British Medical Journal* (24 October 1942), 492–3, 493.
9 These include Deborah Thom, *Nice Girls and Rude Girls: Women Workers in World War 1* (London, 1998); Clare Wightman, *More than Munitions: Women, Work and the Engineering Industries 1900–1950* (London, 1999); Gail Braybon, *Women Workers in the First World War: The British Experience* (London, 1984); Penny Summerfield, *Women Workers in the Second World War: Production and Patriarchy in Conflict* (London, 1984); and Angela Woollacott, *On Her Their Lives Depend: Munitions Workers in the Great War* (Berkeley, 1994).
10 Summerfield, *Reconstructing Women's Wartime Lives.*
11 Dorothy Sheridan (ed.), *Wartime Women: A Mass-Observation Anthology 1937–1945* (London, 2000).
12 Lucy Noakes, *War and the British Identity: Gender and National Identity, 1939–1991* (London, 1997).
13 Rexford-Welch, *The Royal Air Force Medical Services: Vol. 1*, 601.
14 Sonya O. Rose, *Which People's War? National Identity and Citizenship in Wartime Britain 1939–1945* (Oxford, 2003), 107–50.
15 Penny Summerfield and Corinna Peniston-Bird, *Contesting Home Defence: Men, Women and the Home Guard in the Second World War* (Manchester, 2007).
16 D'Ann Campbell, 'Women in Combat: The World War II Experience in the United States, Great Britain, Germany and the Soviet Union', *Journal of Military History*, Vol. 57, No. 2 (April 1993), 301–23.
17 Tessa Stone, 'Creating a (Gendered?) Military Identity: The Women's Auxiliary Air Force in Great Britain in the Second World War', *Women's History Review*, Vol. 8, No. 4 (1999), 605–24, 620.
18 For a selection of works on Florence Nightingale see Mark Bostridge, *Florence Nightingale: The Woman and Her Legend* (London, 2008); and Cecil Woodham Smith, *Florence Nightingale* (London, 1949). Maria Luddy has edited the diaries of the Sisters of Mercy, who were occasionally in dispute with Nightingale. See Maria Luddy (ed.), *The Crimean Journals of the Sisters of Mercy 1854–56* (Dublin, 2004).
19 See Christine Hallett, *Containing Trauma: Nursing Work in the First World War* (Manchester, 2010).
20 See Janet Lee, *War Girls: The First Aid Nursing Yeomanry in the First World War* (Manchester, 2005).
21 See Anne Summers, *Angels and Citizens: British Women as Military Nurses 1854–1914* (Newbury, 2000).
22 See Penny Starns, *March of the Matrons: Military Influence on the British Civilian Nursing Profession, 1939–1969* (Peterborough, 2000).

23 Monica Dickens, *One Pair of Feet* (Harmondsworth, 1956).
24 See Ana Carden-Coyne, 'Painful Bodies and Brutal Women: Remedial Massage, Gender Relations and Cultural Agency in Military Hospitals, 1914–18', *Journal of War and Culture Studies*, Vol. 1, No. 2 (2008), 139–58; Beth Linker, 'Strength and Science: Gender, Physiotherapy and Medicine in Early Twentieth Century America', *Journal of Women's History*, Vol. 17, No. 3 (2005), 105–25.
25 Campbell, 'Women in Combat', 308.
26 *The Times* (3 March 1939).
27 Calder, *The People's War*, 400.
28 *The Times* (10 October 1939).
29 See Harold L. Smith, 'The Problem of "Equal Pay for Equal Work" in Great Britain During World War II', *Journal of Modern History*, Vol. 53, No. 4 (December 1981), 652–72; and Harold L. Smith,' The Womanpower Problem in Britain during the Second World War', *Historical Journal*, Vol. 27, No. 4 (December 1984), 925–45.
30 Smith, 'The Problem of "Equal Pay for Equal Work"', 652.
31 Walter Womersley, 'Differentiation of Rates of Civilian War Injury Compensation as between Men and Women' (1940), CAB 71/10 LP (42) 215, National Archives, London.
32 'Improvements in New Warrant', *The Times* (22 January 1943).
33 Harold L. Smith (ed.), *Britain in the Second World War: A Social History* (Manchester, 1996), viii.
34 Calder, *The People's War*, 267.
35 'Changes in Reserved Occupations', *The Times* (11 October 1941).
36 *Deaf Quarterly News* (January–March 1940), 9.
37 *Interim Scheme for the Training and Resettlement of Disabled Persons* (1941), PL 93/1941, SA/RBC c.8/9, Wellcome Library London.
38 Ibid.
39 Ibid.
40 'Ex-Service Men's Handicraft', *The Times* (8 November 1940).
41 Ms H.B., Interview, 5 April 1992, 12841/2, Imperial War Museum Sound Archive, London.
42 Ibid.
43 'Where Only Deaf are Employed', *British Deaf Times*, Vol. 37, No. 433–4 (January/February 1940), 9.
44 Ms H.B., Interview, 5 April 1992, 12841/2, Imperial War Museum Sound Archive, London.
45 *Deaf Quarterly News*, No. 150 (July–September 1942), 7.
46 'Blind Women Are Job "Viewers"', *Daily Mirror* (4 April 1942).
47 Ms I.H., Interview, 28 January 1999, 18274/4, Imperial War Museum Sound Archive, London.
48 Ibid.

49 Joyce Sheppard, http://www.bbc.co.uk/ww2peopleswar/stories/51/a3817451.shtml.
50 Only 2% of discharges in the ATS were due to injury, although these were more likely to be a result of enemy action. Franklin-Mellor (ed.), *History of the Second World War*, 446.
51 B. Collins, 'Deaf Ex-Service Girl', *British Deaf Times*, Vol. 43, No. 507–8 (March/April 1946), 29.
52 Clemency Greatorex quoted in Mavis Nicolson, *What Did You Do In the War, Mummy: Women in World War Two* (London, 1995), 174–9.
53 'Fine War Work by the Blind at Stoke On Trent', *The New Beacon*, Vol. 25, No. 294 (15 June 1941), 88.
54 'Patriotism of Six Blind Pensioners', ibid.
55 Rose, *Which People's War?*.
56 Norman Longmate, *How We Lived Then: A History of Everyday Life During the Second World War* (London, 2002), 104.
57 'Classified Advertising', *The Times* (7 September 1943).
58 Adrienne Asch and Michelle Fine, 'Introduction: Beyond Pedestals', in Fine and Asch, *Women With Disabilities* (Philadelphia, 1988), 3.
59 'Welfare in the Women's Services', *British Medical Journal* (24 October 1942), 492–3, 492.
60 Report of Auxiliary Territorial Service – *The Wounded and Disabled* (undated), SA/RBC, C.7/5, Contemporary Medical Archives, Wellcome Library, London.
61 'Rehabilitation for ATS', *The Lancet* (15 April 1944), 517.
62 For an example see Julie Anderson, 'Turned into Taxpayers: Paraplegia, Rehabilitation and Sport at Stoke Mandeville 1944–1956', *Journal of Contemporary History*, Vol. 38, No 3 (July 2003), 461–75.
63 Report of the Auxiliary Territorial Service – *The Wounded and Disabled.*
64 T.M. Ling, *Roffey Park Rehabilitation Centre* (pamphlet), FD1/6811 (1943), National Archives, London.
65 'Two Smart Girls', *The Cord*, Vol. 1, No. 4 (1948), 30.
66 National Institute for the Blind, *Annual Report: 1940–1941*, 4.
67 Franklin-Mellor (ed.), *History of the Second World War*, 447.
68 Noakes, *Women in the British Army*, 114.
69 'Welfare in the Women's Services', *British Medical Journal* (October 24, 1942), 492.
70 Howson, *Handbook for the Limbless*, 156.
71 *Report of the Ministry of Pensions Secretary's Conference* (9 November 1948), PIN 15/2888, National Archives, London.
72 Ibid., 3.
73 Rose, *Which People's War?*.
74 R. Langdale-Kelham, 'Amputations and Limb-Fitting', in Cope, *History of the Second World War: Surgery*, 708.

75 Letter from Mrs M.L. to Ministry of Pensions PIN 15/2888 (1948), National Archives, Kew, London.
76 Note C10/FG/366 Mrs M.L., PIN 15/2888 (1948), National Archives, London.
77 Ibid.
78 There are very few details on this particular case. Minute Sheet GEN/1401, PIN 15/2888 (1951), National Archives, London.
79 See Hennessy, *Never Again*.
80 *Report of the Ministry of Pensions Secretary's Conference* (9 November 1948), PIN 15/2888, National Archives, London, 4.
81 R. Harris, 'Re-abling the Physically Disabled Housewife', *Rehabilitation* (Spring 1956), 16.
82 Bourke, *Dismembering the Male*, 66.
83 *The Times* (12 September 1941).
84 'Forces Women – New Pensions', *Daily Mirror* (12 September 1941).
85 *The Times* (22 March 1943).
86 E. Sheppard-Jones, 'More About my Bungalow in Wales', *The Cord*, Vol. 7, No. 2 (September 1954), 32.
87 *The Times* (22 January 1943).
88 'Pensions of the Disabled', *The Times* (22 March 1943).
89 Unpublished autobiography, Ludwig Guttmann, Guttmann Papers, PP/GUT/A.7 Box 4, Wellcome Trust, London, n.d., 187.
90 'Letters', *The Cord*, Vol. 4, No. 2 (Spring 1951), 40.
91 Disabled Persons Employment Act 1944, File C.165, SA/BMA, Wellcome Library, London.
92 Ministry of Labour and National Service, *Training and Resettlement of Disabled Persons* (March 1944), PL 93/1944 (revised) in SA/BMA, C.165, Wellcome Library, London.
93 The scheme was established in 1935 when training was given to disabled women in toy making. Originally, the toys were made from home, but were judged not to be of a sufficiently high standard, so the residential workshop was established in 1948. 'Notes and News', *Rehabilitation*, No. 16 (Winter 1955/56), 30.
94 *The Times* (22 December 1949).
95 Ayrshire and Arran Disablement Advisory Committee, *A Few Interesting Cases of Resettlement of Disabled Persons In the Committee Area* (1949), LAB 18/148, National Archives, London.
96 'Training for Work on the Land', *The Times* (29 August 1946).
97 Campbell, 'Women in Combat', 323.
98 Margaret Randolph Higonnet, Jane Jensen, Sonya Michael and Margaret Collins Weitz (eds), *Behind The Lines: Gender and the Two World Wars* (New Haven, 1987), 266.
99 Gail Braybon and Penny Summerfield, *Out of the Cage: Women's Experiences in Two World Wars* (London, 1987), 1.

7

Nation: rehabilitation and the post-war State

At the formal opening of Egham Industrial Rehabilitation Centre in 1946, the *Manchester Guardian* reported that Minister of Labour and National Service, Ernest Bevin, remarked that after the First World War, disabled people's welfare was left, in the main, to voluntary associations. As a contrast, it was the State's aim after the Second World War to make support 'a public responsibility'.[1] Much of the population hoped the post-war Labour government, elected on a promise to implement the Beveridge Report, would make radical changes to provision for disadvantaged people.

This chapter will focus on the State's role in rehabilitation after the Second World War. The establishment of many rehabilitation centres in the post-war period demonstrates that the State's commitment to rehabilitation did not waver, and in fact, its remit became broader as the administrative systems set up during the war became further entrenched. Similarly to during the war, rehabilitation was used to limit the impact of disability, so disabled people became the primary recipients of rehabilitation services. Following recommendations of the Inter-departmental Committee on the Rehabilitation and Resettlement of Disabled Persons in 1941, legislation was drafted so disabled people had access to a range of services for their rehabilitation, but particularly to job opportunities. Owing to a labour shortage, employment was one of the principal concerns of the post-war government and this interest extended to those with disabilities, many of whom had been employed during the war. Different types of employment were offered to disabled people, including the reworked concept of the sheltered workshop, for those unable to find work on the open market. Complete rehabilitation was achieved only when a disabled person was working.

The chapter will also examine how rehabilitation's inclusive and interdisciplinary nature was demonstrated in post-war legislative reforms. Six pieces of legislation that impacted on disabled people were enacted between 1944 and 1948. They were the Disabled Persons (Employment) Act, the National Health Service Act, the Education Act, the National Insurance Act, the National Insurance (Industrial Injuries) Act and the National Assistance Act. The chapter will focus closely on the Disabled Persons (Employment) Act, but other Acts will be discussed in relation to rehabilitative practices in the period following the war. In addition, discussion of the role of voluntary services and charitable enterprises for disabled people will provide insight into the progression of the negotiated relationship between voluntary associations and the State.

Post-war rehabilitation

The gains in knowledge surrounding rehabilitation practice made during the war were expanded and ratified in legislation after 1945. Administrators and medical professionals, highly trained in rehabilitative practices, converted their expertise to civilian life. Both organisationally and medically, rehabilitation became as vital a part of recovery after injury as it had during the war. Its language, practices and structures became entrenched, and the expertise surrounding the utilisation of manpower through it, ensured that rehabilitation remained central to the process of reconstructing the nation following the devastation of conflict.

Committees were established to continue rehabilitative practices on a national level with government and non-government organisations. In 1945, the British Council for Rehabilitation was set up by a group to coordinate and promote rehabilitation in Britain.[2] The Council expanded administrative aspects of rehabilitation, further developing systems established during the war. In a memo, Reginald Watson-Jones, who continued to work in rehabilitation following from his association with the RAF during the war, noted the British Council for Rehabilitation represented all three phases of rehabilitation: medical and surgical treatment, medical rehabilitation and resettlement in the community. He named a number of professions and their representative organisations, from surgeons to the Institute of Labour Management, who were critical to its success.[3] The Council defined rehabilitation thus: 'Rehabilitation covers the whole range of services from the time of the onset of the individual's disability to the point at which he is restored to normal activity or the nearest possible approach to it.'[4]

In addition to the continuation of its commitment to rehabilitation nationally, Britain became a leader in the international field of rehabilitation in the post-war period. The rehabilitative practices established in the Services and in industry through companies such as Vauxhall Motors were presented at international conferences. One conference organised by the Ministry of Education in 1948 on 'Physical Education, Recreation and Rehabilitation' was attended by delegates from 74 countries.[5] The delegates saw British rehabilitation methods demonstrated by the RAF and the Army.[6] In 1949, the British Council in association with the Ministries of Health, Labour and National Service, and Pensions hosted another international conference. It was organised by surgeon Harold Balme, who advised the Ministry of Labour and National Service on rehabilitation. He stressed the interdisciplinary nature of rehabilitation, and noted in his introduction to the programme:

> It is only by viewing rehabilitation as a continuous process in the field of medical sociology, rather than as a matter of employment technique or of charitable aid, that the problem of disability will be placed upon a scientific basis.[7]

Attendees travelled around the south of England and to Birmingham, Leicester and Wales.[8] They were given a variety of lectures and it seemed rehabilitation affected people in all life stages – Marjory Warren, who established the specialty of geriatrics, gave a paper on 'The Rehabilitation of Elderly Patients'.[9] Faith in rehabilitative methods was so strong that its practice was applied to troublesome groups across society; in 1948 the *Manchester Guardian* reported that tramps would receive mental or moral rehabilitation at centres set up to tackle the problem of vagrancy.[10]

Rehabilitation's international reputation and its success in countries such as Britain impacted on international organisations such as the United Nations. The Relief and Rehabilitation Administration (UNRRA) was established in 1943 with 44 nation members.[11] It was one of the first international organisations created to provide assistance for post-war reconstruction. Britain and the United States took leading positions in this work, no doubt due to the fiscal strength of the United States and the administrative robustness and organisational experience of rehabilitation of Britain. Rehabilitation's reputation for success and its flexible system meant that its phraseology and regimes were adaptable to a number of different situations that could be disabling, including displacement and poverty. In essence, rehabilitation could be applied to any given set of circumstances.

Rehabilitation centres after the war

Despite its flexibility, rehabilitation had a fundamental purpose. The perception was that it had become vital in reducing residual disability, ensuring that people would lead a full life. There was a call for rehabilitation centres during the war, not just for the Forces, but for civilians. A letter in *The Times* noted that few industrial workers were fit owing to poor conditions in homes and factories, insufficient sleep, poor diet and an ignorance of personal hygiene.[12] Some centres were established specifically to treat mental health breakdowns of agricultural workers during the war. Ernest Bevin's work on behalf of the industrial disabled was successful; by 1945 additional rehabilitation centres had been established by the Ministry of Labour and National Service for miners and railway and dock workers.[13]

Rehabilitation centres administered by the Ministry of Labour and National Service provided treatment for a number of disabilities. Due to reduced numbers of locations for rehabilitation centres for civilians after the war, the Army offered some of its Civil Resettlement Units to the Ministry of Labour and National Service.[14] In addition, new residential centres were opened. Farnham Park was opened in 1947,[15] and Garston Manor in 1951.[16] Much early provision was undertaken by industrial companies, but the government also established rehabilitation services and continued to take an active role both during and after the war.[17] Similar to rehabilitation centres established during the war for the Services, these institutions focused on patients' fitness, with rounds of drill, exercise and sport as diversionary therapy. Garston Manor, which was near Watford in Hertfordshire, modelled itself on the highly successful RAF rehabilitation centres.[18] There was little job training; instead, the main focus was exercise. The trainees would spend up to seven hours a day practising activities such as movement to music, building up muscle tone and cycling, swimming, volleyball, golf, cricket and croquet.[19] The role of competition was still as important as it had been during the war. In 1953, the journal *Rehabilitation* noted: 'The competitive spirit which can be induced between groups of even the most seriously disabled has proved to be an important factor in gaining success.'[20]

In addition to the emphasis on sport and competition, occupational therapy and industrial training were provided to assist the rehabilitated to find work. The number of hospitals that offered rehabilitation services was also increased as the National Health Act of 1946 made provision in hospitals for a medical rehabilitation service.[21] Indeed, specialist units for rehabilitation in hospitals increased substantially from 35 in 1943 to 121 in 1946.[22] There was close liaison between medical practitioners and employment services, and some hospitals combined with local industry to provide work experience for patients. After a stay at Roehampton to have two foot prostheses made, a soldier went to a rehabilitation camp for six weeks. He recalled being 'taken to various factories to see if we wanted to take up employment in these industries'.[23] Rehabilitation centres performed two main functions: ensuring minimisation of residual levels of disability through treatment, and finishing the rehabilitative process by procuring employment.

One of the largest rehabilitation centres in Britain was Egham in Surrey. It was officially opened in January 1946, but had operated during the war from 1943 as an experimental rehabilitation centre. It focused on industrial rehabilitation for men between the ages of 18 and 50 and was one of the largest and most successful centres in the south of the country. Training courses at Egham lasted about six to eight weeks. It was designed for the medically fit; a brochure for the centre pointed out that 'the course is of an active character and is therefore not suitable for men who are still in the convalescent stages of the illness'.[24] In addition to those not 'nearly fit', Egham also excluded those with contagious diseases, epilepsy, psychosis, severe symptoms of neurosis, blindness and men with limbs in plaster.[25] A brochure from Egham, *From Illness and Disablement to Health and Vigour and the Road to Re-employment*, highlights the holiday camp surroundings and the mansion's proximity to villages, amenities and the 'playing fields of Eton'.[26] Despite the relative good health of people attending Egham, a full-time medical officer was employed to ensure that the trainees participated in their rehabilitation. This was sanctioned by rehabilitation experts in the Army, who advised that 'the personal and constant supervision of a trained and understanding medical officer is necessary for a course of this kind'.[27] The medical officer and physical training instructor worked closely together. At first one PT instructor was appointed, and another was requested in 1944 after the numbers of trainees increased.[28] Massage and physiotherapy were heavily utilised at Egham; in an average month there were 285 attendances for massage, 297 for electrotherapy, and 246 for Actino-therapy and infra-red ray treatment.[29]

Initially, Egham did not enjoy much success in recruiting trainees. Numbers of men attending were low and it was noted that there was considerable reluctance to go to Egham by disabled ex-servicemen in particular, as they 'have had a lengthy period overseas or in hospital; the preference is to recuperate at home'.[30] In its first year of operation, Egham received 526 applications, the majority of which came from EMS and Service hospitals and referrals from Ministry of Labour and National Service branches.[31] At the beginning of 1945 there were 60 trainees, but that number had increased by the end of the year to 245.[32] In that year, a total of 1,114 men were accepted and of these 815 were disabled ex-servicemen.[33] Training at Egham was not limited to those with war disabilities; those injured in traffic accidents and 'foreigners' were included, even if they were disabled before the war.[34]

Courses of training at the government centres varied widely. Initially, physical therapy, remedial gymnastics and sport in the gymnasium installed in every training centre formed the basis of the course. This was followed by training geared to employment. Even so, remedial exercises were important and formed part of an industrial trainee's daily schedule. Apparatus could be fixed to machinery so they could do exercises while working.[35] Disabled people were trained in building work, shoe repairs and retail distribution.[36] Training for an increased number of occupations was available as the 1950s progressed, which opened new opportunities for disabled people.

Most rehabilitation centres focused on the physical aspects of rehabilitation and centred less on mental health problems. As we have seen from rehabilitation practices during the war, providing activity, competition and a positive outlook was one of the ways that mental health issues were dealt with. Many rehabilitation centres refused to take cases involving mental health breakdowns. It appeared that this was considered a specialist area and also that someone with mental health trouble might affect other patients at a centre. However, Roffey Park in Sussex dealt exclusively with mental health issues arising out of fatigue and nervous disorders. It was opened during the war, and provided rehabilitation for office and industrial workers.[37] Much of the rehabilitative work was agricultural in nature; patients worked in the orchards and vegetable gardens on the property. While there appears to have been little in the way of psychological counselling, the outdoor environment, good nutrition and working on the land were obviously supposed to soothe the 'nervous debility' of stressed office and industrial workers. Roffey Park continued with agricultural rehabilitative therapy after the war.

While training, disabled people were mixed together regardless of disability; however, blind people were an exception. Until the late 1940s, local authorities and voluntary services provided employment training for blind people.[38] Rehabilitation for blind people was highly specific and had to be conducted in an environment conducive to them; learning Braille, typing, learning to move around and promoting self-confidence were part of a blind person's rehabilitation.[39] Furthermore, the majority of training for blind people was conducted in a residential environment. This exception was removed in 1946 when blind ex-servicemen joined the Vocational Training Scheme.[40] The State took over training the civilian blind from local authorities in 1948, but the RNIB continued to place blind people in work throughout the 1950s.[41]

Increasingly, hospitals provided rehabilitation services. By 1946, the number of hospitals providing active rehabilitation to patients had risen to 333 from 150 in 1943.[42] Medicine still played an important part in the initial stages of rehabilitation, and for a number of patients the hospital became a locus of care. Indeed, the hospital became a space for the first stages of the rehabilitation process. An article in *The Hospital* reminded surgeons of their centrality in the rehabilitative process, that they must maintain supervision of patients and that 'rehabilitation is not to be regarded as something secondary to medical and surgical treatment'.[43] Additionally, Medical Interviewing Panels were set up in hospitals to make detailed assessments of patients who were difficult to place in a job.[44]

Hospitals also facilitated the use of sport, setting up gymnasiums and taking over public swimming pools as part of their regimes. Much of the manpower for post-war rehabilitation centres, including hospitals, that devoted themselves to sport derived from ex-Army and RAF physical training instructors. In March 1945, it was estimated that there were 3,000 PT instructors in the Army and 4,000 in the RAF.[45] Owing to the concentration on rehabilitation in post-war Britain, there were a number of positions available. In order to work in civilian jobs in rehabilitation, many underwent training courses in remedial gymnastics. These courses were oversubscribed as trainees opted for roles in rehabilitative practice. At Pinderfields Hospital, which started training courses in 1945, the acceptance letter stressed there were 'many' ex-Service instructors on the waiting list for the course and it would be appreciated if the applicant would notify the hospital as soon as possible if they were unable to attend.[46] By the end of 1946, Pinderfields had trained 114 ex-Service PT instructors, who were placed at various hospitals and rehabilitation centres throughout the country.[47]

The regimes established in the Services formed the basis of the organisation of rehabilitation schemes for civilians. Similarly to the Service-operated rehabilitation centres, rehabilitation was not a passive exercise. There were strong aspects of self-help, and the spirit of competitiveness and encouraging environment that permeated these rehabilitation units ensured that people undergoing rehabilitation took an active part in their treatment.

New sheltered employment: Remploy

Those people whose disability precluded them from finding work on the open job market were included in reforms. The Tomlinson Report recommended that a factory system for severely disabled people be established. In 1945, the Disabled Persons Employment Corporation set up 'British Factories', which were later renamed Remploy. The first factory was established in 1946 in Salford, and by 1948 there were 25, manufacturing a wide range of products from industrial leatherwork to cardboard boxes.[48] Much of the work at Remploy factories was traditional types of work which had been undertaken by disabled people for decades, including woodwork, leatherwork, and mat and brush making. One factory in Bristol and another in Halifax made stump socks for amputees and surgical boots.[49] Sites for factories were difficult to find, and a shortage of materials together with a ban on industrial building slowed the expansion of Remploy. However, special permission was received to continue building factories, so by 1953 90 factories were employing 6,000 disabled people.[50]

These establishments were factories under the Factories Act and were subject to inspections in the same way as other factories, although the Factory Department considered them 'harmless and uninteresting'.[51] Generally, Remploy factories did not employ large numbers of blind people as they had an established system of workshops and government assistance.[52] However, some blind men from St Dunstan's were employed in factories, including two men at the first Remploy factory set up in Salford.[53] Remploy generally concentrated on jobs for those with pulmonary tuberculosis, congenital deformities, heart and lung disease, and epilepsy.[54] The project was beset by problems, including higher costs because buildings had to be erected, high absenteeism due to the health problems of its employees, and difficulties with workers' transport, even though Remploy located factories in areas where significant numbers of disabled people lived.[55] By 1952, there were calls for more Remploy factories. But the Exchequer was funding the losses, so government demurred on spending more money. Instead, it debated concentrating more on improving rehabilitative practices so disabled people could move out of sheltered workshops.[56] Remploy continued to operate at a loss throughout the 1950s despite favourable government contracts, similar to those offered to employers participating in the King's National Roll after the First World War.[57] Providing sheltered workshop employment was a costly exercise, and the types of work on offer were traditional employment opportunities offered to disabled people. Nevertheless, it was part of the regime that the State had adopted as part of the welfare state programme.

As costs for programmes were problematic for a country recovering from a protracted war, State money was also offered for private efforts. At the same time as it was opening Remploy factories, government was providing funds under a Scheme of Grants to Voluntary Undertakings. This included private groups or individuals who provided sheltered workshops for disabled people. Numbers were small: only 700 disabled people were given work from 25 government grants in 1949.[58] Unlike Remploy, these businesses were run at a profit. Establishments such as Michael Works were not willing to accept lower standards of production from their workers.[59] However, there were government concessions for businesses that employed disabled people to reduce costs, such as exemptions from union rates.[60] Other workshops were established at Homes for disabled ex-servicemen, and were well supported by voluntary services. In 1946, The Lord Roberts Memorial Workshops assisted the Star and Garter Home to start a workshop for clock repair and assembly.[61] The enterprise grew, and in 1950 two new workshops were opened.[62]

Getting disabled people to work after the war was important for two reasons. Severe labour shortages meant there were not enough people for available jobs. During the war, disabled people had taken jobs on the home front which enabled others to fight and proved disabled people's value to the wartime economy. Other considerations were merely economic. It was better for disabled people to pay tax and produce goods and services.[63] Britain's economy was in a perilous position after the war; as Correlli Barnett reminds us in *Audit of War*, Britain had 'a ruined export trade, [was] heavily in debt to its bankers (the Sterling Area Commonwealth countries and the United States), and with huge inescapable continuing burdens with regard to the war with Japan'.[64] Despite this, the welfare state became a reality, but welfare for all did not mean that government wished to be burdened with welfare payments for thousands of disabled people.

Rehabilitation, training and employment in the voluntary sector

The State also relied on the voluntary sector to provide rehabilitation services. Voluntary services had often been the only recourse for disabled people to receive assistance, and despite the newly established State systems the voluntary services still maintained an important role in providing support. Finlayson reminds us, 'The voluntary sector grew in the wake of both the limitations and the achievements of the welfare state for it was the achievements that revealed the limitations.'[65]

Severely disabled people were sent to one of three institutions: Queen Elizabeth College in Leatherhead, St Loyes at Exeter and the Sir John Priestman Hospital at Finchdale Abbey near Durham. These centres offered a longer period of rehabilitation than the normal duration of eight week courses offered at government centres such as Egham. Some of the staff at St Loyes were disabled.[66] By 1948, the number of government centres had been reduced to 34, due to a shortage of buildings. However, the Ministry of Labour and National Service overcame this problem by finding more training places with voluntary associations. In 1948, the number of places at the Queen Elizabeth College was increased from 287 to 412.[67]

Voluntary agencies had close associations with disabled ex-servicemen and these close ties continued after the war. Specialised Homes for disabled men who served in the war were set up. In 1947, the National Union of Seamen opened Springbok Village near Alford, a small village in Surrey. Similar to model villages set up for TB sufferers at Papworth, and others established by philanthropic employers such as Saltaire, Bourneville and Port Sunlight, Springbok Village provided Homes for retired merchant seamen and a training and rehabilitation centre for those who were not able to return to sea as a result of war service. Similar to other rehabilitation projects, the land played an important role as a therapeutic space, as the rehabilitation and retraining at Springbok Village centred on farming, and the 400 acres was stocked with animals and poultry.[68] Much of the money was provided from the people of South Africa, who funded the village as a tribute to the support of the Merchant Navy in maintaining shipping lanes during the war.[69] An article in *The Seaman* noted,

> We wanted something alive and vital – a memorial which did not merely record the sacrificial service of seamen who gave their lives that the nation might live; we sought a form of memorial which would benefit the seamen who have survived the privations and perils of the war, and would be of benefit moreover to coming generations of seamen.[70]

Numbers of voluntary associations continued to grow after the war. According to the 1952 Nathan Committee on Charity, there were 110,000 charitable trusts in Great Britain in 1950.[71] During the late 1940s and throughout the 1950s, groups supporting and representing disabled people expanded and specialised; for example, the many interests of blind people were represented by approximately 100 different organisations.[72] In addition, new bodies representing a myriad of groups and interests were also established. The British Epilepsy Association, representing one of the least understood conditions, was established in 1951.[73] Two organisations representing people with cerebral palsy were formed; the British Council for the Welfare of Spastics was established in 1946 and was followed by the Spastics Society in 1952.[74] This second group was set up as parents felt that the British Council for the Welfare of Spastics was not representing the needs of those with cerebral palsy.[75] The Multiple Sclerosis Society was established in 1953, and the Muscular Dystrophy Group was founded in 1954.[76] Other groups with shared interests, which were not disability specific, appeared after the war, including the Invalid Tricycle Association in 1948.[77]

Other voluntary services, which had been working with disabled people for a number of decades, continued their work throughout the 1950s. The Central Council for the Care of Cripples, an established organisation as we saw in chapter two, coordinated other groups working for disabled people.[78] During the 1950s, the Council became interested in disabled people's access to buildings. This reflected the ability of groups representing people to engage in issues as opposed to providing basic services, which were, in the main, provided by the State. Similarly, the Red Cross provided 'comforts' for disabled people, from cigarettes to invalid chairs.[79] Other public organisations, including the BBC, continued charity work on behalf of disabled groups by featuring them on the BBC's Weeks Good Cause Appeal. In June 1950, the British Council of Rehabilitation received £1,000 in donations when its appeal was broadcast.[80]

Part of the reason for expansion of these associations was that the State provided a system of basic care, so organisations were able to broaden their range of activities. As James Walvin reminds us, pleasure became a 'national obsession' in the late 1940s.[81] During the 1950s, there was increasing interest in providing holidays for disabled people, as they were not to be exempt from the pleasures afforded to others. The Central Council for the Care of Cripples and the Red Cross organised holidays for disabled people.[82] Less well-funded associations, including the *National Cripples' Journal*, bought a holiday home for people in iron lungs. This did not limit the role of the State, however, as the National Assistance Act of 1948 ensured that recreational facilities and holidays were provided for people with disabilities.[83]

Ex-servicemen

Ex-servicemen's associations continued to represent their members' interests and maintain their preferential position as heroes to ensure that the government and the public's awareness of disabled ex-servicemen remained high.[84] The British Legion was the most powerful of these organisations, with over one million members between 1946 and 1950.[85] During the war, the Legion managed to rid statute books of the seven year rule, which prevented ex-servicemen from claiming a pension if their disability appeared more than seven years after discharge.[86] After the war, the British Legion maintained pressure on the government so that disabled ex-servicemen continued to receive support. Its campaign to ensure the best support for its members encompassed a number of issues. In May 1946, the British Legion's Employment and Pensions Department wrote to the Secretary of the British Medical Association to protest at doctors charging one pound six shillings to sign certificates proving an ex-serviceman could register as disabled.[87] Indeed, the Legion's influence in Parliament remained strong; MPs Sir Ian Fraser and Sir Brunel Cohen argued constantly in favour of preferential treatment of war disabled.[88] In a letter to *The Times* in 1946, Ian Fraser wrote:

> Should ex-servicemen and women, whose disabilities occur at rare intervals in a nation's life and we may hope, will not occur again, who have been torn away from their homes and have been encouraged to take great risks in our defence, be compensated on a higher scale than those who suffer similar disabilities in civil life?[89]

Support also came from members of the Conservative Opposition who attacked the government on its pension record and the perceived lack of support for disabled ex-servicemen. The government defended itself; in 1948, Minister of Pensions Hilary Marquand pointed out that according to government figures, only 6% of disabled ex-servicemen were unemployed, which mainly came from those judged 100% disabled, and they had 'substantial supplementations'.[90]

In addition to war pensions, there was concern about medical examination for work-based pensions. In 1947, a letter in *The Times* from the National Association of Local Government Officers admitted that this was a problem, but said steps had been taken to rectify this and give 'sympathetic consideration to ex-servicemen who are not up to normal health standards'.[91]

Although special interest groups representing war wounded endeavoured to keep their organisations in the public eye, thereby securing donations, money ran short. One of the best sources of income had been the British Legion Poppy Day, which was inaugurated in 1921. From 1943, Poppy Day had grossed nearly one million pounds a year, which provided St Dunstan's, British Legion Homes and other war charities with operational funds.[92] The British Red Cross provided funds for repairs to and capital expenditure on buildings. However, the tight post-war economy made many of these establishments run short of money. The government supplied funds for some of them; for example, it provided £21,000 toward running the Star and Garter Home in 1947.[93] Since yearly running costs for the Star and Garter were £71,000, voluntary services and private charity had a fundamental role to play in supporting these Homes. The Star and Garter Home made up its shortfall by offering families bed endowments as memorials to those killed in the war.[94] Sports days or exhibitions of disabled ex-servicemen's work carried a small entrance fee which would go to the Home to augment other charitable donations. Smaller charities such as the Not Forgotten Association provided support for ex-servicemen's activities throughout the 1950s. Events that impacted on national life were available for ex-servicemen to experience; for instance, special arrangements were made for disabled ex-servicemen to attend the Festival of Britain in 1951. As noted earlier, holidays had become a feature of British life after the war and ex-servicemen embraced this trend. The British Legion provided money for its members to go on holidays. St Dunstan's also made provision for blind ex-servicemen to go on holiday at its special accommodation near Brighton. Stoke Mandeville sponsored holidays at the Duchess of Gloucester House and Chailey in Sussex for those in wheelchairs, as finding holiday accommodation where a large ungainly wheelchair would fit could be problematic. From 1948 the Ministry of Pensions supplied a small number of cars to disabled ex-servicemen who were 100% disabled. In some cases, cars replaced the motor propelled tricycle that had been the stalwart of many veterans from the First World War. The recipient was responsible for gaining their driver's licence, repairs, maintenance and running costs, although this was offset by a yearly grant, and the Ministry of Pensions paid for road tax and comprehensive insurance.[95] As this percentage of disability applied to blind ex-servicemen, they were provided with cars, but the responsibilities for driving were given to their wives or a friend.[96]

Despite assistance to provide disabled ex-servicemen with support, many of them felt let down by an uncaring State. Direct action became a tool for disabled ex-servicemen. The British Linebless Ex-Servicemen's Association (BLESMA) took action in 1951 when 800 members conducted a Silent Reproach March to Downing Street in protest that pensions had dropped below the cost of living.[97] In 1956, it used the same method to demand increased pensions for elderly war disabled so their standard of care did not diminish.[98] The basic rate of pension for disabled ex-servicemen rose three times between 1948 and 1957.[99] Special concessions awarded to disabled ex-servicemen in addition to different rates of pension caused some resentment, evident from this letter in the *National Cripples' Journal* from 1946:

> You boast of social security, you make 'security from the cradle to the grave' your proud slogan and all the time you ignore thousands of British citizens. You pay pensions to the ex-service invalids, God bless them, you give industrial casualties their just do; old folk receive a rightful reward for a lifetime of hard work, when the ordinary wear and tear of life proves too much for them; if one is 'lucky' enough to be blind instead of crippled a compassionate government grants a pension, but what of the civilian cripple, who is incapable of earning a living?[100]

Welfare state legislation

The National Insurance Act of 1946 provided a system of insurance for contributors which included disabled people. For those unable to work, usually referred to as 'the chronic sick' (although disabilities were not always caused by illness), other means of support were offered. This Act provided disabled people with a subsistence income.[101] It extended the Blind Persons Act of 1920 to include severely physically disabled and deaf people.[102] The Act covered a wide range of provision; for instance Section 29 called for recreational facilities to be provided.[103]

In July 1948 the National Health Service was set up to provide medical care and health services free to all citizens at the point of delivery. What did this mean for disabled people? The NHS provided disabled people with equipment and aids that, for many, were previously unaffordable. Prior to the NHS, disabled people were forced to pay full price directly to manufacturers or go without. With the establishment of the NHS, children were provided with artificial limbs, and did not have to wait until they were fully grown to be fitted with them. Wheelchairs and walking sticks were provided to those who had difficulty in getting around. Huge numbers of corrective glasses and hearing aids were provided for those whose eyesight and hearing were affected through old age.[104] For some deaf people, the Medresco hearing aid could make a lot of difference to life quality. Deaf people were also saved the costly indignity of being swindled by dishonest salesmen who would prey on them, selling them aids that did not provide a miracle cure, despite their promises. Disabled people were provided with associated treatments such as physiotherapy. One disabled woman recalled, 'the NHS changed our lives'.[105] However, demand was great and the State refused to supply some appliances, such as adapted cutlery and walking frames for elderly people. Suggestions were made that either the disabled person pay for aid, or apply to Local Welfare Funds, as they had before.[106]

Transport was also provided by the Ministry of Health. They issued three-wheeled Invacar and AC cars, which were a covered version of the early motorised tricycles. Money was provided for their maintenance, free insurance and a yearly sum of £5 for fuel.[107] While disabled people were satisfied with some form of transport, both AC and Invacars had several drawbacks, making them inferior to four-seater cars provided for ex-servicemen. They were unreliable, unheated and limited to one passenger, so not for family outings.[108] The cars were also very light and could overturn in a gust of wind. A fellow student of Jim Porteous, who had an Invacar at 16, interrupted his chemistry class and said, 'Sir, I'm terribly sorry, but Porteous's car has blown over.'[109] Not all incidences were as amusing or as harmless. One paraplegic lay upside down in a ditch for 14 hours before being found after his Invacar tipped over.[110] Repairs in nominated garages could take months.[111] Despite problems, by 1959 there were approximately 11,300 NHS-owned motor tricycles.[112] In 1960, the House of Commons debated supplying four-seater cars to all severely disabled people and not limiting them to war disabled. Sir Ian Fraser, champion of wounded ex-servicemen argued against this, and Minister of Health, Derek Walker-Smith reminded Parliament that 'a question of costs had to be in their mind'.[113] Cost for alternative transport had to be paid for by the disabled person. While the NHS proved beneficial for a number of disabled people, there remained gaps in provision.

The NHS also took over much of the medical aspects of rehabilitation. By 1951 the NHS was administratively robust and took over many rehabilitation centres previously under the control of other agencies and government departments; for example, the Miners' Rehabilitation Service.[114] The process was gradual and eventually filtered through to affect the war disabled. From 1917, benefits such as hospital and residential care, including rehabilitation, were provided to the war disabled through the Ministry of Pensions. The institutions controlled by the Ministry of Pensions were not fully transferred to the Ministry of Health until 1953, when Pensions was dismantled and amalgamated with National Insurance. Even when the Ministry of Health took over, war pensioners retained some of the preferential treatment they had enjoyed with the Ministry of Pensions. It was noted in a report from the Central Office

Figure 7.1 Outdoor exercises at a miners' rehabilitation centre, led by a member of the Chartered Society of Physiotherapists, 1950s (reproduced with permission of the Chartered Society of Physiotherapy)

of Information that 'hospitals in the National Health Service were asked in 1953 to give priority of admission to war pensioners for treatment of their accepted war disabilities, subject only to the needs of emergency and other urgent cases'.[115]

The Disabled Persons (Employment) Act (1944)

In 1944, the interim scheme which assisted disabled people to find war work was replaced by a permanent piece of legislation. The Disabled Persons (Employment) Act was a breakthrough for disabled people. It was the first piece of legislation which encompassed all people of working age, regardless of their disability and when and where it had occurred. The Act came into effect in 1945, and focused on finding work for disabled people. Disability was defined as, 'on account of injury, disease or congenital deformity [is] substantially handicapped in getting or keeping suitable employment or work'.[116] The Act's purpose was: 'To make further and better provision for enabling persons handicapped by disablement to secure employment, or work on their own account.'[117] The main thrusts of the legislation were the reserved occupation list, systemised registration for disabled people and the quota system. Reserved occupation lists and the quota system, in which companies over a certain size had to provide a percentage of jobs for disabled people, were recommendations of the Tomlinson Report. The Act affected all disabled people in Britain, who were urged to register at their local Labour Exchange. George Tomlinson reminded a meeting in 1944 of the nuance of the Act:

> The Register of Disabled, which is the total from which the quota is made up, is not the sum total of the disabled; it is the sum total of the disabled whose disability is a handicap to them in obtaining and retaining employment.[118]

The Act principally viewed disabled people mainly through their employability. Nevertheless, it was seen as a positive step for disabled people. Prior to the Act, there was little legislation that recognised disabled people's needs, and, as we have seen, much of this related to the education of disabled children. For disabled people to be recognised for their value as employees was seen as a decisive move forward. Support came from many influential people who worked with people with disabilities. Sir Ian Fraser, Chairman of St Dunstan's, approved of the Act. 'I see the possibility of the bill being used for the rebuilding of those who can be rebuilt and for the assistance of those who may have got past rebuilding.'[119] Reginald Watson-Jones, instrumental in developing rehabilitative systems in the RAF, stressed in *The Lancet* that the government was determined 'to create the opportunity for employment of the disabled, not because the country is in peril but because the disabled are capable and worthy of employment'.[120] In the *British Medical Journal* in 1946, as Chairman of the Medical Committee of the National Advisory Council of the Ministry of Labour and National Service, Watson-Jones reminded doctors of their obligations to persuade their disabled patients to register or the 'purpose of the Act will fail'.[121]

Administrative systems were established to advise the government on the progress and impact of rehabilitation. The National Advisory Council on the Employment of the Disabled was established in 1945, and members ranged from professors of public health to nine ex-servicemen and women.[122] The Council was very engaged with the question of publicity to a wider audience to ensure that the rehabilitation and employment of disabled people were disseminated to a large audience. The Council held meetings with leading employers to support the 'Back At Work' exhibitions with films to ensure that the rehabilitation message was received by a wider public.[123] By 1945, over 230,000 people in 6 cities had seen the exhibition.[124] In 1948, the Council approached the Medical Research Council to undertake research into the employment of disabled people, particularly regarding the assessment of individual capacity, job demands analysis, techniques of placing disabled persons and individual disabilities.[125] The MRC produced nine reports in 1951, mainly surveys of the Disabled Persons Register and psychiatric aspects relating to rehabilitation. The examination of the reports led to the Council to call for an enquiry, which was set up in 1953, resulting in the Piercy Committee in 1956.

The Ministry of Education and Ministry of Labour and National Service collaborated to procure employment for a disabled child who left school at 16. The Education Act of 1944 authorised, through Local Committees, to provide services including special schools and vocational training for children with disabilities. The Ministry of Education's Administrative Memorandum No. 94 exhorted all schools to provide details of disabled school leavers, so they might be registered for work.[126] Disabled children's parents were also advised to register children leaving special schools, so the Ministry of Labour and National Service could find them work.[127] The choice of career was made at a meeting with the child, parent, head teacher, juvenile employment officer, school medical officer and social worker.[128] If immediate work was unavailable or unsuitable, the young worker attended Vocational Training Centres run by the Ministry of Labour and National Service.

The Vocational Training Scheme was open to school leavers over 16 and disabled adults. By 1946 there were 67 centres where attendees underwent retraining, often cooperating with industry to ensure that trainees achieved required standards and were suitable for work.[129] Three different types of training were provided: residential training centres, technical colleges and on the job training. More severely disabled adults attended residential centres such as Egham. Industrial rehabilitation units used a combination of methods, including remedial exercises, physiotherapy, occupational therapy and light industrial work. Technical colleges trained school leavers for a range of occupations. Finally, some employers made arrangements with the Ministry of Labour and National Service for industrial training to be held on their premises. However, there were issues surrounding available facilities. Those whom the system purported to help were unable to use facilities provided for them; for example, only three residential training centres would accept disabled people in wheelchairs.[130]

All disabled people were meant to benefit from the Disabled Persons (Employment) Act, Minister of Labour and National Service Ernest Bevin had requested that no preference be given to those disabled in war, and the Tomlinson Report specifically noted that war disabilities may not be a barrier to employment.[131] When negotiations were held with trade unions and the British Employers' Federation on the draft legislation, both sides agreed; since many people were compelled to do war service, there was little merit in discriminating between those injured in battle and those who had become disabled in an industrial or civilian capacity.[132]

However, pressure was applied in Parliament by a group of Members, including Sir Ian Fraser and Sir Brunel Cohen, to ensure the Act gave preference to war disabled.[133] Women who had served in the Forces were also given preferential treatment. Two schemes were established that benefited disabled who had served in the Forces. First, a system of grants was established to set disabled people up in small businesses.[134] There was also a system to provide higher education to disabled ex-servicemen and women through the Further Education and Training Scheme organised by the Board of Education.[135] Indeed, membership of the Services was sufficient to ensure support. A Ministry of Labour and National Service pamphlet stated: 'an ex-Service man who becomes disabled after discharge from Service has the same right to preference as the ex-Service man who was disabled during Service'.[136] Despite his previous misgivings when the legislation was being drafted, publicly Bevin appealed that 'special consideration' in employment be shown to men and women disabled in the war.[137] Immediately following the war, many positions at training centres were filled by disabled ex-servicemen and, in fewer cases, women.

Securing regular work for disabled people was facilitated through three processes. Registration was usually organised at local Labour Exchanges. Secondly, quota systems were set which required every employer with over 20 staff to employ a fixed percentage of disabled workers. Originally set at 2%, in 1946 it was increased to 3%.[138] This system was similar to the King's National Roll, established after the First World War, which provided ex-servicemen with protected employment, and those who employed them with special concessions.[139] Thirdly, the designated employment scheme reserved certain occupations specifically for disabled people; they were lift operator and car park attendant.

There were problems. No system existed to ensure employers kept requisite quotas of disabled people in their employ. If an employer had insufficient numbers of disabled employees, he was merely advised to fill vacancies that occurred with a disabled person.[140] Moreover, disabled people complained that the reserved occupations were low skilled jobs which were not suitable for many disabled people.

Despite problems in the system, clearly skewed toward the needs of war wounded, a lack of suitable protected jobs and insufficient facilities, disabled people still registered. Without registration disabled people did not have access to vocational or industrial training programmes, so it was a vital step to employment. In December 1945 150,000 people registered and by March 1946 numbers had increased to 225,000.[141] Although the register did not reach the 1–1.5 million names predicted by Harold Balme in the *British Medical Journal*,[142] numbers did peak in 1950 at 900,000.[143]

Work was still the best way for disabled people to fully rehabilitate. Public support was sought for awareness and markets for products. As we have seen, after the First World War products made by disabled ex-servicemen were exhibited and sold in shops, and this was repeated after the Second World War. An exhibition called, 'And So To Work' was held in London over a month, showcasing the government's support for disabled people. In addition, a film by the Central Office of Information for the Ministry of Labour was made in support of the exhibition and was shown in the Academy Cinema in Oxford Street, London.[144] The film detailed a disabled man's journey through systematised rehabilitation, where he progresses from feeling as if he will only be useful for 'selling matches' to a job as a mechanical fitter after a course of training at Egham.[145] It also detailed the vital role played by the Disablement Resettlement Officer (DRO) in finding employment for disabled men. The Ministry of Health displayed work by its Social Service Department, types of treatment for disabled people, industrial placement at Pinderfields Hospital and a curative workshop.[146] Markets for disabled people's work were sought among a curious public. Work for disabled people became a wider issue that the public felt they had a stake in, and they made suggestions as to what work disabled people should do. In a letter to *The Times*, one reader proposed that disabled people be given jobs at the football pools.[147] The public were anxious for disabled people to work in some capacity; as long as they were showing independence, which often meant freedom from State assistance. In 1946, Reginald Watson-Jones noted:

> In the case of the vast majority of disabled patients the problem is only to secure the right type of employment; if this is secured the possibility of successful competition with the able-bodied has been proved time and again.[148]

Nevertheless, studies done in the 1950s demonstrated that people with disabilities were still enormously disadvantaged in the job market. One study at a clinic in Glasgow between 1947 and 1951 showed that 17% of attendees remained unemployed and 68% were employed reasonably satisfactorily throughout the period of the study. The report noted that many were in lower skilled jobs than they had been occupied in prior to their disablement, and had to sacrifice levels of expertise in favour of gaining work.[149] In 1948, at a meeting of the National Advisory Council on the Employment of the Disabled, it was noted that unemployment levels were much higher among disabled workers: 8.14% as compared with non-disabled workers at 2%.[150]

As in war, rehabilitation in peacetime required high levels of cooperation by a number of trainees, government departments and voluntary agencies. A by-product of the State-organised rehabilitation process was the establishment of new levels within the civil service. The necessity of arranging services, continuity of care and administration of disabled people's medical care, training and employment required supervision and coordination. The Ministry of Labour and National Service created new positions and appointed DROs who were specially trained to inform disabled people about rehabilitation, training courses offered by the Ministry and assist them in finding work.[151] The DROs worked in hospitals and at local branches of the Ministry of Labour and National Service, where they would advise the patients and work with medical professionals to help with finding a disabled person a job.

There were particular difficulties for the DROs. They had no medical training and did not always understand the full nature of complicated disabilities. Indeed, their three day training course was clearly insufficient. The reason for the short duration of the training course was the shortage of labour following the war and also the speed with which the service was set up.[152] The National Advisory Council on the Employment of the Disabled saw the problem as more fundamental. In 1945 a confidential meeting of the Medical Committee of the Council noted that the reason why the DROs failed was they were recruited from the wrong type and grade, were inadequately trained, worked largely part time and had been given 'an impossible task'.[153] The 'impossible task' referred specifically to skilled medical advice. The DROs were not doctors, they held administrative and organisational positions. By 1948, the Ministry had established another level of administration, the District Disablement Resettlement Officers (DDROs), who oversaw DROs' training. Hospitals also established Medical Interviewing Committees to advise DROs on their clients' medical conditions.[154] DROs could appeal to these committees for assistance should it be difficult to place a disabled person in a job. Despite these improvements, there were still concerns about the Officers' levels of expertise, and training courses became more medical in nature, and were also conducted in a hospital environment.[155] However, by 1956, a DRO's official training period was still only three to four days, and the Standing Committee that advised on rehabilitation recommended this period be extended to four weeks.[156]

Post-war Standing Committees

The Ministry of Labour and National Service established a Standing Committee in 1943 to report on the rehabilitation of disabled people. The purpose of the Committee, which had members drawn from the Ministries of Labour and National Service, Education, Health, Pensions and National Insurance, was to supervise and coordinate rehabilitation services in Britain and essentially to implement the recommendations of the Tomlinson Report of 1943. Reports were produced by the Committee in 1946, 1949 and 1958.

In their 19 meetings, which resulted in the first report, the Committee consolidated rehabilitation's place in the State-supported system. In the first report in 1946, the systems and recommendations set up within the Disabled Persons (Employment) Act were examined and found to be operating. Essentially, the Committee saw its main function in 1946 as one of 'securing co-ordination and an exchange of information between the various Departments'.[157] Its second report in 1949, which was full of illustrative photographs of disabled men undertaking various types of rehabilitative therapy, took account of new legislation that had been fully enacted in the period since 1946, notably the National Health Service Act 1948 and the National Assistance Acts of 1946 and 1948. The Committee noted that the work of medical rehabilitation would be published in the Health Service annual reports which were published by the Chief Medical Officer of the Ministry of Health.[158] The report also noted that rehabilitation, while successful, was affected by a shortage of buildings and a lack of staff in the general hospitals. Space problems were alleviated by the erection of numbers of prefabricated huts for gymnasia and physiotherapy departments.[159]

The final report of the Standing Committee on the Rehabilitation and Resettlement of Disabled Persons was named after its Chairman, Lord Piercy. The Committee was appointed in 1953, and from the outset it was clear that an agenda had been set. It said,

> To review in all its aspects the existing provision for the rehabilitation, training and resettlement of disabled persons, full regard being had to the need for the utmost economy in the Government's financial contribution, and to make recommendations.[160]

Initially, voluntary agencies were asked to provide information to the Committee in order to inform its decisions. This was a confirmation of the importance of the voluntary sector in augmenting State support. As we have seen, voluntary services played a vital role in providing a range of different services for disabled people throughout the century, and their request to the Committee to allow representation was testament to their strength in numbers and expertise. However, before the Committee was established, the government warned funding was not available for sweeping improvements in provision for disabled people.[161] Despite assurances that voluntary services would be consulted, it was agreed that there would be no representation on the Committee, and only government officials would be present because,

> the enormous number of bodies that would think they ought to be represented . . . [they] would be only too disposed to grind its own axe . . . that any report emanating from a body of this kind would almost certainly be full of the most ambitious and expensive projects embarrassing to Ministers and the Chancellor of the Exchequer.[162]

Chancellor R.A. Butler agreed, and wrote to Minister of Labour Sir Walter Monckton in February 1953, explaining, 'inevitably the Committee would make recommendations involving increased expenditure and this is not a result which in present circumstances I can contemplate.'[163]

Despite requests, representatives from voluntary agencies were not allowed on the Committee, nor were they consulted about provision. The Committee sent questionnaires to regional hospital boards, enquiring about facilities and staffing arrangements provided for rehabilitation of disabled people, and by-passed voluntary agencies.[164] When the report was published, it praised the work done by voluntary agencies on behalf of disabled people. However, it also noted that the future of voluntary work lay in 'personal interest and care', which was not provided by the State.[165] The Committee did not plan to increase investment in training and rehabilitation services for disabled people, despite making 43 recommendations throughout the report. The Committee justified its economic restraint:

> It is, moreover, dangerous to assume that more effective services can be brought about solely, or even mainly, by increased expenditure, because some of the best work in the rehabilitation field has been done by relying on the capacity to inspire the disabled to help themselves and the intelligent adaptation of available materials.[166]

The reaction from many agencies that looked after disabled people's interests was disappointment, as without increased spending, few changes would result from the Committee's recommendations. While government was prepared to lean heavily on voluntary agencies to augment its basic services, there was no reciprocal arrangement for voluntary agencies in the allocation of funding. In the following decade, the State was more open to listening to requests for representation by voluntary associations, but until then, requests by agencies to represent disabled people on government policy committees were rejected.

In addition to the Committees that examined services for all disabled people, a number of standing committees and special committees on behalf of voluntary services were established after the war to examine the employment prospects of specific disabilities. Generally, these were

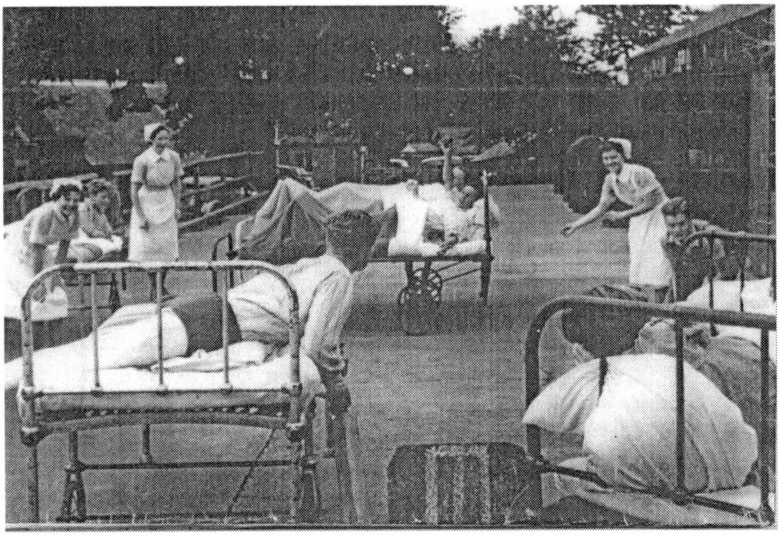

Figure 7.2 Bed cricket at the Royal Orthopaedic Hospital, Birmingham, 1949. Games continued to be used as part of rehabilitation therapy after the war (reproduced with permission of the Royal Orthopaedic Hospital Trust, Birmingham)

interested in ensuring that disabled people were given employment opportunities, thus reducing their demands on a cash-strapped State. A Working Party on the Employment of Blind Persons reported to Parliament in 1951, noting that both blind workers and employers had a commitment to one another and that 'the blind worker can and should do a full week's work in return for a full week's wage'.[167] The relationship between disabled people and their ability to work had been firmly established throughout the war, and through the work of committees and voluntary agencies was maintained and strengthened through the 1950s.

Conclusions

Rehabilitation continued to be important after the war, and the system was transferred from a wartime regime to a civilian one. Rehabilitation had provided a measure of success in returning those fighting to their wartime work as quickly as possible, and limiting the impact of any permanent disability. This, coupled with the long-standing view that employment demonstrated an alternative lifestyle for disabled people and provided a way out of a life of misery and indolence, ensured that rehabilitation programmes were adopted for civilians after the war. As well as its impact on people with disabilities, rehabilitation was applied to others, including the displaced and the indigent.

For those severely disabled, work was available through the reworked concept of the pre-war sheltered workshops. Remploy provided employment for those for whom work in mainstream employment was difficult to procure. Although it can be argued that this was merely a question of expediency, and that rehabilitation and limiting the effects of disability provided a previously underutilised workforce, this labour shortage provided disabled people the space to demonstrate their value as workers. Nevertheless, voluntary services were still important to support disabled people, and their function shifted to provide an additional level of support that augmented the basic provision of the State. The role of charitable and voluntary organisations continued to be important, and during the evolving welfare state their role should not be underestimated.

The Disabled Persons (Employment) Act of 1944, National Assistance Act and National Health Act in particular gave disabled people a level of support that had previously been denied them. The State's responsibility for rehabilitation provision, which had been established during the war, was firmly entrenched in legislation and systems after the war. Ministries continued to cooperate, and hospitals and rehabilitation centres became partners in ensuring that functionality, both physical and mental, was restored to the best of their ability. During the war, doctors and administrators had endeavoured to cooperate, and nowhere was this more evident than in establishing rehabilitation regimes. The lessons of the war were well remembered, and ensured that systems were established, and the nature of cooperation between various bodies continued, so that people who needed rehabilitation after injury and trauma were able to take advantage of the knowledge gained during the war. As an article in the journal *Rehabilitation* noted:

> The ideal all those concerned with rehabilitation should set themselves should be to help the cripple or disabled person *actively* to achieve rehabilitation rather than *passively* to receive treatment which is liable, in such circumstances, to degenerate into mere palliative measures.[168]

Rehabilitation as a practice was extended even further, and formed the basis of post-war methods of getting people back to work. It was argued at that time that health administration would be one of the first activities of the State. Essentially, that was what rehabilitation had become.

It was a technocratic solution which could be applied to the chaotic situation of the post-war world. Rehabilitation had progressed from a medical term that specifically related to reducing the effects of traumatic injury, and broadened into a technical system, with close cooperation between a number of administrative and government bodies, and the voluntary sector, whereby an entire State could be reconstructed.

Notes

1 *Manchester Guardian* (6 January 1946).
2 Member organisations included the British Legion, Central Council for the Care of Cripples, Empire Rheumatism Council, RNIB, RNID, Roffey Park Rehabilitation Centre, St Dunstan's and the Chartered Society of Physiotherapy. *The Lancet* (3 March 1943), 285.
3 Memo, R. Watson-Jones, 'Disablement and Employment' (no date, possibly 1945), LAB 18/218, National Archives, London.
4 Extract from the Constitution of the British Council for Rehabilitation, FD1/6811 (1945), National Archives, London.
5 L.C. Williams, 'International Congress on Physical Education, Recreation and Rehabilitation, 1948', *Journal of Physical Education*, Vol. XL, No. 121 (November 1948), 102.
6 Ibid., 106.
7 The British Council, Conference Programme: *Rehabilitation and Resettlement of the Disabled October 4–26th 1949*, LAB 44/190, National Archives, London.
8 Ibid.
9 Ibid., 9.
10 'Rehabilitation of the Tramp', *Manchester Guardian* (13 September 1948).
11 United Nations Information Organisation, *UNRRA: The Story of the United Nations Relief and Rehabilitation Administration* (London, 1944), 3.
12 'Health In Industry: The Need of Rehabilitation Centres', *The Times* (20 February 1943).
13 Report by Harold Balme, Medical Officer in Charge of Rehabilitation, Ministry of Health, *Rehabilitation in the New Health Services* (1945), FDI 68/10, National Archives, London.
14 Ministry of Labour Conference Minutes (17 June 1945), LAB 18/462, National Archives, London.
15 Eagger A. Austin, 'The Work of Farnham Park', *Rehabilitation*, No. 8 (June 1953), 2.
16 Both men and women attended these centres. Garston Manor provided 10 out of its 55 beds for women. C.J.S. O'Malley, 'Garston Manor Rehabilitation Centre', *Rehabilitation*, No. 13 (Winter 1954/55), 11.

17 Cooter, *Surgery and Society in Peace and War*, 207.
18 Stephen Mattingly, 'Garston Manor: A Comprehensive Medical and Industrial Rehabilitation Centre', *Health Trends*, Vol. 6 (1974), 23.
19 O'Malley, 'Garston Manor Rehabilitation Centre', 11.
20 Austin, 'The Work of Farnham Park', 4.
21 C.J. German, 'State Provision for the Employment of the Handicapped', *Rehabilitation*, Vol. 16 (Winter 1955/56), 23.
22 Overall, hospitals employing rehabilitation had increased to 333 in 1946 from 150 in 1943. Ministry of Labour and National Service, *Report of the Standing Committee on the Rehabilitation and Resettlement of Disabled Persons* (London, 1946).
23 O. Dover, 92/10/1, Imperial War Museum Document Archives, London.
24 Ministry of Labour and National Service, *Egham Centre Industrial Rehabilitation for Men,* FD1/6811 (1943), National Archives, London.
25 Ministry of Labour and National Service, *Proposal,* No. 4691 (29 July 1943), LAB 9/187, National Archives, London.
26 Ministry of Labour and National Service, *From Illness and Disablement to Health and Vigour and the Road to Re-employment* (no date, probably 1946), LAB 12/357, National Archives, London.
27 Ministry of Labour and National Service, *Proposal,* No. 4691 (29 July 1943), LAB 9/187, National Archives, London.
28 Letter from Mr Kettley to Mr Timoney, 'Egham Rehabilitation Staff' (11 August 1944), LAB 12/256, National Archives, London.
29 Ministry of Labour and National Service, *The Experiment of an Industrial Rehabilitation Centre at Egham, Surrey* (31 December 1944), LAB 9/187, National Archives, London.
30 Ibid., 10.
31 Ibid.
32 Ministry of Labour and National Service, *Review of the Work of the Egham Industrial Rehabilitation Centre for the Year Ending 31 December 1945* (1946), LAB 9/187, National Archives, London.
33 Ibid.
34 'British Plan For Training the Disabled', *Monthly Labour Review*, Vol. 54 (February 1942), 407.
35 Buxton, 'Industrial Rehabilitation Units', 541.
36 In 1947 only disabled people were allowed to train for the building trade due to the restrictions on building. Ministry of Labour and National Service, *Second Report of the Standing Committee on the Rehabilitation and Resettlement of Disabled Persons* (London, 1949).
37 Pamphlet: *Roffey Park Rehabilitation Centre*, FD1/6811 (1943), National Archives, London.
38 St Dunstan's cared for the war disabled and the National Institute for the Blind looked after the welfare of civilians.

39 *British Medical Journal* (10 March 1951), 519.
40 St Dunstan's continued to pay for the training. Ministry of Labour and National Service, *Second Report of the Standing Committee on the Rehabilitation and Resettlement of Disabled Persons.*
41 Selwyn Selwyn-Clarke, 'The British Rehabilitation Service', *Rehabilitation*, No. 16 (Winter 1955/56), 22.
42 Ministry of Labour and National Service, *Report of the Standing Committee on the Rehabilitation and Resettlement of Disabled Persons*, 2.
43 'Disabled Person's Employment Act', *The Hospital*, Vol. 42, No. 9 (March 1946), 89.
44 German, 'State Provision for the Employment of the Handicapped', 26.
45 Notes of a Meeting held at the Ministry of Labour, York House, London (16 March 1945), LAB 18/222, National Archives, London.
46 Acceptance Letter, 3rd Rehabilitation Physical Training Course at Pinderfields Hospital, 23/4/46–25/10/46, LAB 18/222 (1946), National Archives, London.
47 Alphabetical List of Ex-Service PT Instructors who Completed a Six Month Remedial Gymnastic Course at Pinderfields During 1945/46, LAB 18/222 (1946), National Archives, London.
48 Ministry of Labour and National Service, *Second Report on the Standing Committee on the Rehabilitation and Resettlement of Disabled Persons*, 15.
49 Memo: Progress of the Disabled Person's Employment Corporation Limited (2 March 1949), LAB 18/148, National Archives, London.
50 'The Work of Remploy', *Rehabilitation*, 9 (1953), 9.
51 Internal Letter to Mr Sisson, Factory Department (11 January 1947), LAB 14/444, National Archives, London.
52 The National Institute of the Blind's workshop made a host of products featuring their logo, including a souvenir for the Festival of Britain, which was soap in a plastic container. *The New Beacon*, Vol. 35, No. 413 (May 1951), 107.
53 'Remploy Factories', *St Dunstan's Review*, Vol. 31, No. 334 (December 1946), 9.
54 Edwards, 'Remploy', 152.
55 Ibid., 151.
56 In 1952 Remploy had a recorded loss of £2,380,399. 'The Work of Remploy', *Rehabilitation*, 9 (1953), 9. Beveridge, *Voluntary Action*, 252.
57 Ministry of Labour and National Service, *Third Report of the Standing Committee on the Rehabilitation and Resettlement of Disabled Persons* (London, 1958).
58 Ministry of Labour and National Service, *Second Report of the Standing Committee on the Rehabilitation and Resettlement of Disabled Persons.*
59 New employees at Michael Works were given three weeks to reach the accepted standard. Failure to do so meant instant dismissal. Clarke, *Disabled Citizens*, 163.

60 Rates for disabled workers were set at 75% of those of the able bodied.
61 *Star and Garter Annual Report* (1947), 9.
62 The workshops were finally finished in 1950. *Star and Garter Annual Report* (1950), 9.
63 Buxton, 'Industrial Rehabilitation Units', 546.
64 Correlli Barnett, *Audit of War* (London, 1986), 37.
65 G. Finlayson, *Citizen, State and Social Welfare in Britain 1830–1990* (Oxford, 1994), 317.
66 Text from 'Return to Action', INF 6/1260 (1947), National Archives, London, 4.
67 Ministry of Labour and National Service, *Second Report of the Standing Committee on the Rehabilitation and Resettlement of Disabled Persons.*
68 Pamphlet: *The Springbok Story*, MT 9/5434 (no date, *circa* 1950), National Archives, London.
69 'South Africa Says "Thank You" With a Village', *News Chronicle* (22 May 1947).
70 Charles Jarman, 'Springbok Village: A Community Centre for Seamen', *The Seaman* (May/June 1945), 69–74.
71 F.K. Prochaska, 'Philanthropy', in F.M.L. Thompson (ed.), *The Cambridge Social History of Britain, 1750–1950, Vol. II* (Cambridge, 1990), 358.
72 Private sources paid approximately £1.5 million per year toward the blind and the government spent about £3 million. Beveridge, *Voluntary Action*, 246.
73 Central Office of Information, *Rehabilitation and Care of the Disabled in Britain* (London: HMSO, 1962), 28.
74 The two did not amalgamate until 1963. Richard Dimbleby, *Every Eight Hours* (London, 1964), 32. See also Alfred Morris and Arthur Butler, *No Feet to Drag* (London, 1972), 42.
75 Special Services General File: Provision for Spastic Children (1954–55), ED 50/565, National Archives, London.
76 Central Office of Information, *Rehabilitation and Care of the Disabled in Britain*, 28.
77 Disabled Drivers' Motor Club, *75th Anniversary Celebration* (Northampton, 1997), 21.
78 Central Council for the Care of Cripples Development Sub-Committee (1957–58), MH 55/2242, National Archives, London.
79 P.G. Cambray and G.C. Briggs, *Red Cross and St John War History 1939–1947* (London, 1949), 132–3.
80 *Rehabilitation*, No. 1 (January 1951), 30.
81 See James Walvin, *Leisure and Society: 1930–1950* (London, 1978), 149.
82 British Red Cross Society, *The Ceaseless Challenge; Souvenir of the Red Cross Centenary* (London, 1964), 79.
83 National Assistance Act, 1948.
84 The King's National Roll was still in operation in 1956 for those who had been disabled in the First World War. *Report of the Committee of Inquiry*

on the Rehabilitation, Training and Resettlement of Disabled Persons (London, 1956), 64.

85 Wootton, *Official History of the British Legion*, 305.

86 This was changed in 1943. Brown, *Red for Remembrance*, 101.

87 Letter from R.H.W. Davidson, Employment and Pensions Department, British Legion, to the Secretary of the British Medical Association (17 May 1946), CMA SA/BMA C.165, Wellcome Trust, London.

88 Wootton, *The Politics of Influence*, 243.

89 Letter from Ian Fraser, 'The Disabled in War', *The Times* (5 January 1946).

90 'Plight of the Disabled', *The Times* (10 July 1948).

91 'Service in the Forces', *The Times* (3 January 1947).

92 Wootton, *Official History of the British Legion*, 317.

93 *Star and Garter Annual Report* (1947).

94 A donation of £1,500 endowed a bed in perpetuity. *Star and Garter Annual Report* (1946).

95 'Free Motor Cars for Some Disabled', *St Dunstan's Review*, Vol. 32, No. 352a (August 1948), 7.

96 'Pensions Minister Presents Car to St Dunstaner', *St Dunstan's Review*, Vol. 32, No. 358 (February 1949), 1.

97 Ryde, *Out On A Limb*, 49.

98 'Disablement Pensions', PIN 59/71 (1956), National Archives, London.

99 Wootton, *The Politics of Influence*, 239.

100 *National Cripples' Journal*, No. 64 (1946), 6.

101 David Owen, *English Philanthropy 1660–1960* (Cambridge, MA, 1965), 532.

102 Central Office of Information, *Rehabilitation and Care of the Disabled in Britain*, 28.

103 Mary G. Thomas, *Party Games for the Blind* (London, 1970), 1.

104 Virginia Berridge, *Health and Society in Britain Since 1939* (Cambridge, 1999), 24.

105 Interview with Peggy Tasker, April 1998.

106 *Report on Appliances* (1958–62), MH 99/83, National Archives, London.

107 The petrol grant ended in 1972. Morris and Butler, *No Feet to Drag*, 78.

108 The police would pull over any driver of an Invacar who was carrying a passenger. Some disabled people found a way to avoid confrontations with the police; for instance, Len Tasker's wife Peggy would sit on the floor of his Invacar so that the police would not see her. Interview with Len and Peggy Tasker, April 1998.

109 Tony Gould, *A Summer Plague: Polio and its Survivors* (New Haven, 1995), 241.

110 German, 'State Provision for the Employment of the Handicapped', 24.

111 *National Survey of Paraplegic and Seriously Disabled Miners* (1955), BX 4/30, National Archives, London.

112 Report: *History of Motor Propelled Tricycles* (no date), BRCS JCM/1/6/3/42 352, Red Cross Archives, London.
113 *The Manchester Guardian* (1 July 1960).
114 Central Office of Information, *Rehabilitation and Care of the Disabled in Britain*, 10.
115 Ibid., 12; *Report on Appliances* (1958–62), MH 99/83, National Archives, London.
116 Pamphlet from the Ministry of Labour and National Service, September 1945, BRCS, Acc 1551/6, Red Cross Archives, London.
117 *Disabled Persons (Employment) Act* (1944), BRCS, Acc 1551/6, Red Cross Archives, London.
118 Speech by George Tomlinson, Parliamentary Secretary, Ministry of Labour and National Service, Ex-Services Welfare Society Annual Medical Conference, 8 February (1944), CMAC SA/RBC c.7/5, Wellcome Trust, London.
119 *The Guardian* (5 February 1944).
120 *The Lancet* (15 April 1944), 521.
121 Letter to the Editor, *British Medical Journal* (16 February 1946), 257.
122 Ministry of Labour and National Service Press Notice, No. 24 (21 December 1944), LAB 18/148, National Archives, London.
123 Minutes, Meeting of the National Advisory Council on the Employment of the Disabled (10 March 1946), LAB 18/148, National Archives, London.
124 The cities included London, Birmingham, Bristol, Manchester, Leeds and Liverpool. The highest number of attendees was 50,000 in Manchester. Memo, National Advisory Council on the Disabled (1945), LAB 18/218, National Archives, London.
125 Special Meeting of Members of the Medical Committee and the Training and Employment Committee, National Advisory Council on the Employment of the Disabled (31 July 1953), LAB 18/146, National Archives, London.
126 Ministry of Education, Administrative Memorandum No. 94, Choice of Employment for Handicapped Children (8 October 1945), CMAC SA/BMA, C.165, Wellcome Trust, London.
127 Ibid.
128 Clarke, *Disabled Citizens*, 142.
129 Ministry of Labour and National Service, *Report of the Standing Committee on the Rehabilitation and Resettlement of Disabled Persons.*
130 These were St Loyes in Exeter, the Queen Elizabeth College, Leatherhead and Portland Training College, Mansfield. *National Survey of Paraplegic and Seriously Disabled Miners* (1955), BX4/30, National Archives, London.
131 The report also suggested that war pensioners should not have the right to automatically register for work. *Report of the Inter-departmental Committee on the Rehabilitation and Resettlement of Disabled Persons*, 1943.

132 Memo: Discussion on the Tomlinson Report (15 September 1943), ADM 1/4615, National Archives, London.
133 Wootton, *Official History of the British Legion*, 269.
134 Pamphlet from the Ministry of Labour and National Service (September 1945), BRCS, Acc 1551/6, Red Cross Archives, London.
135 Ministry of Labour and National Service, *Report on the Standing Committee on the Rehabilitation and Resettlement of Disabled Persons.*
136 Pamphlet from the Ministry of Labour and National Service (September 1945), BRCA Acc 1551/6, Red Cross Archives, London.
137 'Jobs For Disabled Service Men', *The Times* (9 February 1945).
138 Statutory Rules and Orders and Statutory Instruments Revised – Disabled Persons (Employment) Act (31 December 1948), CMAC SA/BMA C.165, Wellcome Trust, London.
139 For a discussion on the King's National Roll see Meaghan Kowalsky, '"This Honourable Obligation"': The King's National Roll Scheme for Disabled Ex-Servicemen, 1915–44', *European Review of History*, Vol. 14, No. 4 (December 2007), 567–84.
140 Clarke, *Disabled Citizens*, 162.
141 Barry Turner and Tony Rennell, *When Daddy Came Home: How Family Life Changed Forever in 1945* (London, 1995), 10.
142 *British Medical Journal* (9 February 1946), 215.
143 Morris and Butler, *No Feet to Drag*, 56.
144 Script: 'Return to Action' (1947), INF 6/1260, National Archives, London.
145 Ibid., 1.
146 Executive Committee Minutes, PEA, 1/8 (17 January 1947), Physical Education Association Records, Liverpool University, Special Collections and Archives.
147 Letter to the Editor, *The Times* (17 October 1947).
148 'Work for the Disabled', *British Medical Journal* (17 August 1946), 237.
149 T. Ferguson and A.N. McPhail, *Hospital and Community* (London, 1954), 117.
150 Minutes, National Advisory Council on the Employment of the Disabled: Medical Committee (17 March 1948), LAB 18/148, National Archives, London.
151 Ministry of Labour and National Service, *Report of the Standing Committee on the Rehabilitation and Resettlement of Disabled Persons.*
152 Ibid., 7.
153 National Advisory Council on the Employment of the Disabled, Confidential Report of the Medical Committee on Disablement Resettlement Officers, NAC 26 (28 November 1945), LAB 18/148, National Archives, London.
154 Ministry of Labour and National Service, *Second Report of the Standing Committee on the Rehabilitation and Resettlement of Disabled Persons*, 9.

155 Ibid., 9.
156 Ministry of Labour and National Service, *Third Report of the Standing Committee on the Rehabilitation and Resettlement of Disabled Persons.*
157 Ministry of Labour and National Service, *Report of the Standing Committee on the Rehabilitation and Resettlement of Disabled Persons*, 15.
158 Ministry of Labour and National Service, *Second Report of the Standing Committee on the Rehabilitation and Resettlement of Disabled Persons*, 1.
159 Ibid., 2.
160 Statement in Parliament on the establishment of the Piercy Committee, DP 1096/1952, MH 55/2158 (1952), National Archives, London.
161 For an overview see Kevin Jeffreys, *Retreat From New Jerusalem: British Politics, 1951–1964* (Basingstoke, 1997), chapter 6.
162 Minute Sheet, PSO 209, MH 55/2158 (15 November 1952), National Archives, London.
163 Letter to Walter Monckton from R.A. Butler (14 February 1953), MH 55/2158, National Archives, London.
164 Memo to all Regional Hospital Boards from Tom Nicole, Joint Secretary, Ministry of Health, MH 55/2158 (1954), National Archives, London.
165 Ministry of Labour and National Service, *Third Report of the Standing Committee on the Rehabilitation and Resettlement of Disabled Persons*, 7.
166 *Report of the Committee of Inquiry on the Rehabilitation, Training and Resettlement of Disabled Persons*, 3.
167 'Blindness and Employment', *British Journal of Nursing*, Vol. 99 (1951), 22.
168 'The British Rehabilitation Service', *Rehabilitation*, Vol. 16 (Winter 1955/56), 26.

Conclusions

This book traces the history of rehabilitation in the first half of the twentieth century and contextualises it within systems both in peacetime and in war, including State intervention, industry, voluntary agencies and society. It also attempts to historically locate disabled people, who were often recipients, whether willing or not, of State support, restricted employment opportunities and medical treatments.

From the outset, it was clear that fresh air, good food and physical exercise were important. The State and medical practitioners collaborated in their plan for a healthier population. Prescribing a combination of preventative measures was a less costly way for the State to improve the nation's health and to ensure that health problems would not develop later, and also impact on the State's coffers. Disabled children were supplied with some government assistance through programmes such as the School Medical Service. Fears over degeneration after the First World War and the rise in popularity of eugenics were also responsible for this new wave of preventative treatment and efforts to limit the effect of disability.

After the First World War, numbers of disabled people increased dramatically. Young, previously fit men had suffered the disastrous impact of war, joining the already large number of disabled people in Britain. With no experience of how to reintegrate them into society, the disabled soldier returning from the Great War relied on government assistance and different charities were established for his benefit. A new Ministry was set up in order to deal with pensions and assistance for disabled ex-servicemen.

Associations such as St Dunstan's were an early example of the assistance that blind soldiers received, but also their preferential treatment in relation to other disabled people that would last for many years. One of the ways that disabled soldiers could return to their normal lives was to enjoy the pastimes and recreations that they had practised before the war. Sport was introduced for these disabled ex-servicemen, to improve their morale and physical standard, and to provide them with something familiar to fall back on, a revisiting of their masculine self. Sports developed competitively, either at different associations, like St Dunstan's, at individual hospitals like Roehampton or at institutions such as the Star and Garter Home. This was more easily accomplished with groups of reasonably well fed, fit ex-servicemen than it was with groups of undernourished, tired children, and the war disabled continued to receive the most sympathy and fiscal support.

The influx of permanently wounded soldiers after the First World War compelled state intervention. Not only did this manifest itself through State aid, but also within the voluntary sector there were societies and workshops where disabled ex-servicemen gained assistance in finding employment. All of the other disabled groups were marginalised in favour of the war disabled. At the 1920 Conference on the Care and Cure of Crippled Children, it was remarked that this provision for the war disabled had caused 'an appalling amount of suffering' among other disabled people.[1] People disabled in industry, particularly mining, gained concessions from employers; for example, mining companies were pressured by unions and provided remedial exercises and retraining for those injured at work. The National Insurance Scheme was established to provide support for a worker who was injured, but this was not an option for those whose incapacity lasted longer than 26 weeks, or who were unemployed.

While some would argue that the advent of the welfare state ensured that there was adequate treatment for everybody, and no doubt the situation for disabled people improved markedly, ex-servicemen continued to have priority over all groups of disabled people. Nonetheless, State interest in disabled people's condition grew throughout the 1930s, and with it developments in material aid, albeit at varying and low rates. During the 1930s, Factory Acts and medical committees concerned themselves with workers' health and accident prevention. Disabled children were better off as they were provided with education (of varying quality), even if it was only to prepare them for work, and were more likely to receive charitable support due to a combination of vulnerability and response to training. They also responded well to medical interventions, mainly fresh air and exercise, which became standard methods of treatment from early in the century. Maintaining a healthy body and creating good character were popular with the State, medical professionals and employers, and promoted after the First World War. The threat of war in the 1930s also led to increased concentration by the State and voluntary services to improve the fitness of potential soldiers.

During the Second World War, advances in medicine increased survival chances for injured people. It was in this period that rehabilitation therapies became the backbone of physical medicine. Rehabilitation was a holistic therapy that blended medical, employment and social techniques that ensured that those injured, both combatants and civilians, were provided with support to ensure they made the best possible recovery. Total war provided the perfect environment for numbers of men trained in modern business techniques, who entered the Services and used their expertise to improve levels of efficiency. As an exercise in staff retention, rehabilitation was a system where these theories were conceptualised, and played out within the context of bodily usefulness. Residual disability was no barrier to employment and did not always result in discharge from the Forces. Rehabilitation was a successful system for returning those in the Services back to the front line, and disabled people's bodies were redeployed to assist in the war effort in industry; those who had been injured and discharged, or those who were disabled before the war.

Rehabilitation signified an important change in attitude; it made government, industry and medicine reassess its attitude toward people with disabilities. This repositioning of disabled people from societal drain to valued workers was largely due to the demands of a wartime economy; nevertheless, disabled people did make important contributions to the war effort, as citizens and workers. The efforts of the Tomlinson Committee's report published during the war enabled rehabilitation regimes to proliferate, providing a number of specialist centres which would provide the backbone of rehabilitations centres after the war.

The book concentrates on two case studies to contextualise two of the main aims of rehabilitative therapy. The first case study centres on the RAF as their fitness was required from a number of perspectives. The RAF provided the highest quality rehabilitative therapy and the successes of the RAF in rehabilitation and its medical treatment were held up to others as an example of excellent quality care. The RAF utilised two types of rehabilitation that were vastly different in scope. Social rehabilitation was generally more psychological than physical. For aircrew who had suffered burns, the typical round of rehabilitative therapy was not suitable, as the delicate medical condition of burns patients did not allow them to participate in tough sporting competition practised in the rehabilitation centres established for those with orthopaedic injury. Instead, parties and outings replaced PT and sports. The methods of rehabilitative therapy were not prescriptive when it came to restoring the vital services of the RAF. The rehabilitation centres that specialised in orthopaedics were staffed with the highest quality medical practitioners. Consultant surgeons such as Archibald McIndoe and Reginald Watson-Jones were able to run their medical services independently. The RAF did not follow the usual rules relating to discharge, generally ignoring the rules adopted by the other Services and 'turning a blind eye' to those that stayed in the Service longer than they should have under the rules. The specialists who provided medical expertise to the RAF colluded in its unique position and gained concessions unavailable to those in other Services. Both Watson-Jones and McIndoe used the special nature of the RAF to break standard military rules, such as the wearing of uniforms while recovering in hospital. The notion that they would receive excellent medical care should they be injured alleviated the problem of fear in aircrew.

The second case study focused on the rehabilitation regime of Stoke Mandeville, which was a combination of the physical and social rehabilitation that was practised at RAF rehabilitation hospitals and centres. Rehabilitation at Stoke Mandeville was a structured method reaching disabled people as the spinal paralysed had previously been judged beyond medical intervention. Nonetheless, the war presented medical professionals with the ability to apply established rehabilitative techniques to the spinal paralysed. Rehabilitation had proved that it could be applied to all types of injured bodies, and could be restructured to gain specific results. Due to Guttmann's single-minded pursuit of results, and the cheerful and competitive atmosphere, which worked particularly well with its majority of young ex-servicemen, Stoke Mandeville was rated highly as a successful rehabilitation centre. Games were developed to assist the men to withstand the strains on their bodies associated with paraplegia. On the whole, men in the Services responded well to its tough competitive regime. This was a way of regaining, or refashioning a sense of masculine identity, a hyper-masculine sporting identity that could be juxtaposed with their tendency toward health breakdowns. The meanings associated with sport, with fitness and the male body gave Stoke Mandeville a spectacular opportunity to reinvent a recognisable notion of the self and a vision of the whole man vital to physical and mental health. However successful Stoke Mandeville was in its rehabilitation methods, it experienced less success in gaining employment for the men there, but there may have been a number of reasons for this, including transport problems and issues of accessibility in large ungainly wheelchairs. Stoke Mandeville's real legacy was the development of international disability sport.

Although their stories are more difficult to reveal than those of men, rehabilitation services were also provided for women. Rehabilitation methods that had been applied to men were less successful for women, and the Ministry of Pensions had to rethink the way that injured women were rehabilitated. Should their injury result in permanent disability, disabled women were allowed to share some of the preferential treatment that injury in war afforded to men, although they were not as well recompensed by the pension system. Nevertheless, the State, through its government departments, altered its male dominated systems and assisted women with a range of medical issues, including fertility and sterilisation, and also appreciated women's desire to consider the aesthetic. Disabled women participated in the war in a number of capacities, and enjoyed freedom from gendered roles as much as their able-bodied counterparts. For those that were disabled as a result of the conflict, State support became more available and women enjoyed many of the benefits afforded to disabled men, including some means to manage their disability in relation to the demands of family, work and social life. However, when the war was over, women returned to lives centred once more around home and family, which was problematic for disabled women. Unlike their able-bodied counterparts, disabled women were less inclined to be cast in the role of carer and mother; instead, the perception was that they occupied a more passive position, cared for rather than being carers. The Ministry of Pensions did not devise ways to assist disabled women with their families. Instead it assisted them to limit the size of their families, thereby reducing their dependence on the State. For some unmarried disabled women, their choices were limited to returning to the family home or remaining institutionalised, as their disability and lack of fiscal support through inadequate work opportunities or low pension rates, forced them to remain dependent on the State.

Owing to the work of the Tomlinson Committee and its wide influence, rehabilitation continued to be important after the war, and the system transferred easily to the civilian context. Rehabilitation had proved successful in redeploying people disabled by injury, whether temporarily or permanently, to work, and the centralised system had been established already, so it was just a matter of readjusting the system to peacetime. This was coupled with the long-standing view that employment demonstrated an improved situation for disabled people, both physically and mentally, and in addition provided a way out of a life of poverty and indolence. Remploy provided jobs for those for whom work in mainstream employment was problematic. However, numbers of disabled people were employed outside the sheltered workplace. It can be argued that employment for disabled people was merely a question of expediency, and that rehabilitation and limiting the effects of disability merely identified a previously underutilised workforce. In short, the labour shortage provided disabled people the space to demonstrate their value as workers. Nevertheless, voluntary services were still important to support disabled people, and their function shifted to provide an additional level of support that augmented the basic provision of the State. The role of charitable and voluntary organisations continued to be important, and despite the burgeoning welfare state, voluntary associations continued to proliferate and became more focused on a single disability, or provided alternative services to what the State was able to supply.

Legislation including the Disabled Persons (Employment) Act, National Assistance Act and National Health Act gave disabled people a level of support that had not previously been available to them. Ministries continued to cooperate to ensure that rehabilitation took place, and hospitals and rehabilitation centres became partners in ensuring that functionality, both physical and mental, was restored in the main to injured workers, who were the new focus of rehabilitation therapy. Nevertheless, criticisms were still levelled at the State for demonstrating preference for the disabled from the war. This time, the lessons of the war were remembered, and ensured that systems were established and the nature of cooperation between various bodies continued, so that people who needed rehabilitation after injury and trauma were able to take advantage of the knowledge gained during the war.

Rehabilitation as a practice was extended even further, forming the basis of post-war methods of getting people who had been injured and those with permanent disabilities back to employment. Rehabilitation was a technocratic practice that had progressed from a medical term that specifically related to reducing the effects of traumatic injury, and broadened to a technical system, with close cooperation between a number of State agencies, industry and the voluntary sector.

Finally, what this study essentially demonstrates is the need for more work on disabled people, their experiences and their history. Historians of disability specialise in this field but often disabled people are missing from studies that cover more general historical topics. In addition to concentrating on histories which focus on disabled people's past within any given period of time, work should be undertaken to ensure that disabled people feature as part of overarching historical studies. A study of the welfare state, for example, should not be considered complete unless the story of disabled people is woven into the text. This research has endeavoured to rectify the way history and historians have largely ignored approximately 10% of the British population.

Note

1 *Report of the Central Committee for the Care of Cripples* (London, 1921), 18.

Select bibliography

Primary sources

BBC archives

- BBC News Archives, various reports 1945–70.

British Red Cross archives

- Disability – Acc 0167/12, Acc 599/3, Acc 750/5/11(2)/, PT 3, Acc 961/3/7/1, Acc 961/1/23, Acc 961/1/24, Acc 961/1/27, Acc 961/1/28, Acc 1551/6, Acc 0167/12(a).
- Joint Committee Archives – JWO/3/1/4, JCM/1/6/3/42 352, JCM/1/6/3/48(357).
- Publicity, Photographs and Press Cuttings – PH7, PH11, PH15.

Central Council of Physical Recreation archives, London

- Correspondence between John Wolfenden and Ludwig Guttmann.

Contemporary Medical Archives Centre, Wellcome Library, London

- PP/HUN, Personal Papers of Donald Hunter – C.2/179, F.5.
- SA/BMA, British Medical Association – Files C.507, C.509, f.98.
- SA/CSP, Chartered Society of Physiotherapy – Box 192, Files P.4/1/10–11, P.4/1/1/4, P.4/1/1/2.
- SA/HVA, Health Visitors' Association – File G.1/18.
- SA/RAMC, The Royal Army Medical Muniment Collection – File O/539.778.
- SA/RBC, Research Board for the Correlation of Medical Science and Physical Education – Files C.7/3, C. 7/4, C.7/5, C.8/3, C.8/9.

Imperial War Museum document collection

- Diaries – Dover 92/10/1, Ferne 91/16/1, McCall 81/15/1, Sanders 79/15/1.

Physical Education Association records

- Minutes of Executive Meetings 1942–70.

National Archives London

- Admiralty – ADM 1/4615.
- Air Ministry – AIR 2/250, AIR 8/796.
- Cabinet – CAB 117/145.
- Coal – COAL 75/4024, BX 4/30.
- Colonial Office – CO 968/138/8.
- Foreign Office – FO 371/181/107.
- Medical Research Council – FD 1/6810, FD 1/6811, FD 1/3986, FD 1/4167, FD 1/4168, FD 1/6809, FD 4/141, FD 4/20, FD 4/61, FD 4/219, FD 4/61, FD 4/246, FD 4/88, FD 4/243, FD 4/237, FD 4/221, FD 4/199, FD 4/89, FD 68.
- Mining BX – BX 4/30.
- Ministry of Education – ED 113/48, ED 124/4, ED 136/910, ED 169/73, ED 169/74, ED 24/2097, ED 50/249, ED 50/563, ED 50/565, ED 62/76, ED 62/178, ED 927.
- Ministry of Health – MH 120/8, MH 160/376, MH 99/83, MH 55/2158, MH 55/1088, MH 55/2242, MH 55/590, MH 55/1034.
- Ministry of Information/Central Office of Information – INF 6/1260.
- Ministry of Labour and National Service – LAB 9/187, LAB 12/357, LAB 14/444, LAB 18/148, LAB 18/222, LAB 18/462, LAB 18/469, LAB 20/1.
- Ministry of Pensions – PIN 15/2888, PIN 15/3097, PIN 15/3098, PIN 20/458, PIN 59/71.
- Ministry of Transport – MT 9/5434.

Queen Mary's Roehampton Hospital archives

- Leaflets and Press Cuttings 1915–43.
- Photographs sports and recreation 1915–20.

Royal National Institute for the Blind

- Annual Reports 1931–61.

Royal Star and Garter Archives

- Annual Reports 1938–70.
- House Committee Agenda Books 1940–59.

- Photographs of activities and special events 1900–1970.
- Press Cuttings and programmes from events 1920–70.

Oral Interviews

Conducted by J. Anderson

- Len and Peggy Tasker, The Midlands Centre for the Disabled and Able-Bodied, Tile Hill, Coventry, April 1998.

Imperial War Museum sound archive

- Interviews – Baines 12481/2, Gleave 10084/3, Guttmann 4596/03, Hobby 18274/4, MacLean 10788/3.

Journals and Newspapers

The Athletic News.
The Beacon.
British Deaf News.
The British Deaf Times.
British Medical Journal.
Bucks Herald.
The Cord.
Cripples Journal.
Deaf News.
The Deaf News Quarterly.
Deaf Quarterly News.
Health Trends.
Hearing.
The Lancet.
Manchester Guardian.
National Cripples Journal (became *Voice of the Disabled* in 1969).
The New Beacon.
Rehabilitation.
The Silent World 1924–25 became magazine of the NID 1946–63 (renamed *Hearing* in 1964).
Special Schools Journal.
Special Schools Quarterly.
St Dunstan's Review.
St Mary's Hospital School of Physiotherapy Magazine (Swedish Institute).
Star and Garter Magazine.
The Teacher of the Deaf.
The Times.

Contemporary reports

Board of Education, *Syllabus of Physical Training for Schools 1933* (London: HMSO, 1933).

Central Council for the Care of Cripples, *The Care and Cure of Cripple Children* (Bristol: John Wright, 1924).

Central Office of Information, *Rehabilitation and Care of the Disabled in Britain* (London: HMSO, 1962).

Department of Health and Social Security, *National Health Service: Twentieth Anniversary Conference* (London: HMSO, 1968).

Disabled Living Foundation, *Sport and Physical Recreation for the Disabled: An Enquiry by the Disabled Living Foundation* (London: Disabled Living Foundation, 1970).

Garston Manor, *Garston Manor: Combined Medical and Industrial Rehabilitation Centre near Watford* (Garston: Garston Manor, 1970).

International Society for the Welfare of Cripples, *The Disabled in the Modern World: Proceedings of the Fifth World Congress of the International Society for the Welfare of Cripples* (London: J.B. Shears, 1951).

International Society for the Welfare of Cripples, *Planning for Victory Over Disablement: Proceedings of the Seventh World Congress of the International Society for the Welfare of Cripples* (London: Central Council for Care of Cripples, 1958).

Invalid Children's Aid Association/Central Council for the Care of Cripples, *The Welfare of Cripples and Invalid Children* (London: Invalid Children's Aid Association and Central Council for the Care of Cripples, 1935).

Ministry of Health, *Final Report of the Inter-departmental Committee on the Rehabilitation of Persons Injured by Accidents* (London: HMSO, 1939) (Delevingne Committee).

Ministry of Health and Central Health Council, *Rehabilitation of the Sick and Injured* (London: HMSO, 1959).

Ministry of Labour and National Service, *Disabled Persons (Employment) Act, 1944* (London: HMSO, 1945).

Ministry of Labour and National Service, *Report of the Standing Committee on the Rehabilitation and Resettlement of Disabled Persons* (London: HMSO, 1946).

Ministry of Labour and National Service, *Second Report of the Standing Committee on the Rehabilitation and Resettlement of Disabled Persons* (London: HMSO, 1949).

Ministry of Labour and National Service, *Third Report of the Standing Committee on the Rehabilitation and Resettlement of Disabled Persons* (London: HMSO, 1958) (Piercy Committee).

Ministry of Pensions, *The Disabled Soldier's Handbook* (London: HMSO, 1918).

Biographies and contemporary experiences

Brickhill, Paul, *Reach for the Sky: The Story of Douglas Bader* (London: Companion Book Club, 1955).

Brown, Christy, *My Left Foot* (London: Secker and Warburg Ltd, 1989).

Dean, Vera, *Three Steps Forward* (London: Faber and Faber, 1957).

Douglas, Percy O., 'Aboard an Ambulance Train 1915–1918', in Samuelson, Pauline (ed.), *I Owe My Life: British Red Cross Celebrating 125 Years* (London: Bloomsbury, 1995).

Fraser, Ian, *Whereas I was Blind* (London: Hodder and Stoughton, 1942).

Fraser, Ian (ed.), *Conquest of Disability* (London: Odhams Press, 1956).

Hillary, Richard, *The Last Enemy* (London: Macmillan and Co., 1961).

Hodgkinson, Colin, *Best Foot Forward: The Autobiography of Colin Hodgkinson* (London: Odhams Press, 1957).

Housden, Dr Leslie, *Healthy, Happy Children, Britain Advances #15* (London: Sir I. Pitman and Sons, 1944).

Hunt, Agnes, *Reminiscences* (Shrewsbury: Wilding and Son, 1935).

Hunt, Paul (ed.), *Stigma: The Experience of Disability* (London: Geoffrey Chapman, 1966).

McBryde, Brenda, *A Nurse's War* (London: Sphere Books Ltd., 1980).

Priestley, J.B., *Postscripts* (London: William Heinemann, 1940).

Scrymgeour, James Tindal, *Reminiscences of St. Dunstan's* (Devon: Arthur H. Stockwell, 1920).

Simpson, William, *The Way of Recovery* (London: Hamish Hamilton, 1944).

Welch, Denton, *A Voice Through a Cloud* (London: Readers' Union, 1951).

Articles

Alan, S. and Malkin, S., 'The Conquest of Disability', *Annals of the Royal College of Surgeons of England* (Vol. 20, 1957).

Andrew, D.R., 'The Guinea Pig Club', *Aviation Space and Environmental Medicine* (Vol. 65, No. 5, May 1994).

Baker, Norman, 'A More Even Playing Field? Sport During and After the War', in Nick Hayes and Jeff Hill (eds), *'Millions Like Us?' British Culture in the Second World War* (Liverpool: Liverpool University Press, 1999).

Berridge, Virginia, 'Health and Medicine', in F.M.L. Thompson (ed.), *The Cambridge Social History of Britain 1750–1950, Vol. II* (Cambridge: Cambridge University Press, 1990).

Borsay, Anne, 'Disciplining Disabled Bodies: The Development of Orthopaedic Medicine in Britain, c. 1800–1939', in David M. Turner and Kevin Stagg (eds), *Social Histories of Disability and Deformity* (Abingdon: Routledge, 2006).

Bredberg, Elizabeth, 'Writing Disability History: Problems, Perspectives and Sources', *Disability and Society* (Vol. 14, No. 2, 1999).

Buxton, W.L., 'Industrial Rehabilitation Units: A British Experiment', *International Labour Review* (Vol. 67, 1953).

Callaghan, John, 'The Welfare State: A New Society?', in Jim Fyrth (ed.), *Labour's Promised Land? Culture and Society in Labour Britain 1945–51* (London: Lawrence and Wishart, 1995).

Campbell, D'Ann, 'Women in Combat: The World War II Experience in the United States, Germany, Great Britain and the Soviet Union,' *Journal of Military History* (Vol. 57, No. 2, April 1993).

Casson, Elizabeth, 'Occupational Therapy', *After-Care and Rehabilitation* (London: Eyre and Spottiswoode, 1943).

Charles, J.A., 'Rehabilitation', *Health Education Journal* (Vol. 1, 1943).

Cooter, Roger, 'Medicine and the Goodness of War', *Canadian Bulletin of Medical History* (Vol. 7, 1990).

Country Life, 'Roehampton House as a Hospital', *Country Life* (Vol. 38, No. 971, 14 August 1915).

Ebner, Maria, 'The Place of Heavy Ball Exercises in Rehabilitation', in Olive F. Guthrie-Smith (ed.), *Rehabilitation, Re-education and Remedial Exercises* (London: Balliere, Tindall and Cox, 1949).

Edwards, J.L., 'Remploy: An Experiment in Sheltered Employment for the Severely Disabled in Great Britain', *International Labour Review* (Vol. 77, 1958).

Elsey, Ena, 'Disabled Ex-servicemen's Experiences of Rehabilitation and Employment after the First World War', *Oral History* (Vol. 25, No. 2, Autumn 1997).

Englander, David, 'Soldiers and Social Reform in the First and Second World Wars', *Historical Research* (Vol. 67, No. 164, 1994).

Fraser, Ian, 'Employment of the Disabled', *Occupational Therapy and Rehabilitation* (Vol. 22, December 1943).

Gibbs, Denis, 'Rickets and the Crippled Child: An Historical Perspective', *Journal of the Royal Society of Medicine* (Vol. 87, No. 12, December 1994).

Gleeson, B.J., 'Disability Studies: A Historical Materialist View', *Disability and Society* (Vol. 12, No. 2, 1997).

Griffiths, H.E., 'Rehabilitation After Fractures', *After-Care and Rehabilitation* (London: Eyre and Spottiswoode, 1943).

Guthrie-Smith, O.F., 'Rehabilitation Exercises', *Journal of Massage and Medical Gymnastics* (October 1940).

Guttmann, Ludwig, 'The Significance of Sport in the Rehabilitation of the Disabled', in International Society for the Welfare of Cripples (ed.), *Planning for Victory Over Disablement* (London: Central Council for the Care of Cripples, 1958).

Guttmann, Ludwig, 'Services for the Treatment and Rehabilitation of Spinal Paraplegics and Tetraplegics in Great Britain', *Trends in Social Welfare* (Oxford: Pergamon Press, 1965).

Guttmann, Ludwig, 'Reflections on Sport for the Physically Handicapped', *Staff Publications* (No. 1, 1966).

Hackenbroch, M., 'Physiological and Clinical Aspects of Sport for the Disabled', in International Society for the Welfare of Cripples (ed.), *Planning for Victory Over Disablement* (London: Central Council for the Care of Cripples, 1958).

Hardy, Anne, 'Rickets and the Rest: Child-care, Diet and the Infectious Children's Diseases 1850–1914', *Social History of Medicine* (Vol. 5, No. 3, December 1992).

Harris, Jose, 'War and Social History: Britain and the Home Front during the Second World War', *Contemporary European History* (Vol. 1, No. 1, 1992).

Harrison, Mark, 'The Medicalization of War – the Militarization of Medicine', *Journal of the Society for the Social History of Medicine* (Vol. 9, No. 2, August 1996).

Herrick, C.E.J., 'The Broken Soldier, the Bonesetter and the Medical Profession: Manipulating Identities During the First World War', in Bertrand Taithe and Tim Thornton (eds), *Themes In History: War* (Stroud: Sutton Publishing, 1998).

Hirsch, Karen, 'Culture and Disability: The Role of Oral History', in Robert Perks and Alistair Thomson (eds), *The Oral History Reader* (London: Routledge, 1998).

James, Theodore, 'A History of the Medical Branch of the Royal Air Force Part 2', *Adler Museum Bulletin* (Vol. 10, No. 3, 1984).

James, Theodore, 'A History of the Medical Branch of the Royal Air Force', *Adler Museum Bulletin* (Vol. 10, No. 2, 1984).

King, Rex M., 'A "Break" for the War Wounded', *Hygeia* (22 July, 1944).

Kny, E. Cecil, 'Rehabilitation of Cripples', in Invalid Children's Aid Association/ Central Council for Care of Cripples (ed.), *The Welfare of Cripples and Invalid Children* (London: Invalid Children's Aid Association/Central Council for Care of Cripples, 1935).

Koven, Seth, 'Remembering and Dismemberment', *American Historical Review* (October 1994).

Kramer, R., 'Voluntary Agencies in the Welfare State: An Analysis of the Vanguard Role', *Journal of Social Policy* (Vol. 8, No. 4, October 1979).

Lanckenau, Nellie I., 'Occupational Therapy and Rehabilitation', in O.F. Guthrie-Smith (ed.), *Rehabilitation, Re-education and Remedial Exercises* (London: Balliere, Tindall and Cox, 1949).

Leneman, Leah, 'Lives and Limbs: Company Records as a Source for the History of Industrial Injuries', *Social History of Medicine* (Vol. 6, No. 3, December 1993).

Lewis, Jane, 'The Voluntary Sector in the Mixed Economy of Welfare', in David Gladstone (ed.), *Before Beveridge: Welfare Before the Welfare State* (London: IEA Health and Welfare Unit, 1999).

Lewis, Jane, 'Health and Health Care in the Progressive Era', in Roger Cooter and John Pickstone (eds), *Companion to Medicine in the Twentieth Century* (London: Routledge, 2003).

Littlewood, Mary, 'Rehabilitation in the Gymnasium: Some Strong Exercises Suitable for Rehabilitation of Patients as Individuals or Groups', in O.F. Guthrie-Smith (ed.), *Rehabilitation, Re-education and Remedial Exercises* (London: Balliere, Tindall and Cox, 1949).

Lorenzen, H., 'The Limits of Athletic Activity for the Disabled', *World Veterans' Federation Rehabilitation Bulletin* (No. 10, January 1956).

Lowerson, John, 'Stoolball and the Manufacture of "Englishness"', in Gertrud Pfister, Toni Neiwerth and Gerd Steins (eds), *Games of the World: Between Tradition and Modernity, Proceedings of the Second Annual ISHPES Congress*, Berlin 1993 (Sankt Augustin: Academia Verlag, 1993).

Luis, Leon, 'Recent Adaptations in the Treatment of Arm Amputations, Kineplastic Surgery and Arm Prostheses', *Annals of the Royal College of Surgeons of England* (Vol. 3, November 1948).

MacNicol, John, 'Eugenics and the Campaign for Voluntary Sterilization in Britain Between the Wars', *Social History of Medicine* (Vol. 2, No. 2, 1989).

Mennell, James, 'Physiotherapy in Post-operative Convalescence', *After-Care and Rehabilitation* (London: Eyre and Spottiswoode, 1943).

Mitchell, W.R.D., 'The After-Care of Amputation', *After Care and Rehabilitation* (London: Eyre and Spottiswoode, 1943).

Monthly Labour Review, 'British Plan for Training the Disabled', *Monthly Labour Review* (No. 54, February 1942).

Moran, Joe, 'Crossing the Road in Britain, 1931–76', *Historical Journal* (Vol. 49, No. 2, 2006).

Morris, Sharon, '"Human Dregs at the Bottom of Our National Vats": The Interwar Debate on Sterilization of the Mentally Deficient', in David M. Turner and Kevin Stagg (eds), *Social Histories of Disability and Deformity* (Abingdon: Routledge, 2006).

Munroe, Donald, 'Rehabilitation of the Totally Paralysed Below the Waist with Special Reference to Making them Ambulatory and Capable of Earning their Own Living', *New England Journal of Medicine* (233, 18 October 1945).

Neushul, Peter, 'Fighting Research: Army Participation in the Clinical Testing and Mass Production of Penicillin During the Second World War', in Roger Cooter, Mark Harrison, and Steve Sturdy (eds), *War, Medicine and Modernity* (Stroud: Sutton Publishing, 1998).

Noakes, Lucy, 'Review Article: Gender, War and Memory: Discourse and Experience in History', *Journal of Contemporary History* (Vol. 36, No. 4, 2001).

Ohry, Abraham, 'Historical Perspectives of Medical Rehabilitation', *Koroth* (Vol. 8, Nos 1–2, June 1981).

Petter, M., '"Temporary Gentlemen" in the Aftermath of the Great War: Rank, Status and the Ex-Officer Problem', *Historical Journal* (No. 37, 1994).

Phelps, Winthrop M., 'The Rehabilitation of Cerebral Palsy', *Journal of the Southern Medical Association* (Vol. 34, No. 7, July 1941).

Pickard, J.A.A., 'The Special Problem with the Child in Connection with Street Accidents More Particularly from the Point of Prevention', in Invalid Children's Aid Association/Central Council for Care of Cripples (ed.), *The Welfare of Cripples and Invalid Children* (London: Invalid Children's Aid Association/Central Council for Care of Cripples, 1935).

Pierson, Ruth Roach, 'Beautiful Soul or Just Warrior: Gender and War', *Gender and History* (Vol. 1, No. 1, Spring 1989).

Powell, M., 'An Expanding Service: Municipal Acute Medicine in the 1930s', *Twentieth Century British History* (Vol. 8, No. 3, 1997).

Prochaska, F.K., 'Philanthropy', in F.M.L. Thompson (ed.), *The Cambridge Social History of Britain 1750–1950, Vol. II* (Cambridge: Cambridge University Press, 1990).

Production and Engineering Bulletin, 'Employing Limbless Workers', *Production and Engineering Bulletin* (No. 3, January 1944).

Pullen, Gloria and Sutton-Spence, Rachel, 'The British Deaf Community During the 1939–1945 War', in Renate Fischer and Harlan Lane (eds), *Looking Back: A Reader on the History of Deaf Communities and their Sign Language* (Hamburg: Signum Press, 1993).

Reidy, J.P., 'The Formation and Early History of the Stoke Mandeville Plastic Surgery Unit', *British Journal of Plastic Surgery* (Vol. 39, 1986).

Roberts, Lawrence, 'The After-Care of Pulmonary Tuberculosis with Special Reference to Tuberculosis Colonies', *After-Care and Rehabilitation* (London: Eyre and Spottiswoode, 1943).

Robinson, K.P., 'Historical Aspects of Amputation', *Annals of the Royal College of Surgeons of England* (Vol. 73, 1991).

Rosen, Norman B., 'The Role of Sports in Rehabilitation of the Handicapped Part 3: The Wheelchair Games', *Maryland State Medical Journal* (Vol. 22, Pt. 11/12, 1973).

Sakula, Alex, 'That the Blind May Read: The Legacy of Valentin Hauy, Charles Barbier, Louis Braille and William Moon', *Journal of Medical Biography* (Vol. 6, No. 1, February 1998).

Schneider, William H., 'Blood Transfusion in Peace and War 1900–1918', *Social History of Medicine* (Vol. 10, No. 1, April 1997).

Scruton, Joan, 'Sir Ludwig Guttmann: Creator of a World Sports Movement for the Paralysed and Other Disabled', *Paraplegia* (Vol. 17, No. 1, May 1979).

Silbey, D., 'Bodies and Cultures Collide: Enlistment, the Medical Exam and the British Working Class, 1914–1916', *Social History of Medicine* (Vol. 17, No. 1, 2004).

Smith, Harold L. (ed.), 'The Effect of the War on the Status of Women', *War and Social Change: British Society in the Second World War* (Manchester: Manchester University Press, 1986).

Smyth, J.L., 'Industrial Accidents and Rehabilitation', in Invalid Children's Aid Association and the Central Council for Care of Cripples (ed.), *The Welfare of Cripples and Invalid Children* (London: Invalid Children's Aid Association and the Central Council for Care of Cripples, 1935).

Stack, Prunella, 'National Fitness', in Joseph Mayers and Bernard Spiers (eds), *Where Do We Go From Here?* (London: Frederick Muller, 1938).

Thane, P., 'The Debate on the Declining Birth Rate in Britain: The "Menace" of an Ageing Population 1920s–1950s', *Continuity and Change* (Vol. 5, No. 2, 1990).

Webster, Charles, 'Healthy or Hungary Thirties?', *History Workshop Journal* (No. 13, 1982).

Webster, Charles, 'Health, Welfare and Unemployment During the Depression', *Past and Present* (No. 109, 1985).

Welshman, John, 'Physical Education and the School Medical Service 1907–1939', *Social History of Medicine* (Vol. 9, No. 1, April 1996).

Weston, Simon, 'The Royal Star and Garter Home', in Pauline Samuelson (ed.), *I Owe My Life: British Red Cross Celebrating 125 Years* (London: Bloomsbury, 1995).

Whiteside, Noel, 'Counting the Cost: Sickness and Disability Among Working People in an Era of Industrial Recession 1920–1939', *Economic History Review* (Vol. 40, No. 2, May 1987).

World Veterans' Federation, 'Sports and the Disabled', *World Veterans' Federation Rehabilitation Bulletin* (No. 16, 1959).

Secondary sources

Alper, Helen (ed.), *A History of Queen Mary's University Hospital Roehampton* (Roehampton: Richmond, Twickenham and Roehampton Healthcare NHS Trust, 1997).

Anderson, Joan, *A Record of Fifty Years' Service to the Disabled 1919–1969* (London: Central Council for the Disabled, 1969).

Armstrong, David, *Political Anatomy of the Body: Medical Knowledge in Britain in the Twentieth Century* (Cambridge: Cambridge University Press, 1983).

Bailey, Henry Hamilton, *Surgery of Modern Warfare*, Vols 1–5 (Edinburgh: E & S Livingstone, 1944).

Balme, Harold, *The Unfit Made Fit: Britain Advances*, No. 4 (London: Sir I Pitman and Sons, 1943).

Bamji, Andrew, *Queen Mary's Sidcup 1974–1994: A Commemoration* (Sidcup: Queen Mary's, 1994).

Barclay, Jean, *In Good Hands: The History of the Chartered Society of Physiotherapy 1894–1994* (Oxford: Butterworth-Heinemann Ltd, 1994).

Barnes, C., *Disabled People in Britain and Discrimination* (London: Hurst and Company, 1991).

Barnett, Correlli, *The Audit of War* (London: Papermac, 1986).

Barry, Jonathan and Jones, Colin (eds) *Medicine and Charity Before the Welfare State* (London: Routledge, 1991).

Beaver, Patrick, *A Tower of Strength* (Lewes: The Book Guild Ltd, 1992).

Berridge, Virginia, *Health and Society in Britain Since 1939* (Cambridge: Cambridge University Press, 1999).

Best, S.H., *The Story of the British Red Cross* (London: Cassell and Company Ltd, 1938).

Beveridge, Lord William, *Voluntary Action: A Report on Methods of Social Advance* (London: George Allen and Unwin Ltd, 1948).

Beveridge, Lord William and Wells, A.F., *The Evidence for Voluntary Action* (London: Allen and Unwin, 1949).

Blaxter, Mildred, *The Meaning of Disability: A Sociological Study of Impairment* (London: Heinemann, 1976).

Bolderson, Helen, *Social Security, Disability and Rehabilitation: Conflicts in the Development of Social Policy 1914–1946* (London: Jessica Kingsley Publishers, 1991).

Borsay, Anne, *Disability and Social Policy in Britain Since 1750* (Basingstoke: Palgrave, 2005).

Bourke, Joanna, *Dismembering the Male: Men's Bodies, Britain and the Great War* (London: Reaction Books, 1996).

Bourke, Joanna, *An Intimate History of Killing: Face-to-Face Killing in Twentieth Century Warfare* (London: Granta, 1999).

Boyce, Anthony J., *The History of the Yorkshire Residential School for the Deaf 1829–1979* (Doncaster: Doncaster M.B.C. Museums and Arts Services, 1999).

Brereton, Frederick S., *The Great War and the R.A.M.C.* (London: Constable and Company, 1919).

Bridgen, Paul and Lowe, Rodney, *Welfare Policy Under the Conservatives* (Kew: PRO Publications, 1998).

Briggs, Asa, *The BBC: The First Fifty Years* (Oxford: Oxford University Press, 1985).

Brown, Antony, *Red for Remembrance: The British Legion 1921–1971* (London: Heinemann, 1971).

Calder, Angus, *The People's War: Britain 1939–1945* (London: Pimlico, 1992).

Cambray, P.G. and Briggs, G.G., *Red Cross and St John War History 1939–1947* (London: Red Cross, 1949).

Campbell, Jane and Oliver, Michael, *Disability Politics* (London: Routledge, 1996).

Carden-Coyne, Ana, *Reconstructing the Body: Classicism, Modernism and the First World War* (Oxford: Oxford University Press, 2009).

Carr-Saunders, A.M., Caradog Jones, D. and Moser, C.A., *A Survey of Social Conditions in England and Wales* (Oxford: Clarendon Press, 1958).

Cartwright, Frederick F., *A Social History of Medicine* (London: Longman, 1977).

Catterall, Peter (ed.), *Britain 1918–1951* (Oxford: Heinemann, 1994).
Central Statistical Office, *Fighting With Figures* (London: HMSO, 1995).
Clarke, Joan Simeon, *Disabled Citizens* (London: George Allen and Unwin, 1951).
Clarke, K.W., *A Review of the First Ten Years in the National Health Service 1948–1958* (Aylesbury: Royal Buckinghamshire and Associated Hospitals, 1959).
Committee for Research on Apparatus, *Aspects of Rehabilitation* (London: National Fund for Research into Crippling Diseases, 1968).
Cooter, Roger, *Surgery and Society in Peace and War: Orthopaedics and the Organisation of Modern Medicine 1880–1948* (Basingstoke: Macmillan Press, 1993).
Cooter, Roger, Harrison, Mark and Sturdy, Steve (eds), *War, Medicine and Modernity* (Stroud: Sutton Publishing, 1998).
Cope, Sir Zachary, *History of the Second World War: Surgery* (London: HMSO, 1953).
Crew, F.A.E., *Army Medical Services: Campaigns Vol. II* (London: HMSO, 1957).
Crew, F.A.E., *Army Medical Services: Campaigns Vol. IV* (London: HMSO, 1962).
DeGroot, Gerard J., *Blighty: British Society in the Era of the Great War* (London: Longman, 1996).
DePauw, Karen P. and Gavron, Susan J., *Disability and Sport* (Champaign, IL: Human Kinetics, 1995).
Devine, Edward T., *Disabled Soldiers' and Sailors' Pensions and Training* (New York: Oxford University Press, 1919).
Dimbleby, Richard, *Every Eight Hours* (London: Hodder and Stoughton, 1964).
Dimmock, Arthur F., *Aurthur James Wilson 1858–1945* (Feltham: British Deaf History Society, 1996).
Doherty, William Brown and Runes, Dagobert D., *Rehabilitation of the War Injured: A Symposium* (London: Chapman and Hall, 1945).
Dormandy, Thomas, *The White Death: A History of Tuberculosis* (London: The Hambledon Press, 1999).
Ellis, John, *The Sharp End: The Fighting Man in World War II* (London: Pimlico, 1990).
Farrant, David S., *The Queen Alexandra Hospital Home for Disabled Ex-Servicemen* (Worthing: Queen Alexandra Hospital Home, 1997).
Finlayson, G., *Citizen, State and Social Welfare in Britain 1830–1990* (Oxford: Clarendon Press, 1994).
Fletcher, I., *Queens Mary's Hospital Roehampton 1915–1965* (Roehampton: The Trustees, Roehampton, 1965).
Franklin-Mellor, W. (ed.), *History of the Second World War: Casualties and Medical Statistics* (London: HMSO, 1972).

Fraser, Ian, *Learning to be Blind: Britain Advances* (London: Sir I Pitman and Sons, 1943).

Frazer, W.M., *A History of English Public Health 1834–1939* (London: J.B. Lippincoff, 1950).

George, V., *Social Security: Beveridge and After* (New York: Routledge and Kegan Paul, 1968).

Gilbert, Bentley B., *The Evolution of National Insurance in Great Britain: The Origins of the Welfare State* (London: Joseph, 1966).

Gilbert, Bentley B., *British Social Policy 1914–1939* (London: Batsford, 1970).

Goldenson, Robert M. (ed.), *Disability and Rehabilitation Handbook* (New York: McGraw-Hill Book Company, 1978).

Goodman, Susan, *Spirit of Stoke Mandeville: The Story of Sir Ludwig Guttman* (London: Collins, 1986).

Gosden, P.H.J.H., *Self-Help: Voluntary Associations in the Nineteenth Century* (London: B.T. Batsford Ltd, 1973).

Grant, Brian, *The Deaf Advance: A History of the British Deaf Association 1890–1990* (Edinburgh: Pentland Press, 1990).

Grayzel, Susan R., *Women's Identities at War: Gender, Motherhood and Politics in Britain and France during the First World War* (Chapel Hill: University of North Carolina Press, 1999).

Guthrie, Douglas, *A History of Medicine* (London: Thomas Nelson and Sons, 1945).

Guthrie-Smith, Olive F., *Rehabilitation, Re-education and Remedial Exercises* (London: Balliere, Tindall and Cox, 1949).

Guttmann, Sir Ludwig, *Spinal Cord Injuries: Comprehensive Management Research* (Oxford: Blackwell, 1973).

Guttmann, Sir Ludwig, *Textbook of Sport for the Disabled* (Aylesbury: HM & M Publications, 1976).

Hales, Gerald, *Beyond Disability: Towards an Enabling Society* (London: Sage Publications, 1996).

Hardy, Anne, *Health and Medicine in Britain Since 1860* (Basingstoke: Palgrave, 2001).

Harland, Kathleen, *A History of the Queen Alexandra's Royal Naval Nursing Service* (London: The Journal of the Royal Naval Medical Service, n.d.).

Harris, Garrard, *The Redemption of the Disabled* (New York: D Appleton & Company, 1919).

Hennessey, Peter, *Never Again: Britain 1945–1951* (London: Vintage, 1993).

Hobson, Elvira, *Physiotherapy in Paraplegia* (London: J & A Churchill, 1956).

Holt, Richard, *Sport and the British* (Oxford: Clarendon Press, 1992).

Howson, G. (ed.), *Handbook for the Limbless* (London: Disabled Society, 1922).

Humphries, Steve and Gordon, Pamela, *Out of Sight: The Experience of Disability 1900–1950* (Plymouth: Northcote House, 1992).

Hunter, Donald, *The Diseases of Occupations*, 6th edition (London: Hodder and Stoughton, 1978).

Illingworth, W.H., *History of the Education of the Blind* (London: S. Low, Marston and Co. Ltd, 1910).

Jackson, Peter, *Britain's Deaf Heritage* (Edinburgh: Pentland Press, 1990).

Jeffreys, Kevin, *Retreat From New Jerusalem: British Politics 1951–1964* (Basingstoke: Macmillan, 1997).

Jones, Helen, *Health and Society in Twentieth Century Britain* (London: Longman, 1994).

Jones, Robert and Hunt, Agnes, *The Heritage of Oswestry 1900–1961* (Oswestry: Robert Jones and Agnes Hunt Orthopaedic Hospital, 1961).

Keeble, Ursula, *Aids and Adaptations* (London: The Social Administration Research Trust, 1979).

Kershaw, John D., *Handicapped Children* (London: William Heinemann, 1961).

Kessler, Henry H., *Cineplasty* (Springfield, IL: Charles C. Thomas, 1947).

Kimmins, C.W., *Chailey Heritage 1903–1948* (London: Baynard Press, 1948).

Klopsteg, Paul E. and Wilson, Philip O., *Human Limbs and their Substitutes* (New York: McGraw Hill, 1954).

Land, Andrew, Lowe, Rodney and Whiteside, Noel, *The Development of the Welfare State 1939–1951* (London: HMSO, 1992).

Le Gros Clark, F., *National Fitness* (London: Macmillan and Co., 1938).

Lee, Janet, *War Girls: The First Aid Nursing Yeomanry in the First World War* (Manchester: Manchester University Press, 2005).

MacKay, *The Test of War: Inside Britain 1939–1945* (London: UCL Press, 1999).

MacKenzie, Robert Tait, *Reclaiming the Maimed: A Handbook of Physical Therapy* (New York: Macmillan Company, 1918).

McAllister, Gilbert, *Houses That Are Homes: Britain Advances No. 22* (London: Sir I Pitman and Sons, 1944).

McBride, Earl D., *Crippled Children: Their Treatment and Orthopaedic Nursing* (London: Henry Kimpton, 1931).

McKibbin, Ross, *Classes and Cultures: England 1918–1951* (Oxford: Oxford University Press, 1998).

McLoughlin, M.G., *A History of the Education of the Deaf in England* (Gosport: Ashford Colour Press, 1987).

Mann, Ida and Pirie, Antoinette, *The Science of Seeing* (London: Pelican, 1946).

Marquand, David and Seldon, Anthony, *The Ideas that Shaped Post-War Britain* (London: Fontana Press, 1996).

Mason, Tony, *Sport in Britain: A Social History* (Cambridge: Cambridge University Press, 1989).

Medical Department, United States Army, *Surgery in World War II: Vol. II, Neurosurgery* (Washington: DC Office of the Surgeon General, 1959).

Mitchell, David T. and Snyder, Sharon L. (eds), *The Body and Physical Difference: Discourses of Disability* (Ann Arbor: University of Michigan Press, 1997).

Morgan, Kenneth O., *The People's Peace: British History Since 1945* (Oxford: Oxford University Press, 1999).

Newman, Sir George, *The Building of a Nation's Health* (London: Macmillan and Co., 1939).

Noakes, Lucy, *War and the British Identity: Gender and National Identity, 1939–1991* (London: IB Tauris, 1997).

Noakes, Lucy, *Women in the British Army: War and the Gentle Sex, 1907–1948* (Abingdon: Routledge, 2006).

North, Barry, *Something to Lean On: The First Sixty Years of the British Polio Fellowship* (South Ruiship: British Polio Fellowship, 1999).

O'Connell, Sean, *The Car in British Society: Class, Gender and Motoring 1896–1939* (Manchester: Manchester University Press, 1998).

Oliver, Michael, *Understanding Disability: From Theory to Practice* (Basingstoke: Macmillan, 1996).

Oliver, Michael and Barnes, Colin, *Disabled People and Social Policy: From Exclusion to Inclusion* (London: Longman, 1998).

Oliver, M. et al., *Walking into Darkness: The Experience of Spinal Cord Injury* (London: Macmillan, 1988).

Overy, R.J., *The Air War 1939–1945* (London: Europa, 1980).

Owen, David, *English Philanthropy 1660–1960* (Cambridge, MA: Belnap Press of Harvard University Press, 1965).

Pater, John E., *The Making of the NHS* (London: King Edward's Hospital Fund for London, 1981).

Pember-Reeves, Maud, *Round About A Pound A Week* (London: Virago Press, 1999).

Phillips, Gordon, *Best Foot Forward: Chas A. Blatchford and Sons Ltd. 1890–1990* (Cambridge: Granta Editions, 1990).

Porter, Dorothy, *Health, Civilization and the State: A History of Public Health From Ancient to Modern Times* (London: Routledge, 1999).

Porter, Roy, *The Greatest Benefit to Mankind* (London: HarperCollins, 1997).

Pritchard, D.G., *Education and the Handicapped 1760–1980* (London: Routledge and Kegan Paul, 1983).

Rackham, Kate, *The Invalid Children's Aid Association: The First Ninety Years* (London: The Invalid Children's Aid Association, 1977).

Rathbone, Josephine L. and Lucas, Carol, *Recreation in Total Rehabilitation* (Springfield, IL: Charles C. Thomas, 1959).

Rexford-Welch, S.C., *The Royal Air Force Medical Services: Vol. 1: Administration* (London: HMSO, 1954).

Rose, June, *Changing Focus: The Development of Blind Welfare* (London: Hutchinson and Co., 1970).

Rose, Sonya O., *Which People's War? National Identity and Citizenship in Wartime Britain 1939–1945* (Oxford: Oxford University Press, 2003).

Royden, Michael W., *Pioneers and Perseverance: A History of the Royal School for the Blind, Liverpool (1791–1991)* (Liverpool: Liverpool Countywise/Royal School for the Blind, 1991).

Rusk, Howard A. and Taylor, Eugene J., *New Hope for the Handicapped: The Rehabilitation of the Disabled from Bed to Job* (New York: Harper, 1949).

Ryde, Peter, *Out On A Limb: A Celebration of the British Limbless Ex-Servicemen's Association Golden Jubilee 1932–1982* (London: British Limbless Ex-Servicemen's Association, 1982).

Sainsbury, Sally, *Registered as Disabled – Occasional Papers on Social Administration #35* (London: G Bell and Sons, 1970).

Saunders, Hillary St. George, *The Red Cross and the White: A Short History of the Joint War Organisation of the British Red Cross Society and the Order of St. John of Jerusalem During the War 1939–1945* (London: Hollis and Carter, 1949).

Scruton, Joan, *Stoke Mandeville: Road to the Paralympics* (Aylesbury: Peterhouse Press, 1998).

Seaton, Derek, *From Strength to Strength: The History of the First 100 Years of the Leicester, Leicestershire and Rutland Guild of Disabled People 1898–1998* (Leicester: The Leicester, Leicestershire and Rutland Guild of Disabled People, 1998).

Sheridan, Dorothy (ed.), *Wartime Women: A Mass-Observation Anthology 1937–1945* (London: Phoenix Press, 2000).

Smith, Harold L., *War and Social Change* (Manchester: Manchester University Press, 1986).

Smith, Harold L. (ed.), *Britain in the Second World War: A Social History* (Manchester: Manchester University Press, 1996).

Smith, Sheila, *Still Unique After All These Years: A History of Blanche Nevile School, formerly Tottenham School for the Deaf 1895–1995* (London: Blanche Nevile School, 1995).

Southern Regional Association for the Blind, *Chronological Summary: Legislation Relating to the Blind*, 3rd edition (London: The Southern Regional Association for the Blind, 1965).

Spencer, Clive, *Directory of Goalball* (Worcester: Worcester College, 1986).

Stafford, George Thomas, *Sports for the Handicapped* (New York: Prentice-Hall, 1939).

Starns, Penny, *March of the Matrons: Military Influence on the British Civilian Nursing Profession 1939–1969* (Peterborough: DSM, 2000).

Stone, Deborah, *The Disabled State* (Basingstoke: Macmillan, 1985).

Story, Geoffrey O., *A History of Physical Medicine: The Story of the British Association of Rheumatology and Rehabilitation* (London: Royal Society of Medicine Services, 1991).

Summerfield, Penny, *Reconstructing Women's Wartime Lives* (Manchester: Manchester University Press, 1998).

Surtees, John, *Chaseley: A Home from Home* (Eastbourne: Chaseley Project Management Ltd, 1997).
Taylor, Eric, *Front-Line Nurses: British Nurses in World War II* (London: Robert Hale, 1997).
Thomas, David, *The Experience of Handicap* (London: Methuen, 1982).
Thomas, Mary G., *Party Games for the Blind*, revised edition (London: RNIB, 1970).
Thompson, F.M.L. (ed.), *The Cambridge Social History of Britain 1750–1950, Vol. II* (Cambridge: Cambridge University Press, 1990).
Timmins, Nicholas, *The Five Giants: A Biography of the Welfare State* (London: Fontana Press, 1996).
Titmuss, Richard M., *Problems of Social Policy* (London: HMSO, 1950).
Tomlinson, Jim, *Employment Policy and the Crucial Years 1939–1955* (Oxford: Clarendon Press, 1987).
Topliss, Eda, *Provision for the Disabled* (Oxford: Basil Blackwell, 1975).
Tranter, Neil, *Sport, Economy and Society in Britain 1750–1914* (Cambridge: Cambridge University Press, 1998).
Turner, Barry and Rennell, Tony, *When Daddy Came Home: How Family Life Changed Forever in 1945* (London: Pimlico, 1995).
Varrier-Jones, P.J., *Papers of a Pioneer* (London: Hutchinson and Co., 1943).
Vincent, David, *Poor Citizens: The State and the Poor in Twentieth Century Britain* (London: Longman, 1991).
Vitali, Miroslaw, Robinson, Kinglsey P., Andrews, Brian G. and Harris, Edward E., *Amputations and Prostheses* (London: Bailliere Tindall, 1978).
Walvin, James, *Leisure and Society: 1930–1950* (London: Longman, 1978).
Watson, Frederick, *Civilization and the Cripple* (London: John Bale Sons and Danielsson Ltd., 1930).
Watson, Lavinia, *The Story of St David's: The Ealing Home for Disabled Ex-servicemen* (Shipley: Lavinia Watson, 1977).
Webster, Charles, *The Health Services Since the War: Vol. I, Problems of Health Care: The National Health Service Before 1957* (London: HMSO, 1988).
Webster, Charles, *The Health Services Since the War: Vol. II, Government and Health Care: The National Health Service 1958–1979* (London, HMSO, 1996).
Wicksteed, Jane, *The Growth of a Profession* (London: Edward Arnold and Co., 1948).
Williams, J.G.P., *Medical Aspects of Sport and Physical Fitness* (Oxford: Pergamon Press, 1965).
Wilmot, Frances and Saul, Pauline, *A Breath of Fresh Air: Birmingham's Open-Air Schools 1911–1970* (Chichester: Phillimore and Co., 1998).
Wilson, Elisabeth, *Women and the Welfare State* (London: Tavistock Publications, 1977).
Wilson, John Rowan, *Margin of Safety: The Fight Against Polio* (London: Collins, 1963).

Woodford, Doreen E., *Homerton 1900–1921* (Feltham: British Deaf Society Publications, 1998).

Woodhead, Sir G. and Varrier-Jones, P.C., *Industrial Colonies and Village Settlements* (Cambridge: Cambridge University Press, 1920).

Wootton, Graham, *The Official History of the British Legion* (London: Macdonald and Evans, 1956).

Wootton, Graham, *The Politics of Influence: British Ex-Servicemen, Cabinet Decisions and Cultural Change 1917–1957* (London: Routledge and Kegan Paul, 1963).

Wootton, Graham, *Pressure Groups in Britain 1720–1970* (London: Allen Lane, 1975).

Unpublished theses

Elsey, Ena, *The Rehabilitation and Employment of Disabled Ex-Servicemen After the Two World Wars*, PhD Thesis, University of Teesside, 1997.

Index

Page numbers in italic refer to illustrations

accidents 14, 18, 23, 33, 34, 74, 90, 105, 113, 142, 181, 211
amputees 25, *45*, 56–58, 62, *88*, 92, 104, 120, 154, 167, 169, 183
archery 32, 141–143, 162
Army
  ex-service 85
  medical 75, 84, 104, 121, 123
  physical training 55, 77, 78, 182
  rehabilitation 121, 178–180, 182
artificial limbs 25, *45*, 47, 57, 77, 120, 165, 190
Auxiliary Territorial Service (ATS) 78, 152, 155, 160–162, 164, 170

Bader, Douglas 104, 120, 154
Balme, Harold 86, 178, 195
Beveridge Report 166, 176
Bevin, Ernest 85, 90, 157, 164, 176, 179, 194
blind 16, 42
  children 18, 19, 21
  employment 92, 159, 160, 163, 182, 183, 200
  ex-servicemen 43, 182, 188, 189
  schools 20, 21, 93
  sports 31, 32, 163
Blind Person's Act 21, 28, 189
Blind Person's March 28, 29
blood transfusion 75
Braille 20, 49, 182
British Council for Rehabilitation 144, 177
British Ex-Servicemen's Limbless Association (BLESMA) 189
British Legion 8, 47, 48, 52, 58, 64, 138, 141, 168, 187, 188
burns 9, 11, 75, 76, 103, 105, 109, 113–116, 118, 119, 123, 212
Butler, R.A. 199

Cairns, Hugh 116, 133, 134
cars 144, 169, 189, 190
Central Council for the Care of Cripples 15, 26, 27, 186, 187
Central Office of Information 195
cerebral palsy 19, 94, 186
Chailey Heritage 22, 30
charities 5, 15, 23, 32, 44, 170
  children 19, 30
  war 8, 11, 46, 54, 64, 188, 210
  see also voluntary associations
Chaseley Home 139
Churchill, Winston 115

civilians 1, 7, 8, 10, 11, 14, 15, 25–28, 31, 33, 34, 83, 89, 153, 158, 163, 179, 183, 201, 212
class 21, 22, 23, 52, 58, 65, 106, 107
coal 24
  Coal Mines Act 24
  injuries 24
  miners 142
Cohen, Brunel 187, 194
conscription 78
  disabled people 91
  women 157, 158
Constant Attendance Allowance 46, 167
Cripplecraft 27
Cripple's Journal 23, 26, 27, 32, 33, 187, 189

Dawson Report 16
deaf 189
  children 18–21
  employment 92, 159, 160
  ex-servicemen 43
  institutions 15
  schools 93
  women 91, 159
Delevingne Committee 24, 90
degeneration 14, 16, 210
Disabled Person's (Employment) Act 10, 139, 145, 169, 177, 192, 194, 198, 201, 215
Disablement Resettlement Officers 170, 196, 197
disease 7, 14, 15, 17, 18, 24, 93, 180
  occupational 24, 25
  soldiers 44, 46, 160
  venereal 75
drill 179
  schools 29, 31, 34
  servicemen 59, 78, 106, 107
  women 162
Duchess of Gloucester House 139, 168, 188

East Grinstead 11, 75, 109, 113–115, 118, 143
education 4, 18–23, 25, 26, 34, 94, 192, 194, 211
  Board of Education 16
  Ministry of Education 193
Education Acts 177, 193
  Elementary Education Act 19
Egham 83, 85, 144, 176, 180, 181, 185, 194, 196
Emergency Medical Service 73, 77, 79
employment 4, 27, 73, 89, 91–94, 176, 180–185, 192, 193, 195, 196, 199, 200, 210, 212, 215
  ex-servicemen 47, 48, 65, 84–86, 138–140, 143–145, 195, 211, 214
  women 10, 152, 157, 158, 160, 161, 169, 170
Enterprise Club 32, 33
epilepsy 180, 183, 186
eugenics 14, 16, 33, 210
  British Eugenics Education Society 16
exhibitions 28, 158, 193
  sporting 63, 188
experiments 23, 78, 103, 111, 116, 133, 144, 180

factories 23, 27, 34, 85, 90, 91, 120, 154, 158, 159, 179
Factories Act 183
Farnham Park 179
Festival of Britain 188
fitness 8, 14–16, 29, 31, 33, 78, 80, 81, 83, 179
  depots 77–79
  ex-servicemen 55, 57, 65, 140, 143, 144
  RAF 103, 104, 106, 107, 111
  soldiers 34, 212
  war work 158, 159
  women 163

fractures 24, 25, 44, 76, 80, 86, 105, 107, 117
Fraser, Ian 50, 52, 61, 65, 89, 187, 190, 192, 194

Garston Manor 144, 179
Gillies, Harold 44
Gleave, Tom 114
Guinea Pig Club 116
Guthrie-Smith, Olive 81
Guttmann, Ludwig 133–140, 142–145, 213

Headley Park 121
hearing aids 22, 190
Hillary, Richard 114, 115
Hodgkinson, Colin 104, 120
holidays 187, 188
hospitals 25, 73, 77, 81, 84, 86, 87, 93, 95, 180, 182, 197, 198, 201
  field 76
  military 102, 104, 113, 117
  mining 24, 90
  sport 57, 182, 183
Hunt, Agnes 23, 27
Huskinson, Commodore 104

Interdepartmental Committee on Physical Deterioration 16
Interdepartmental Committee on the Rehabilitation and Resettlement of Disabled Persons 88, 89, 91, 158, 176
Invacar 190
Invalid Children's Aid Association 15, 19

Jefferson, Geoffrey 116, 133, 134
Jones, Robert 23, 27, 80

King's National Roll 47, 184, 195
Kytes Estate 139

Lest We Forget Association 46
Lord Robert's Memorial Workshops 46, 184
Lyme Green 139

Marquand, Hilary 142, 188
masculinity 50, 56, 115, 131, 153
  sport 43, 55, 57, 58, 64, 81
massage 19, 21, 76, 77, 80, 106, 112, 132, 180, 181
McIndoe, Archibald 75, 76, 109, 113, 115, 116, 118–120, 123, 213
Medical Research Council (MRC) 17, 24, 133, 193
mental health 9, 78
Michael Works 184
Ministry of Education 178, 193
Ministry of Health 16, 190, 191, 196, 198
Ministry of Labour and National Service 73, 84, 85, 87, 92, 143, 144, 153, 158, 164, 169, 178, 179, 181, 185, 193, 194, 196, 197
Ministry of Pensions 8, 10, 43, 46, 47, 73, 84, 137, 139, 144, 188, 189, 191
  women, 153, 164–166, 169, 171
Monckton, Walter 199
Mongewell Park 109, 121

Nathan Committee 186
National Advisory Council on the Employment of the Disabled 119, 193, 196, 197
National Assistance Act 187, 198, 201
National Health Service 166, 190, 198
National Institute for the Blind *see* Royal National Institute of the Blind
National Insurance Acts 23, 177, 189
National Insurance (Industrial Injuries) Act 177
Navy 84, 121

neurosurgery 76, 133
Not Forgotten Association 46, 63, 188
nurses *21*, 64, 115, 138, 156, 164

occupational therapy 76, 80, 81, 111, 113, 132, 180, 194
one-armed golfers 31
open air schools 20
orthopaedics 9, 16, 27, 103, 107, 117, 213
  surgery 23, 134

paralysis *see* paraplegia
paraplegia 62, 131, 132, 134, 135, 138, 139, 166–169
Pearson, Arthur 50–52, 55, 58, 59, 65
penicillin 74, 75, 136
Penley 142
pensions 15, 188
  war 34, 45, 46, 48, 168, 189
physical training 29, 55, 59, 77, 78, 84, 106, 107, 114, 122, 180, 182
physiotherapy 76–78, 81, 82, 85, 106, 132, 136–138, 180, 190, 194
Piercy Committee 193, 198
Pinderfields Hospital 182, 183, 196
plastic surgery *see* burns
polio 121–123
Poppy Day 48, 188
Portal, Charles 117–119
Priestley, J.B., 102, 152, 153, 154

Queen Elizabeth Training College for the Disabled 27, 169, 185
Queen Mary Roehampton *see* Roehampton

Red Cross 49, 53, 86, 139, 162, 186–188
Remploy 183–185, 201
Riddoch, George 133
rickets 17, 20
Roehampton 25, *45*, 49, 180
  sport 56, 57, *88*
Roffey Park 85, 162, 181, 182
Royal Air Force 102–129
Royal Army Medical Corps 133
Royal National Institute for the Blind 163, 182
Royal National Orthopaedic Hospital 27

sheltered workshops *see* workshops
St Dunstan's 28, 49–53, 83, 152, 163, 183, 188
  sport 58–62
St Loyes College 27, 185
spinal carriage 132, 137
sport *see* fitness and entries under institutions
Springbok Village 185
Stack, Prunella 14
Star and Garter Home 53–55, 64, 65, 139, 184, 188
  sport 62–64, 81, 142
Stoke Mandeville 130–151, 162, 163, 168, 188
  Festival of Sport 142
Stoke Mandeville Bed Cycle 136, *137*
Sub-standard Recruits Physical Development Depots 77–79
sulphanilamide 74
Sunlight League 20, 27
Sunshine Homes for Blind Babies 20

Thistle Foundation 139
Thomas, Hugh Owen 20
Tomlinson, George 1, 88, 92
Tomlinson Committee 73, 79, 95, 212
tuberculosis 17, 19, 20, 46, 91, 93, 159, 160, 166, 183

Vocational Training Scheme 182, 194
Voluntary Aid Detachment (VAD) 53, 160
voluntary associations 5, 15, 25, 44, 176, 185, 186, 199, 215

Warren, Marjory 178
Watson-Jones, Reginald 107, 108, 111, 113, 116–120, 122–124, 17, 193, 196, 213
Weeks Good Cause 186
wheelchairs 22, 54, 132, 137, 140, 163, 188, 190, 194
  motorised 54, 169
  polo 140, 141
  sport 62, 137, 140–142, 162
women 26, 64, 91, 144
  blind 31, 83
  League of Health and Beauty 55
  Services 82, 84, 85, 144, 152–175, 194
  sport 141, 142
  sterilisation 166
  war workers 78, 85, 91
Women's Land Army 91, 159
Womersley, Walter 157
workshops *see* Remploy
  sheltered 22, 184, 201

CPSIA information can be obtained at www.ICGtesting.com
Printed in the USA
BVOW04s1725150516

448061BV00007B/40/P

9 781784 993498